Michelle challenges professionals and caregivers to think more deeply and practice more consciously in helping individuals with ASD acquire and apply social knowledge in their lives. In building on her seminal work in social thinking, Michelle argues effectively for an important and more thoughtful alternative to behaviorally based social skill "training" approaches, which are so limited in honoring the complexity of individuals with ASD."

Barry M. Prizant, PhD, CCC-SLP
Director, Childhood Communication Services
Adjunct Professor, Center for the Study of Human Development, Brown University

A compelling tour with a long overdue destination! With some of the most difficult questions surrounding the social challenges in ASD as a point of departure, Michelle charts an informed rationale for social learning strategies. Dispelling myths in the way of social understanding, she connects behavior to thought, mistakes to insight, and confusion to direction. This is a trip worth taking!

Carol Gray
Specialist of persons with ASD, author, and creator of *Social Stories*™

Why Teach Social Thinking?

Questioning Our Assumptions About
What It Means to Learn Social Skills

By
Michelle Garcia Winner

Think Social Publishing, Inc.
Santa Clara, California

Why Teach Social Thinking?

Michelle Garcia Winner

ISBN: 978-1-936943-13-5

A version of this book was previously published under the title:
A Politically Incorrect Look at Evidence-based Practices and Teaching Social Skills: A Literature Review and Discussion (former ISBN: 978-0-9792922-5-5)

Think Social Publishing, Inc.
404 Saratoga Avenue, Suite 200
Santa Clara, CA 95050
Tel: (408) 557-8595
Fax: (408) 557-8594

This book was printed and bound in the United States by Think, Inc.

TSP is a sole source provider of Social Thinking products in the U.S.

Books may be purchased online at www.socialthinking.com

Contents

About the Author vii

Acknowledgments ix

Foreword xi

Abstract xxi

Ch. 1. Introduction to Social Thinking and Social Skills 1

Ch. 2. What Are Social Skills? 23

Ch. 3. What Are the Origins of Social Development? Is There
an Age When Our Social Development Stops? 27

Ch. 4. In What Areas of Social Thinking Do Students with
Social Cognitive Challenges Struggle? The ILAUGH Model
Remodeled 33

Ch. 5. What Impact Do Weaknesses in Social Conceptual
Information Have on Learning the Common Core State
Standards? 59

Ch. 6. When Do We Use Social Thinking and Related Social
Skills? How Do We Approach Teaching These Skills? 72

Ch. 7. How Can Cognitive Behavior Therapy Address Teaching
Social Thinking and Related Social Skills? 85

Ch. 8. Do All Those with ASD-SCD Benefit from the Same Teachings? The Social Thinking-Social Communication Profile (ST-SCP).. 91

Ch. 9. Who Is Responsible for Creating and Teaching Social Thinking and Related Social Skills? Is the Same Set of Teaching Techniques Relevant for All Persons with ASD and Related Social Learning Challenges? 160

Ch. 10. What Is a Framework for Teaching Social Thinking and Related Social Skills?.. 175

Ch. 11. What Are Some Guidelines for Teaching Social Thinking and Related Skills to Groups of Students? Best-Practice Teaching Guidelines for Social Thinking 193

Ch. 12. How Does Social Teaching Fit into What We Typically Call "Education"?.. 207

Ch. 13. What Are Evidence-Based Practices? How Do They Apply to Teaching Social Thinking and Related Social Skills?........ 215

Ch. 14. Summary: We End at the Beginning.............................. 242

References. 248

Appendix A. Study Guide 274

Index.. 305

About the Author

Michelle Garcia Winner, MA, CCC-SLP, is a speech language pathologist who specializes in the treatment of individuals with social cognitive deficits at the Social Thinking Center, her clinic in San Jose, CA. She works with clients who range from children to adults in individual and group settings. She also consults with families, schools, and businesses and is a prolific writer and speaker.

She coined the term Social Thinking® in the mid-1990s and developed the treatment framework that today includes information, vocabulary, curriculum, and strategies that help individuals with social learning challenges become better social thinkers. Her approach led GreatSchools.org, a leading national nonprofit organization, to call Michelle, "the leading expert in the field of social skills."

The heart of Michelle's work illuminates the often illusive and intangible world of social thinking. She focuses on the development of practical strategies that can be easily used by parents, educators, and service providers to teach social thinking and social skills across different environments. Her work is now being applied not only to persons with higher functioning autism, Asperger's Syndrome, attention deficit disorder (ADD)/attention deficit hyperactivity disorder (ADHD), and related social cognitive deficits but also more broadly to students in mainstream classrooms and to adults in vocational and professional settings in the U.S. and abroad.

Michelle has written or co-authored more than 20 books on Social Thinking. She travels internationally, speaking on a variety of Social Thinking topics, and repeatedly receives accolades for her educational, energetic, and enthusiastic workshop presentations.

She's been invited to train psychiatrists, psychologists, counselors, parents, educators, and state policy-makers on the importance of social thinking. Her goal is to raise awareness among administrators, educators, and parents about the critical role social thinking and social skills play in every student's life, not just in achieving academic success but for success in adulthood and life in general. In 2008, she was awarded a Certificate of Special Congressional Recognition for developing the Social Thinking treatment approach.

Michelle lives in San Jose, CA with her partner. She has two daughters, Heidi and Robyn, who continue to keep her very humble.

Acknowledgments

This project started as a challenge, and I've never been one to shy away from a stimulating challenge. Andrea Walker, the director of the Orange County, California S.U.C.S.E.S.S. Project (a county-wide training program for educators of students on the autism spectrum), met with me in San Jose, California. She literally trapped me in a corner in my house and forced me into a discussion about the evidence-based practice movement. There was a powerful movement underfoot, she told me, and it was time I got my head out of the sand and voiced a response to the movement, no matter how complicated the resulting argument might turn out to be. Thank you, Andrea, for that wake-up call.

Her timing was impeccable, or maybe it was fate that I'd also just finished reading the book *Freakonomics* (Levett & Dubner, 2005). The authors posed the thesis that if we ask a different question, we may get a whole different set of answers. The light bulb went off in my brain, and I realized that within the realm of education we don't ask enough questions. In relation to my own work and this new exploration into evidence-based teaching, the relevance was startling. What if we asked the question, "What are social skills?" before we started to measure our success in teaching them?

In the world of academia, Dr. Patricia Prelock stands tall as one of my heroes. I'm honored that she is willing to take me under her wing and offer academic guidance. She was extremely helpful in streamlining my thinking process about this book and gently prodding me to make a more powerful statement. Her endless encouragement accomplished its goal.

My work is further empowered by the dedication of Veronica Zysk toward making my thoughts and ramblings sound more intelligent.

But the true undercurrent of this project, the force that makes me do what I do, is my father, Max Rodrigues Garcia, a Holocaust survivor from Amsterdam, Holland, and the spirit of my mother, my personal teacher, Priscilla Thwaits Garcia. These exceptional people raised my siblings and me to always use our brains, to think and question, to never accept what people lay in front of us as the way it should be.

Mom and Dad—I've taken that message to heart.

—Michelle Garcia Winner

Foreword

Patricia A. Prelock, PhD, CCC-SLP

....

Theory of mind and the range of perspective taking needed for meaningful social experiences require a synergistic set of communication, social, and behavioral skills that the literature reports is often lacking in the repertoire available to individuals with autism spectrum disorders (ASD) (Baron-Cohen, 1995; Baron-Cohen, Leslie, & Frith, 1985; Happé, 1994; Perner, Frith, Leslie, & Leekam, 1989; Prior, Dahlstrom, & Squires, 1990). The ability to understand your own thoughts as well as those of others anchors your social thinking and related social skills that clearly impact behavior. Unfortunately, clinicians and researchers lack a common vocabulary and understanding of what is really meant by social skills, which compromises our ability to assess the underlying knowledge base needed to be successful social partners. In this book, however, Michelle Garcia Winner raises our awareness of the complex issues related to social skills by guiding our thinking across 12 questions, from defining social skills to determining the evidence-based practices for social learning.

Winner challenges her readers to reconsider how we "think" about social skills, reminding us that being "social" is a complex experience that requires more than just learning isolated social skills. This challenge includes a consideration that we enhance our understanding about the well-documented social impairment in autism (American Psychiatric Association, 2000; Lord, 1993; Volkmar,

1987; Volkmar & Klin, 1990) to consider what is behind that impairment and required for success as a "social being." She suggests it may be less about learning individual social skills and more about social cognition and social learning. In fact, she begins her discussion of the issues in Chapter 1 by asking us to more carefully consider how we think and reason socially. Winner suggests we may be initiating social instruction with children with ASD at a level that is not well matched to their foundational skills or in a way that is so segmented that there is no real way for children to build on the skills they are learning. She highlights the value of executive function as leading the way to supporting joint attention and theory of mind understanding—important skills to developing active learning that allows us to effectively coexist across social situations. In addition, she reminds the reader of the emotional skills necessary for successful social learning including self-awareness, self discipline, and empathy.

Winner continues to pose important questions about the use of traditional behavioral approaches to developing social skills and facilitating social interaction. Although these are evidence-based approaches, they may be focused on the wrong goals, i.e., changing a behavior vs. attending to a child's underlying thoughts, perceptions, motives, and beliefs. Targeting inappropriate behavior is not likely to promote, for example, the ability to think in social contexts or increase self-awareness and social perception—which is at the heart of what Winner believes is the core social challenge for individuals with ASD. She posits that for us to establish truly successful social teaching programs, we must appreciate the individual nature of the social and emotional behavior of individual students with ASD. She asks an important question of clinicians: are we providing the foundational information children with ASD can actually use to problem solve their own social dilemmas?

In Chapter 2, Winner questions traditional ways of thinking about social skills. She suggests it may not be the individual social skills that are critical to teaching children with ASD but rather the ability to engage in social thinking. She offers important food for thought because survival in a variety of social contexts, such as the classroom, requires an understanding of the unspoken social "dos' and don'ts." It becomes clear that no specific set of social skills drives all instruction. It is important that we assess a child's understanding of the social environment and provide intervention that considers a varying social context.

The origins of social development are discussed in Chapter 3, reminding us of early voice and face recognition in infants that supports joint attention and an emerging theory of mind where children begin to understand that their thoughts and feelings may be different than others. The developmental trajectory of social learning is important to our understanding of why limited social opportunities for young children with ASD compromise their social development. As children with ASD approach school age, their challenged social understanding impacts their narrative language development, both understanding the thoughts and feelings of story characters as well as describing the mental states and perspectives of others in oral or written narratives (Capps, Losh, & Thurber, 2000; Diehl, Bennetto, & Young, 2006; Losh & Capps, 2003; Loveland, McEvoy, Tunali, & Kelley, 1990; Norbury

& Bishop, 2003; Tager-Flusberg, 1995). Intervention, then, needs to build on principles of social thinking and theory of mind that can be applied flexibly in a dynamic social environment.

In Chapter 4, Winner presents her innovative ILAUGH Model of Social Cognition but remodels her framework in the context of the developing social mind. She describes five key components in the development of social thinking that are compromised in individuals with ASD: central coherence theory, theory of mind, executive function, emotion regulation, and sensory integration. She explains that the lack of concept formation that is typical of individuals with central coherence challenges can be both a strength and a challenge for individuals with ASD. On the one hand they exhibit a strong memory for details of events yet lack the gestalt or "gist" of the situation, leading to missed social information. Their poorly developed joint attention and theory of mind keep them from being able to predict what others are going to do based on their desires and beliefs. Because executive function requires an ability to plan, organize, and problem solve, individuals with ASD struggle to define, manage, and work toward meaningful social goals. The combination of central coherence and executive function challenges is particularly problematic as individuals with ASD too often miss the "gist of social relatedness" and are unable to structure their thoughts or ideas in a coherent manner. Emotion processing or emotional regulation is another area of challenge as individuals with ASD have difficulty calming themselves in times of stress and anxiety and are challenged to identify their emotions. The final area impacting social thinking that Winner describes is the limitations individuals with ASD have in processing sensory information, which affects their ability to cope with a complex social world. Winner believes all five factors interface synergistically to complicate social thinking and social relatedness although she is careful to point out that a strong science base is absent for connecting these concepts and the social thinking of children with ASD. Her clinical experiences and work with children with ASD in educational settings have led her to speculate that the ILAUGH Model can begin to explain breakdowns in school performance and social behavior. Her remodeled approach suggests the original ILAUGH components need a central focus upon which individual components can be built. She proposes perspective taking and gestalt processing as central features of social processing that are supported by learning to initiate communication, listen with your eyes and brain, abstract and inference from information provided, and establish human relationships.

Chapter 5 provides an interesting discussion about how challenges in social concept development impact a student's ability to learn the Common Core State Standards that states have established as benchmarks for student success. As an example, she highlights the social knowledge required to manage the Common Core State Standards in language arts but reminds us that often teachers make assumptions about the level of competence students possess in their social thinking. Often, foundational skills are not taught or explicitly modeled, which places children with ASD at a distinct disadvantage as they are now trying to maneuver not only the academic environment but the social environment as well. This raises several questions regarding approaches to service delivery. How do we help them build a capacity for learning socially abstract information that most students get intuitively? Can we assume that a child with ASD will know when to ask for help, will know how to participate in a group, or understand different perspectives? Can we simultaneously teach both the academic and social curriculum?

In Chapter 6, Winner revisits when we use social thinking approaches to support learning in educational settings. She provides a number of examples where it becomes clear that social thinking, or the lack thereof, impacts language arts, social studies, and history, to name a few academic areas. Often, children with ASD struggle to grasp social-emotional concepts important to their understanding of story characters as well as their ability to recognize what others may be thinking. When confusion sets in, children with ASD often experience emotional dysregulation and struggle to get back on track. Behavioral intervention approaches often fall short in ensuring students transfer "learned skills" beyond the specific context in which they were taught. The question must be asked, then, how do we get children to relate the specific language skills they are taught to their underlying social knowledge? Winner offers an important example to illustrate this point. She suggests that poor eye contact is more than just lacking a specific skill. She explains it as a lack of intuitive social cognitive connections with others. Winner encourages us to be thoughtful in our approach to treating social skills. Teaching separate skills creates a risk of removing the skills children need for social communication from the larger framework for learning and thinking.

Winner offers one approach to teaching social thinking that works to change the way a child behaves. In Chapter 7, she describes the role of cognitive behavior therapy (CBT), which focuses on changing perceptions and increasing self understanding. CBT increases children's awareness of how their behavior impacts not only them but others. Winner recognizes that not all children benefit from the same intervention but we do need to have some way to profile the social thinking and social communication of children with ASD so that we can make good decisions about the most appropriate intervention methods.

Chapter 8 describes a Social Thinking-Social Communication Profile (ST-SCP) that is used to identify treatment groups based on levels of social functioning to guide an intervention team in their educational planning for children with ASD. She cautions that the ST-SCP framework is not research-based, but it is grounded in clinical experience and matches the social communication elements highlighted in the DSM-5. The ST-SCP helps predict student academic learning challenges linked to social learning for six different social communication treatment groups: 1) significantly challenged; 2) challenged; 3) emerging; 4) nuance challenged (weak interactive and socially anxious); 5) neurotypical; and an alternative category 6) resistant. Assignment to a particular group is determined by several aspects of social functioning such as understanding one's own and others' perspective (social radar), emotional coping, social problem solving, peer interaction, self awareness, academic skills, bullying and mental management, and lying and cognition. Understanding a child's strengths and challenges in each of these aspects helps to determine the most appropriate intervention approach. Thus, Winner provides a way to profile the social communication of children with autism and use that profile to guide treatment.

As we think about intervention planning for children with ASD, it is important to consider who has a role. In Chapter 9, Winner suggests everyone has a role and responsibility to address the social communication needs of children with ASD. Each of us brings a unique perspective to an intervention team but it is critical that we function as an interdisciplinary team if we hope to have the greatest impact on addressing the social thinking and understanding of this population.

So, how do we do this? What is the framework for intervention that is likely to be the most successful in teaching social thinking and related social skills? In Chapter 10, Winner challenges providers to not make assumptions regarding our children's understanding about underlying social concepts. It is important that children become active thinkers about the social learning process. At the core of ensuring social thinking is the development of frameworks for explaining abstract information in more concrete, meaningful terms. Winner is a master at developing and implementing frameworks for social understanding such as her Four Steps of Perspective Taking and Four Steps of Communication. Both frameworks are designed to help students recognize the synergy involved in social thinking and the dynamic processes involved in making a social encounter meaningful and successful.

In Chapter 11, guidelines for teaching social thinking are presented. These are important considerations for developing an intervention plan that will make a difference for children with ASD. For example, Winner highlights the importance of evaluating a child's level of social thinking, individualizing the intervention, starting with the basics, and teaching without assumptions about prior social knowledge. In addition, she encourages providing multisensory learning opportunities, teaching flexible thinking, using a team-oriented approach, and ensuring the intervention is meaningful to the student. Importantly, she reminds providers that everyone is accountable for the intervention success including the child with ASD.

How does this all fit within the context of education? In Chapter 12, Winner explains that communication enables the child with ASD to make sense of the curriculum, such as interpreting the thoughts and beliefs of characters in a story read in the classroom. To increase children's opportunities for social success, we must help them develop an ability to adapt to a variety of social contexts that will prepare them for independence and adulthood. This begins at home and carries into school, work, and the community.

The role of evidence-based practice in the service delivery to children with ASD is the focus of Chapter 13. Winner explains the importance of advancing our knowledge and understanding of the learning styles of children with ASD, recognizing it is not an easy task because of the variability in strengths, challenges, and needs that characterize children with ASD. She provides some considerations for implementing meaningful research, such as recognizing the diverse set of skills that characterize children with ASD, the age of children involved, and related mental health concerns. She also suggests providers should consider what children need to survive in the real world that will facilitate their social interactions with family and other children.

In the final chapter, Winner ends where she began, reminding us that children with ASD do not enter their educational environment with intact social systems and will require thoughtful, dynamic, and meaningful intervention. Throughout her text, Winner provides provocative examples of social adaptations we make as social beings and the likely challenges for those with less sophisticated social thinking. She emphasizes the importance of teachers knowing and understanding the complex nature of social thinking, the impact of this construct on classroom culture, and the social content interwoven throughout the curriculum. Fortunately, Winner does not leave the reader to start the social thinking and implementation process without a foundation for assessment and intervention. She provides a synergistic approach to guiding the development of practical treatment methods for both social and academic improvement. Her Social Thinking frameworks can be used by parents and professionals and are founded on what we have learned in the research about ways children learn, think, and socialize. Coordinating what children know from their past experience with their current experience and utilizing those experiences to understand the intentions and expectations of others requires something more than teaching isolated social skills.

Abstract

The concept of teaching social skills misrepresents the dynamic and complex process that's at the heart of social skill production. Before we can act socially, we need to be able to think socially. However, in general, the fields related to education and counseling of school-aged students have failed to study the complexity of teaching social learning. Instead, they've applied behavioral teachings in an attempt to tidy up "inappropriate behavior" without exploring whether, and to what extent, the behavior itself is caused by weak social thinking.

Students who are challenged in the areas of social thinking and social skills—individuals diagnosed with autism spectrum disorders (ASD), social (pragmatic) communication disorder (SCD), nonverbal learning disorders (NLD), attention deficit hyperactivity disorder (ADHD), and those with related social learning issues—struggle daily within an education system that is, at present, ill-suited to meet their needs. Our current education of children (both students who have disabilities and those who don't) is based on the assumption that all students enter school with basic social thinking abilities in place. And therein we fail our students before they even arrive at our classrooms.

We assume students understand that people have thoughts that may differ from their own. We assume students know how to learn by watching others. We assume students understand that knowledge can be gleaned not just from verbal communication and textbook content but also from the vast realm of nuance, innuendo, nonverbal communication, and environmental influences that are integral parts of our social world. Furthermore, we assume not only that this social know-how is in place, but that students have learned how to use basic social thinking to regulate their own behavior in a group.

Complicating matters is federal public educational policy—No Child Left Behind (NCLB)—which calls for schools to use "evidence-based" practices in teaching students, especially students with disabilities. The reality of today's world is that strategies abound for teaching social thinking and related social skills, and many of these strategies are resulting in significant gains for our students. However, few—if any—meet the criteria for being evidence-based. As an educational community, we haven't yet defined what we mean by "social skills" or agreed on which types of curriculum to use with different types of students to teach social skills. We also haven't collectively agreed upon a host of other definitions that must first exist before evidence-based practices can become a reality.

This lack of common vocabulary and terminology about social skills does little to help our students become better social thinkers and to prepare them for the real-world experiences they encounter daily. Further, if we group students together for treatment based only on their diagnosis, without taking into consideration social learning strengths and weaknesses as well as emotional coping mechanisms, we fail to use best practices that will result in real social learning improvement.

We pat ourselves on the back when a student masters an isolated skill such as waiting in line appropriately, but we fail to appreciate the bigger picture—the importance of teaching a student to apply social thinking and related social problem-solving across a range of diverse contexts. We have put the proverbial cart before the horse.

By exploring the following 12 questions, this book attempts to raise awareness of the many complex and interrelated issues that are at the core of teaching social skills.

- What are social skills?

- What are the origins of social development? Is there an age when our social development stops?

- In what areas of social thinking do students with social cognitive challenges struggle? The ILAUGH Model remodeled (Winner, 2000)

- What impact do weaknesses in social conceptual information have on learning the Common Core State Standards?

- When do we use social thinking and related social skills? How do we approach teaching these skills?

- How can cognitive behavior therapy address teaching social thinking and related social skills?

- Do all those with ASD-SCD benefit from the same teachings? The Social Thinking-Social Communication Profile (ST-SCP)

- Who is responsible for teaching social thinking and related social skills? Is the same set of teaching techniques relevant for all persons with ASD and related social learning challenges?

- What is a framework for teaching social thinking and related skills?

- What are some guidelines for teaching social thinking and related skills to group of students?

- How does social teaching fit into what we typically call "education"?

- What are evidence-based practices? How do they apply to teaching social thinking and related social skills?

There are no easy, clearly defined answers to these questions. Each question will invariably raise other questions. But the questions are a starting place, a launching pad for discussions among educators, parents, school administrators, and the state and national education professionals who create policy and standards.

While we wait for public policy to catch up with the ever-present and growing needs of our students, this book will open doors to a new understanding for parents, teachers, service providers, and administrators about effective ways to teach social thinking and related social skills. Our idea of what constitutes evidence-based practice within the realm of teaching social skills may shift and change. However, what remains constant is our collective goal to equip our students with the knowledge and skills to become as independent as possible while also contributing as members of society and the world at large. In this shared goal, we're truly united.

NOTE:
A Study Guide is included at the end of this book. It includes Self-Assessment Forms (pre and post reading of the book) and discussion questions for each chapter of the book.

Chapter 1

Introduction to Social Thinking and Social Skills

People think that if something feels easy to do, the mechanisms behind it must be simple.

—Cosmides

Our understanding of the cognitive and learning challenges of persons with disabilities—especially those on the autism spectrum—has evolved immensely over the last two decades. Today it's generally accepted that formal social skills training is germane to any treatment program for this population, starting from early infancy and continuing into adulthood. Within this diverse population of people with social learning weaknesses, social impairment is a hallmark struggle, and the challenges for this group aren't just within the realm of social actions. Irrespective of the intellectual capacities of these individuals, weak social learning strikes to the very core of their social awareness—impacting their ability to think and reason on a social level.

Relatively little has been done by the educational community to explore the depth and complexity of social skills instruction to those not born intuitively with these abilities. We make assumptions and recommendations on treatment from our own highly social frame of reference. We seldom stop and analyze the very different social processing mechanisms at work in the brains of these individuals. When our instructions fail and these children or adults stumble along with hit or miss social learning, we continue to attribute their failures to their disability. In reality it's we who sometimes fail our students and children by our inability to step outside our own innate social functioning and consider a new paradigm of teaching. In essence, to teach social thinking and related social skills, we need to understand how social thinking develops in neurotypical individuals, strip off the resultant preconceived notions about social development to get at the core of social teaching, and then build from there. Too often we let our assumptions guide our instruction and end up starting at a level too advanced for many of these individuals, or we offer piecemeal instruction unaware of missing information that thwarts learning. Without the requisite foundation of social knowledge to build upon, our students bob along, adrift at times, in a sea of social misunderstandings related to their weaker innate capacity for social learning.

Generalizing Social Development

By exploring what other fields have learned about social development in people and society, we, as educators can make more informed decisions and create a range of treatment programs that are effective for students with differing social knowledge.

The fields of sociology, linguistics, and anthropology explore how we develop and utilize our social skills to function as greater members of society (Allman, 1995a). Professionals in these disciplines have "repeatedly demonstrated the systematicity of various forms of communication across a host of languages and cultures" (Simmons-Mackie & Damico, 2003). What this means is simple—although communication is complex, many systems of communication transcend culture. The knowledge gained by these disciplines provides us with a better lens with which to view our students within the culture of the school and home day. Furthermore, the emerging field of cognitive science is actively exploring how neurological development from the beginning of life is responsible for our social and language development (Hirsh-Pasek, Golinkoff, & Eyer, 2003).

The overall conclusion from researchers is that the study of social development in neurotypical populations is overwhelmingly complex, regardless of how "simple" or "intuitive" the application of these social systems is perceived to be on a daily basis. Cosmides states, "People think that if something feels easy to do, the mechanisms behind it must be simple" (Allman, 1995b). We think it's exactly the other way around. Things seem simple because evolution has crafted amazingly complicated mental machinery that's up to the task and makes it seem easy.

Three critical advances in social development theory have paved the way toward a better understanding of how social thinking unfolds: executive function theory (EF), central coherence theory (CCT), and theory of mind (ToM). These developmental processes typically start in infancy and evolve throughout our years of development and into adulthood (Marshall & Fox, 2006). This chapter provides a brief introduction to these theories—they're discussed again in Chapter 4 as some of the areas of difficulty for students who have social cognitive challenges.

ToM is defined as our ability to infer a full range of mental states, which in turn cause actions, beliefs, desires, intentions, imagination, emotions, and so on (Baron-Cohen, 2000). The emergence of ToM is viewed as one of the key elements in social development (Sabbagh, 2006). Without ToM or its more basic cousin, joint attention, social development falters or is halted altogether.

The Complex Nature of Social Learning

Our social development encompasses far more than our ability to participate in conversations or other active prosocial relations. Social thinking and appropriate social actions help us navigate a world shared by other people—people with differing thoughts, motives, beliefs, desires, and perceptions. Our world is built on social structures, structures that aren't always clearly defined and are often open to subjective interpretation. Further complicating matters, social knowledge is age and situation dependent. What's an acceptable and appropriate social faculty at age three may be viewed as immature or inappropriate at age ten. For example, when teaching a preschooler to cross a street, we tell the child to first look to see if a car is coming and then wait until the car passes before stepping into the street. As a preschooler evolves into a fifth grader, the student's social awareness expands intuitively, and he learns that when crossing a street he doesn't have to wait until a coming car passes before he can cross. Instead, the fifth grader looks to see whether the driver of the approaching car sees him and recognizes the possibility of a crossing attempt. If the student thinks the driver is considering his motive to cross, he has no hesitation in stepping out into the intersection and expecting the car to slow down accordingly.

Seemingly simple social skills are, in reality, quite complex networks of interdependent thoughts and actions, supported by an equally complex organizational structure. Once again, this structure develops without effort or concrete teaching in the neurotypical child. It's a normal part of the child's social development. This isn't so for the child with social challenges. Without a structure that helps this child organize and make sense of social learning, she drifts even further without this innate compass to guide her thoughts and actions. This social organizational structure is called executive function (EF) skills, which help individuals cope with the changing demands of different situations (Barkley, 2012; Yeager & Yeager, 2013). EF skills are "required to prepare for and execute complex behavior, including planning, inhibition, mental flexibility and mental representation of tasks and goals" (Ozonoff & Griffith, 2000). They include "the cognitive processes that serve to monitor and control thought and action, such as self-regulation, planning, response inhibition and resistance to interference" (Eslinger, 1996). Executive functioning across contexts may be more appropriately termed *social executive functioning*, which contributes to an individual's ability to process complex social information conveyed through ToM. Social information processing is a multilayered process through which comprehension, pragmatic knowledge, central coherence, ToM, and EF intersect (Twachtman-Cullen, 2000).

It's not enough for an individual to have social knowledge. The student or adult must be able to systematically coordinate prior social knowledge within the context of the current situation, reading both verbal and nonverbal cues from the environment and people within it—whether or not verbal conversation is taking place. For example, a child standing alone during recess must still employ social reasoning skills, even though there's no interaction with any other kids. Social rules that govern his behavior are at play in this—and every—setting. Likewise, an adult walking into a new job site for the first time is also expected to have a certain level of social knowledge based on prior work history that she can transfer to this new setting. And it's expected that she can quickly compare her historical knowledge to the present situation and adapt the social rules that do—and don't—apply to the new setting. The ability to conceptualize our surroundings and glean the gist of what's happening through observation and language processing is critical; this core concept is referred to as central coherence theory. The critical ability to organize meaning by seeking coherence in our social observation and participation is also a critical factor in the development of social competence (Happé & Frith, 2006).

This is EF in real-life terms. Developmentally it appears EF leads the way into the development of joint attention and ToM (Pellicano, 2010). However, multiple complex skills, including language development, are also mutually beholden to the progressive further development of ToM (Landa & Goldberg, 2005). These concepts work hand-in-hand, each synergistically and dynamically encouraging the other toward higher levels of sophistication. As ToM, EF, and language skills (and likely CCT) evolve, the individual is better able to code language using increasingly sophisticated linguistic devices and becomes more adept at understanding the nuances of others' minds (De Villiers, 2000). For example, a student entering college for the first time draws on his knowledge of past education to help him understand the new and somewhat different educational environment of the college campus. The college freshman on his first day of classes would know from previous experience that he'd be getting homework in every class, so he wouldn't ask the teacher, "Do I have homework?" Instead he'd say, "Where do you post the homework?" To ask the former question would sound ignorant and cause the teacher to have a negative thought about the student. However, the latter question demonstrates a desire to succeed and shows forethought on the part of the student. To understand language in a social perspective, we need to understand the intentions and consider what we know about the previous experience of the communicative partners.

Social intelligence is but one of many types of intelligences that work collaboratively to help individuals cope and function in the world (Levine, 2002). Howard Gardner (1993) developed the multiple intelligence model of learning, identifying these seven distinct intelligences people use to interpret the world around them: language, logical mathematical analysis, spatial representation, musical thinking, the use of the body to solve problems or make things, an understanding of other individuals, and an understanding of ourselves. Gardner recognized that all people can be seen as having developmental strengths and weaknesses based on how these intelligences play out.

"While some individuals are 'at promise' in an intelligence, others are 'at risk.' In the absence of special aids, those at risk in an intelligence will be most likely to fail tasks involving that intelligence. Conversely, those at promise will be most likely to succeed. It may be that intensive intervention at an early age can bring a larger number of children to an 'at promise' level."

As Gardner points out, learning can occur through different pathways. However, active learning that arises from using one's social intelligence is a major contributor toward our ability to coexist effectively with others across a range of situations. Daniel Goleman in Emotional Intelligence (1995) and David Brooks in *The Social Animal* (2011) draw on behavioral and brain research to postulate that it isn't IQ that matters most in achieving success in the world but rather an interrelated set of emotional skills encompassing self-awareness, self-discipline, and empathy—all part and parcel of social development. Yet social skills need to be learned "on the job" through meaningful interaction with others. And herein is the Catch-22 for social development within individuals with ASD. They lack a full maturational development of social processing and responding relative to their other intellectual strengths. Without these concepts intact, they miss the opportunities to practice and hone their abilities. Without the practice, their social skills fail to fully develop.

In typical children, social cognitive processing evolves steadily, with little fanfare, through active social learning as a child grows and works through experience after experience. Although all parents and pediatricians are quick to celebrate a child walking and talking, few realize the enormous party that should be thrown when a child has established joint attention by the age of 12 months. This is one of the most pivotal and world-expanding social skills a child will learn.

On the flip side, the educational approach toward teaching students with social learning challenges is often greatly oversimplified. As Gardner (1993) also points out, "Our educational system is heavily biased toward linguistic modes of instruction and assessment and, to a somewhat lesser degree, toward logical-quantitative modes as well." We're linear thinking when it comes to education, and we usually adopt a one-method-for-everyone teaching style. Furthermore, educators and therapists erroneously assume social intelligence exists and develops in direct proportion to one's *intelligence quotient* (IQ). Based on this false assumption, why should educational systems make the time to teach something they think everyone should have learned intuitively if they're smart enough?

Even with those educators who recognize the need for formal social skills teaching, the emphasis is often toward the production of social skills in the absence of additional instruction on the social thinking that supports these skills. This is especially true for those "milder" students with ASD as well as those with social communication disorders (referred to here as ASD-SCD) who have near normal to above normal verbal IQs. We assume they "get it" socially because of their extensive vocabulary or possibly their ability to expound elaborately on a favorite subject. Research demonstrates students can learn to produce discrete social skills but often in the absence of generalization of the learned skill into other environments (Minne & Semrud-Clikeman, 2011; Rao, Beidel, & Murray, 2008; White, Keonig, & Scahill, 2007). In 2007, I theorized that a significant part of the educational problem related to teaching students social skills in isolation from larger social knowledge is that many professionals assume the students have the prerequisite social knowledge from which the skills should have originated (Winner, 2007b). For example, we teach students the steps involved in giving a compliment, assuming students understand how to apply that skill with different people in different contexts, including the possibility that we can use this skill to get our own larger desires met.

Although much has been written about social complexity from the standpoint of sociologists, linguists, cognitive psychologists, and anthropologists, relatively little of this information has been integrated into efforts to teach the metacognitive dynamics of social understanding. Knowledge gained from these disciplines is helpful toward developing treatment models and related plans for persons with social learning challenges. It's time to move beyond defining and discussing the complexity of social development and to start creating a workable and meaningful curriculum to teach social thinking and related social skills through differing lessons based on students' differing social learning abilities.

History of Social Skills Teaching

Historically, the idea of teaching social skills arose from the recognition of persons with autism—a diagnostic condition characterized by impaired social development and social abilities. When

Kanner first recognized autism in 1943, persons given this label displayed marked impairment not only in social growth but also in cognitive and language development. This triad of deficiencies led professionals to create early teaching programs that were strongly based on behavioral methods. Typical social communication skills, such as making eye contact or communicating simple requests, were identified as missing by the educator or therapist and then taught through the application of behavioral reward systems. It was assumed that basic behavioral principles—such as shaping, repetition, and reinforcement—would result in the student's improved ability to learn basic concepts.

It became common practice to use applied behavior analysis (ABA) to teach students not just appropriate behavior, but language, communication, and social skills as well. ABA has proven to be successful in helping children with autism develop increased basic social competencies. This type of teaching program is now broadly used with toddler and preschool-aged children and is often referred to as "early intensive behavioral intervention." ABA is a set of principles that governs treatment programs, and professionals vary widely in their application and execution of these principles. ABA program models include the more regimented, structured format of Discrete Trial Training (DTT), similar to the formats created by O. Ivar Lovaas (1987), but also now include more naturalistic ABA teachings such as Pivotal Response Therapy (PRT) (Koegel & Koegel, 2006) and Picture Exchange Communication System (PECS) (Bondy & Frost, 2002). Because it has empirical research to support its efficacy, ABA is considered a sound teaching methodology to use with individuals with ASD-SCD. Clearly measured improvement has been witnessed in the majority of students with autism using these different techniques (Perry & Condillac, 2003). However, we must take into consideration how and by what standards we define "improvement." Behavior-based methods seek to change behavior and may not necessarily attend to the underlying thoughts, perceptions, motives, and beliefs from which behavior arises. Although ABA can improve behavior—a monumental step in improving the lives of children and adults with ASD—historically we've focused on the behavior action itself rather than on behavior change arising naturally from an internal shift in self-awareness and social perception on the part of the individual with autism. An ongoing challenge within behaviorally-based research is the difficulty students have generalizing the social skills they've learned in one environment to a new but similar situation.

As the number of children diagnosed on the autism spectrum has continued to grow, in recent years in alarming proportions, our efforts to better understand and define this increasingly heterogeneous community of individuals have also evolved. Our behavioral treatments are being reexamined and refined to become more child-focused and flexible enough to adapt to the different learning styles of individuals with ASD-SCD.

Teaching social skills through behavioral methods is best when teaching social rules, yet our social world seldom operates within such a prescribed and rigid framework. Exceptions are often more common than the rules. Although the use of social rules may help improve social behavior in individuals with severe to moderate social learning challenges, such rule-based social information is unable to capture the essence of refined social communication. Social nuance and sophistication are at the heart of neurotypical peer-based relationships starting in school and continuing into adulthood. The subtle lift of an eyebrow may question whether the speaker's information is credible; the nuanced tilt of the head may serve to greet another person or perhaps provide a signal for the direction a person should turn next. The ability to discern meaning from almost imperceptible social signals requires active reading of people in context. Instead of teaching students to adhere to a singular social rule, we need to teach our students to think and respond to multiple processes in multiple ways to be considered socially sophisticated. These higher level social lessons are accessible to some of our students with more subtle but significant social learning challenges. However, they'll fail to be lessons we can teach others with ASD and related disabilities who are born to more challenged social neurology.

The Call for Evidence-Based Practice

In the mid-1990s, the increasing numbers of students with autism and Asperger's Syndrome in our school systems resulted in widespread concern as teachers unfamiliar with the disorder and its manifestations were forced to attempt to learn "on the fly" how to work effectively with these students. Instruction manuals were nonexistent, and it wasn't until the late 1990s that published books on teaching students with ASD could easily be found. Some educators adapted and were able to modify their teaching methods and curriculum to present material in a way that made sense to their students. Others struggled, without proper training and administrative support, left alone to deal with students who didn't respond to traditional teaching methods and "the way we always do it" mentality. It was at best a hit or miss way of teaching students.

However, as time passed, workable strategies from in-the-trenches teachers and professionals made their way into curriculum guides, books, and workshops specifically for educators who were seeking to learn. Information available via the Internet opened up a new avenue for sharing effective ideas. Both parents and educators began to realize that many of these students were assisted by the more robust use of visual and concrete explanation of social information that benefited their academic as well as their social learning abilities. Hope was revived within the ASD-SCD community that these students could be taught. However, it was also recognized that many of the concepts and skills the students needed to learn related to more practical information than that typically taught in an academically-based classroom. Lessons on social problem solving and life skills were critical for those with social learning challenges.

Then in 2001 the education climate shifted with the passage of the No Child Left Behind Act (NCLB). NCLB called for more scientifically-based research (SBR) to be paired with our educational teachings (NCLB, 2002). "Evidence-based practices"—education practices grounded in research—became the new buzzword in schools and boardrooms across the nation.

What a tight spot for teachers everywhere to be in! To date, the only method with SBR to support its use for teaching individuals with ASD-SCD is ABA. Many bright, curious, creative teachers had discovered alternative methods for teaching students with ASD-SCD, but their teaching strategies weren't SBR. The alternative methods, which included in part relationship development, sensory integration, and Social Thinking hadn't been formally studied or had double-blind, placebo-controlled studies backing up their efficacy. Thus began the dilemma of teachers everywhere of how to meet the requirement imposed on them by NCLB involving using only evidence-based practices. The only evidence-based practice for this population of students was ABA, and even some methods within ABA weren't even evidence-based, such as methods for teaching social communication.

As the heterogeneous nature of individuals with ASD-SCD became more and more evident, so did the appreciation that one instruction method wasn't appropriate for all students with ASD. The principles of ABA may facilitate some level of learning for all spectrum students. However, ABA doesn't adequately address the whole treatment program for students with ASD or like disabilities who have higher cognitive and linguistic abilities (Simpson, 2005). Teaching pragmatics—the social use of language—and associated verbal and nonverbal social communication skills through behavior analysis discounts the core synergistic conceptual problems associated with having weak social cognition. Social skills can't be isolated and taught apart from their context, from the executive functioning skills that support them, or from the social thinking strategies that preclude the action. Furthermore, many studies now confirm that those who function on the higher end of the autism spectrum or with a range of social communication diagnoses often have comorbid mental health challenges such as anxiety and depression (Abell & Hare, 2005; Bellini, 2004; Farrugia, & Hudson, 2006; Hedley & Young, 2006; Reaven et al., 2009; Stewart, Barnard, Pearson, Hasan, & O'Brien, 2006). This indicates that social emotional support goes hand-in-hand with social pragmatic treatments.

Addressing the complexity of each student's needs, based on her personal social cognitive and social emotional challenges, is a precursor to developing effective and appropriate treatment for this group of students. Also, social rules and nuance evolve with age, and the academic curriculum requires students to use more sophisticated social knowledge to discern meaning from their language arts curriculum or to understand how to relate to their peers to meet educational standards related to science lab participation. One size doesn't fit all; one method isn't appropriate for all. My clinical experience has led me to conclude that successful programs are those that appreciate the individual nature of each student and base treatment on the student's unique combination of social, behavioral, and emotional needs in addition to considering the student's temperament and developmental age.

Richard Simpson (2006) points out that the requirement of using scientifically-based research, while well intended, is difficult if not impossible to apply, given the complex and varied makeup of individuals with ASD. Simpson urges more thought be given at the national level to how we define evidence-based practice and the criteria we use to prove a treatment technique is of sound practice. At the same time, Simpson also encourages the community of educational care providers to take a deeper look at establishing treatment programs for students with ASD, based on key features specific to this population, that will help persons with ASD cope better with their learning challenges.

It's also important to note that even now definitions for evidence-based practice vary from field to field. The American Speech-Language-Hearing Association (ASHA) defines evidence-based practice as an approach that considers client-family values in combination with treatment evidence provided by experienced clinicians (ASHA, 2005).

One size doesn't fit all; one method isn't appropriate for all. Successful programs are those that appreciate the individual nature of each student.

In spite of the disagreement over what constitutes evidence-based practice and the immaturity of our instruction programs in general for students with ASD, public school system administrators are aggressively pursuing social skills programs that are evidence-based. In doing this, they're failing to appreciate the very complex nature of their quest as it applies to students with a range of social learning challenges. Few have stopped to ask pressing and highly relevant questions such as these:

- What's meant by the term *social skills program*?

- How can we relate this treatment need to evidence-based practices?

- Is it reasonable to assume there can be one social skills treatment program for all students diagnosed with social learning challenges?

- Is it even feasible to gather research evidence solely on social skills performance, which by definition, is highly subjective, fluid, and changing from context to context?

Relevant Questions Rarely Asked

The underlying reason to pursue evidence-based measures is to clearly define, as much as is possible, sound, effective treatment and education programs for persons with ASD-SCD. If we're to respond to requests or government imposed regulations that require their use, it behooves those professionals upon which this responsibility lies to first fully consider the nature of ASD-SCD in general, and social skills specifically, to answer pivotal questions upon which these treatments will be formulated. Not all life-relevant learning can be neatly parceled out into discrete units that can be uniformly

Is it even feasible to think that evidence-based practices can be developed for teaching social skills?

defined and then broken down sufficiently into teachable segments for this diverse group of social learners. That reality, in and of itself, poses a huge challenge when teaching social thinking and related social skills to individuals with ASD-SCD. Is it even feasible to think that SBR can be developed for teaching social competencies? Other, equally important questions merit discussion before any evidence-based treatment program can be created, questions such as: What, specifically, needs to be treated in these students? What's involved in the treatment process? What outcome is expected from the treatment? What challenges might the student continue to have across the life span?

To assume there will be no lingering problems for this population post-high school, that any evidence-based practice will be sufficient to remediate autism, is to assume we can cure people with ASD-SCD. Our current understanding of those diagnosed with ASD-SCD is that this is a lifelong disorder that involves varying degrees of symptom amelioration that fluctuate from individual to individual. Even if we could "cure" people of their autism, the larger ethical question arises—should we? A very vocal and growing group of adults on the spectrum suggests that not all persons with ASD want that option. Keep in mind, many of our society's most notable inventions have been created by the highly focused, intelligent minds of people with social learning challenges, such as those individuals highlighted in the book *Scholars with Autism Achieving Dreams* (Perner, 2012).

Yet we must begin someplace. Both parents and professionals seek best practices when it comes to helping individuals with ASD-SCD learn and achieve at their highest functional capacity in the world. As the educators and clinicians who take on the responsibility of designing such programs, our job is to continually investigate and question existing assumptions about persons with ASD-SCD and the manner in which we teach and treat them. If we seek evidence-based practices for teaching social skills and social thinking, our first step is to thoroughly define the issue, then use this information to formulate intervention strategies that eventually will be researched.

It's time to abandon the quest for a singular program to treat individuals with ASD–especially within the realm of social skills, and start focusing on patterns of thinking and processing that point us to common ground within the spectrum.

In essence, we need to explore curriculum development and learning principles. We also need to "take data" on whether or not our teaching methods are able to provide our students with information upon which they can further problem solve their own social dilemmas. If not, we may need to rethink our methods, adapt, and try something new. Success won't be instantaneous, nor will it be at all likely that one program will emerge that's equally effective across the board for individuals with ASD-SCD. The very nature of the disorder—one that's characterized by a broad spectrum of strengths and challenges—precludes this. It's time to abandon the quest for a singular teaching program to treat individuals with such a wide range of social learning challenges—especially within the realm of teaching social skills. We need to start focusing on patterns of thinking and processing in our students that will steer us toward creating more relevant treatments for those with ASD-SCD. By asking different questions, we may discover subsets among this population for which one type of program achieves more success than does another. Before we can look for research-based clinical evidence, we have to clearly define what we're teaching, to whom, and why. We want evidence-based practice now (or yesterday), but starting today we need to discuss what treatment techniques we should measure in the first place and how to meaningfully take data to assess their effectiveness.

The remainder of this book poses many of the seldom-asked but vital questions that underscore the development of sound social skills teaching programs. These questions ask us to explore and consider the depth and complexity of teaching social skills to those born with limited social insight. Answers to these questions come in the form of relevant information from both research and clinical practice. These answers will hopefully broaden our perspectives enough to spur more creative thought toward treatment. We can also begin to map out a continuum of services that's more reliant on ABA at one end and cognitive behavior therapy and related mental health services at the other end. Perhaps this will emerge as the basis for what can eventually become evidence-based social skills programs that can be formed for those individuals with higher cognitive and linguistic skills. At minimum, these questions steer us to think much more about how to teach social thinking and related social skills before we decide how best to approach working with a specific person with social learning challenges. The reader may also find this information helps to rethink how we teach all students about social learning to help each person understand what it means to relate well to others.

....

Chapter 2

What Are Social Skills?

T alk to five different adults, and each will probably have a different definition of social skills. Probe further, and each will probably have different ideas of what constitutes "good" and "bad" social skills. Take this exercise to a community of Latino or Hindu families, and the answers will again be somewhat different. When we talk about social skills, we often describe individual problematic skills rather than explore the topic conceptually. How are we to develop educational and mental health programs dedicated to helping students with "poor social skills" when we, as parents and professionals, lack agreement as to what this all means? To develop more meaningful social skills programs, we need to explore how we define social skills and the other concepts that help us figure out how to use and maintain appropriate social skills with diverse people and contexts.

Weak social thinking and related social skills generally arise from two sources. The first is an inability to communicate effectively, to express oneself in verbal and nonverbal ways. The second is an inability or weakness to figure out how to engage in the process of social thinking and understanding one's own and others' emotions which impairs effective adaptations of one's behavior in different contexts. Some individuals are strong verbal communicators but lack the ability to know when, where, why, and how to apply their interpersonal skills. They just don't fit in, despite their obvious academic intelligence and verbal capabilities.

In real life, these social learning challenges play out continually. For instance, to participate in a classroom with reasonable success requires more nonverbal know-how of generally accepted social dos and don'ts and contextual cues than active verbal communication. This is true the majority of the time we interact with our world. Most instances where we have to monitor and possibly modify our social presentation occur in the absence of direct social communication. When we step onto an elevator filled with strangers, we adapt our behavior by stepping to the side and silently staring at the elevator door or floor numbers. It's generally accepted as what we do when riding an elevator. Contrast this with the social contextual requirements of joining a large dinner party. In this setting, even though the room is filled with unfamiliar people, each participant is expected to actively engage socially. The uncommunicative wallflower is seen as socially odd, unable to fit in, and less likely to be invited back again. Instances requiring social understanding and social adaptation exist by the thousands during any typical day. An individual who struggles is easily overwhelmed by this multilayered process, one which was learned innately by neurotypical peers.

Effective adaptation to a situation shared by other people happens on the fly, off the cuff. As much as we may rehearse appropriate social skills, encounters with people are fluid exchanges, requiring flexibility in thought and action. No two encounters unfold in exactly the same way. In any given situation, we consider what we know about the context (formal or laid-back; boisterous or subdued) and the people within that set-

> Social thinking is the master key that unlocks all the other social doors.

ting (strangers, acquaintances, family, longtime friends) to gauge what we can say and do to gain entry into the group. Our ability to engage in this social algebraic equation is done at a minimally con-scious level, often in nanoseconds of time. To complicate things, social adaptation isn't only about engaging. Sometimes the appro-priate or preferred social response isn't to directly interact or com-municate. Lightning quick thoughts and sensory input give us the clues we need to make a decision to act or not act, speak or remain silent, engage or walk away.

Social thinking is the master key that unlocks all the other social doors.

Employing pragmatics—the social use of language and appropriate social interpretation of spoken messages—is no less challenging. Brown and Yule (1983), researchers about teaching and assessing effective spoken communication, explore in great detail the mul-tifunctional nature of communication, even at the level of spoken language. There are few specific language utterances that are inter-preted exactly the same way by all.

Ultimately, the application of social thinking and expected social skills is a complex, active, fluid process that goes far beyond adherence to a set of behavior rules related to a specific context. Social expectations evolve in nuance and sophistication with age. Appropriate social actions stem from an inner social understanding that takes into account the individual, the social partners (if any), the environment, the cultural norms of that context within a specific community, and each participant's knowledge, affiliation, and impressions of the other persons in the environment.

To teach these concepts, we as educators must interpret what we're teaching much more broadly than we have to date; there can be no one set of social skills that drives all instruction. Educators should understand the complex nature of social behavior and teach within a framework that's highly driven by context and social understanding. We need to go beyond simply helping students learn the overt and hidden rules of social conversations or practice step-by-step social actions. A student who can't adapt effectively to the nonverbal expectations of the classroom will have little social success in or outside the classroom setting. Peers interpret, respond to, and remember each other's social behavior from the beginning of their play group experiences and certainly throughout their school-age years. Social skills are life skills. We must integrate social teaching early and view this as continual, ongoing instruction.

Chapter 3

What Are the Origins of Social Development?

Is There an Age When Our Social Development Stops?

The 1990s were designated the "Decade of the Brain" by President George H.W. Bush to enhance public awareness of the benefits to be derived from research on the brain. The impact of this research and understanding of the brain overflowed into the realm of social development. Advances in neuroimaging coupled with an increasing interest in exploring the subtleties of the mind have resulted in more research attention to social thinking and social relatedness. In fact, this interest spawned a new field called social cognitive neuroscience (Adolphs, 2003).

We now know more than we ever have about the origins of social development. Social development starts prior to birth through embryonic neurological formations. Social functioning emerges as babies actively pursue learning through their experiences. Multiple books are devoted to revealing the research detailing critical and intuitive social growth milestones (Gopnik, Meltzoff, & Kuhl, 1999; Hirsh-Pasek et al., 2003; Marshall & Fox, 2006). In just 36 hours of life, babies can distinguish between facial expressions (Field et al., 1983); by seven months babies can match vocal expressions of emotion to facial expression (Walker, 1982). Prelinguistic infants may also be able to understand that people's actions are motivated by internal mental states, an early developmental feature of theory of mind (Kuhlmeier, Wynn, & Bloom, 2003).

By age one, most infants are pointing to show what interests them or to indicate what they desire. Language development begins in earnest around this time. Typically developing children talk about things of interest in their world as well as what they desire. As they learn to express themselves, they also continue to explore what others are thinking and feeling. Meltzoff (1995) demonstrated that 18-month-old infants will follow through to complete an action they saw an adult intend to do, although the adult failed to complete it. Children start to use emotional words such as "mad," "happy," and "scared" at around two years of age (Bloom, 1998).

Marshall and Fox (2006) define multiple components working together in early development toward social engagement. These include perceiving and identifying social stimuli, the processes involved in the experience of emotion, and developing shared affective experience, such as joint attention.

A range of social, emotional, and behavior regulation skills emerges through infancy and early childhood leading to shared imaginative play and ultimately cooperative play. As children's minds move into more abstract thinking, their play shifts from concrete (a car is a car) to more abstract play (a car can be an airplane). As they continue to evolve in their social thinking, they also incorporate other children into their play, first by sitting near them when they play (parallel play) and then by playing more directly with peers. By four years of age, children aren't only playing together but are pretending together.

A typically developing child's mind becomes highly socially attuned toward group participation by the preschool years. Social thinking and related social skills are critical for a child to succeed in most future academic and social learning environments—kindergarten, elementary, middle or junior high school, and high school, not to mention the college campus or job site.

Language, social and emotional thought, and perception of a situation appear to work synergistically on the same social cognitive team, moving us along in social development. As these abilities evolve during the early years, more abstract social communicative skills emerge, such as narrative language (Franke & Durbin, 2011; Rooney Moreau, 2010). Narrative thinking and narrative-language skills allow us to conceptualize and share ourselves and our personal stories with the world around us. These are fundamental skills in forming social, emotional, communicative, and academic connections in life. Children quickly learn to modify their narrative language, based on the context of the environment. For example, they need to share far less descriptive detail when talking to a family member about the vacation they experienced together as compared to explaining the same event to a friend who hadn't been on the vacation. Determining the level of information, emotions, and the sequence of events one speaker needs to provide to the other depends heavily on the level of prior knowledge about each other shared by the communicative partners.

We're all active learners of social information throughout our life span.

Students who have difficulty with narrative thinking or conceptualizing temporal or causal aspects of events and describing them with increasing syntactical complexity may be unable to use narration as a tool for the kinds of thinking and the assignments routinely required in school (Miller, Gillam, & Pena, 2001). Narrative thinking is critical for the ability to produce coherent written expression. If one doesn't understand how to sequence written information to help the reader follow the writer's thoughts, narrative problems will result. Good narrative language requires the writer to consider the reader and what the reader needs to know and to organize sentences and content in a coherent manner. Even though writing is often done in isolation, it's an act predicated on social thinking.

This complex evolution of social emotional adaptation and social communication continues as we get older. It contributes in large measure to what we call "maturation" and "wisdom." Our social emotional development never stops; there's no ceiling to what we can learn socially. Therefore, it's ineffective and impractical to view social skills instruction as a stand-alone curriculum or a singular set of rules independent of age, experience, and setting. Social rules change as we age. Third grade marks a developmental shift in social functioning—from the black and white realm of "right" and "wrong" actions into social behavior based on nuance and sophistication. The social behaviors we accept as normal for dealing with a conflict as a four-year-old aren't those we deem acceptable during elementary school, teen years, or young adulthood.

We're all active learners of social information throughout our life span. Therefore, successful treatment programs for persons with social cognitive learning challenges are built on principles that grow with the child.

These programs are:

- Dynamic: They're driven by the unique needs and challenges of each individual, rather than a one-size-fits-all approach.

- Flexible: They're constantly changing based on the age, situation or context, and social and cognitive problem-solving abilities of the person.

- Ongoing: Our social responsibilities increase in complexity as we age. It's unreasonable to think that early social learning instruction will result in students who have no need of services as they move into adolescence and young adulthood.

  It's also daunting—and unproductive—to think we can "catch a child up" to normal or typical social learning. Although it's true that our students can show remarkable progress in their social thinking, their neurotypical peer group is always pushing ahead due to their innate ability for intuitive social learning. We can lessen the gap between these two diverse peer groups; however, we shouldn't set goals or expect children with social weaknesses to think on a par with their neurotypical peers. That said, we can't be teaching the social conventions of yesterday. Our teaching needs to keep up with the shifting perceptions, morals, and cultures of our students' peer group and larger community if our goal is for our students to fit into the world as it exists today.

In What Areas of Social Thinking Do Students with Social Cognitive Challenges Struggle? The ILAUGH Model Remodeled

Many top researchers in the field of social cognition have described key concepts that appear to be pivotal in the development of the social mind—central coherence, theory of mind, executive function, emotion regulation, and sensory integration. Several of these concepts have been identified as significantly contributing to the social, communicative, and self-regulation processing problems experienced in varying degrees by all persons with ASD-SCD. This chapter first summarizes each of these concepts and its relevance to students with social cognitive challenges. The chapter then presents the ILAUGH Model of Social Cognition, a framework designed to help guide the development of treatment strategies for social and academic improvement for school-aged students and adults (Winner, 2000).

Central Coherence Theory (CCT)

As mentioned in Chapter 1, central coherence theory (CCT) explains a weakness in concept formation. Persons with challenges in building central coherence tend to focus more on the facts or details rather than the conceptual whole. Many students and adults with high-functioning autism or Asperger's Syndrome have explained that they never know what a book or movie is about, but they enjoy the details in the story. A person with more classic autism may play with the wheels of a car for hours yet never recognize the object (a toy car) or its function. Other students with high-functioning autism may check off steps in a sequence (get bread, jelly, and peanut butter; open jars; spread jelly on one slice of bread) as they accomplish them but not realize the overall purpose of doing the related sequential steps (to make a peanut butter and jelly sandwich when you're hungry). Concept formation is the infrastructure supporting most aspects of our academic curriculum (reading comprehension, written expression, and organizational skills). It's also the foundation of social relations and the ability to live independently as adults through adaptive life skills (cleaning an apartment, paying bills, shopping for food as part of meal planning, and so on).

Central coherence is the term used to describe one's ability to think conceptually—to form gestalts we then deconstruct to arrive at the related details. Uta Frith, a developmental psychologist, introduced this theory in the late 1980s to describe the ability of neurotypical children and adults to derive meaning from more global information. This is in contrast to persons with ASD, who appeared to have a stronger tendency to attend to and remember the details and surface structure but demonstrated weaker ability to "see the big picture." Frith (1989) hypothesized that this lack of conceptualization of information was at the heart of the social issues experienced by persons with ASD.

CCT gained a lot of attention and related research, which Happé and Frith (2006) reviewed to explain their more current thinking, in which they explore central coherence as a perceptual process that may be seen as both a weakness and strength for persons with ASD. Their strength is a tendency toward superior local or detailed focused processing, which then leads directly to the weakness of poor global, conceptual processing. This type of functioning suggests these individuals have a processing bias or cognitive style that's more detail focused. This can be overcome to some extent when they're given information in a manner that helps them to explicitly see the connections between the details and related core concepts. There are neurotypical people with this processing bias (think about some engineers, scientists, or doctors) who don't have the larger presentation of social cognitive learning challenges. Hence, more recently weak central coherence isn't seen as a primary cause of symptoms related to ASD but as an important contributing factor. Furthermore, those with social learning challenges who have poor central coherence struggle with generalization of learning from one situation to another. Generalization is the ability to learn how to do something in one situation and then apply what was learned in another situation. Applying similar skills across situations requires students to have extracted the gist of what they learned and be able to effectively transition that information into a new situation where all the details aren't the same, but where they can still understand how to apply the core concepts of their learning. Students who learn skills through rote memorization of details related to a specific situation will struggle much more to transition their learning across environments (Hume, Loftin, & Lantz, 2009; Plaisted, 2001). Dr. Peter Vermuelen, in his book *Autism as Context Blindness* (2012), further addresses the depth and complexity of CCT and how a weakness in this area can have profound impact on how persons interpret and respond to the information they perceive or fail to perceive.

Joint Attention and Theory of Mind (ToM)

Our earliest social developmental milestones, if we know to pay attention to them, have to do with connecting with others' minds. By the time most children are nine to fourteen months old, they've established joint attention—the ability to look at a person's eyes and track his eye gaze to see what he's looking at. This provides the opportunity to figure out what others are thinking about (Baron-Cohen, 2010; Jones & Carr, 2004). The development of this critical skill, which lies as a foundation of social communication and social emotional growth, is acquired intuitively through the steady progress of the neurotypical infant's emerging mind. Early developing aspects of joint attention begin to emerge in children from three to six months old, with more sophisticated elements that require integrated social coordination of attention and communication with social partners occurring as late as eighteen months of age (Baron-Cohen, Baldwin, & Crowson, 1997; Tomasello, Carpenter, Call, Behne, & Moll, 2005).

As children establish basic joint attention, they're making their first predictions about what people are thinking about and what they may do next.

The amazing evolution of the social mind continues and by the end of neurotypical children's fourth year, they can engage at a reasonable level of cooperative, negotiated, shared imaginative play while communicating and regulating their own emotions in the presence of others. At this point children are learning that not everyone shares their perspective—some like to play differently from others—but that doesn't mean that children can't figure out how to play together.

However, some individuals have a weakness in theory of mind, the cognitive process in which we consider our own and others' thoughts, beliefs, prior knowledge, intentions, and personalities. ToM is often a significant contributing factor as to why persons with ASD-SCD don't learn to communicate, play, or converse as effectively as their neurotypical peers. Throughout our lives we engage in a nearly unending process of trying to determine the mental states of others—their emotions, desires, beliefs, and intentions (Flavell, 2004; Westby, 2012). Recent research has begun to explore the very early emergence of ToM, beginning in infancy, and the prerequisite acquisition of joint attention for the fuller development of ToM. Like CCT, ToM operates most often in our daily functioning below the level of fully conscious thought or reasoning, whether we're actively engaged in social interaction or thinking about a response to a past or future interaction.

Frith and Frith (2010) describe that the social brain has a ToM, which enables us to predict what others are going to do on the basis of their desires and beliefs. They go on to explain that we read intention into each other's movements even when the person we're observing is an unintentional communicative agent.

Early development of ToM begins with the emergence of joint attention and evolves in nature to a point where we can measure specific basic stages of ToM development in preschool and early elementary school neurotypical children.

The first stage beyond joint attention is referred to as first-order ToM; this is marked by a child understanding and then being able to verbally describe knowing her thoughts are different from another person's. Most children have developed this capacity by four to five years of age.

The second stage beyond joint attention is called second-order ToM, which marks when children engage in false beliefs and have a solid understanding that people may lie, cheat, and steal through the ability to manipulate others' minds. This is developing solidly in neurotypical children in their sixth year. Although the ability to describe a mental process, such as the different stages of theory of mind with language, may not emerge until ages four to six, clever researchers have been able to demonstrate that this knowledge is emerging in much younger children even though the children aren't able to verbally describe what they're thinking (Repacholi & Gopnik, 1997). However, for children with ASD-SCD it appears this early learning process is delayed or disordered to different degrees for different children on the social learning continuum. Some of our students with ASD-SCD appear to have severe limitations in their understanding of these basic ToM concepts, and these limitations last throughout their lives in spite of strong treatment interventions to assist with their social learning. Many individuals with ASD-SCD who we refer to as "higher functioning" (in that they have functional language, a reasonably strong academic cognition, and have acquired two basic stages of ToM) still demonstrate weaknesses in perspective taking.

A challenge for researchers has been to identify more sophisticated stages of ToM to help us understand the difficulties we observe in our higher functioning adolescents and adults as they attempt to participate in social interactions. The researchers have noted that though the higher functioning group can pass tests related to social knowledge, social problem solving, and social communication, a significant discrepancy exists between their high test scores and how they actually function socially (Klin, Jones, Schultz, & Volkmar, 2003). As a result, researchers developed two "advanced ToM" tests: the Strange Stories Test and the Faux-Pas Test (Spek, Scholte, & Van Berckelaer-Onnes, 2010). The Strange Stories Test (Happé, 1994) provides vignettes that present everyday situations in which people say things they don't mean literally. The person taking the test has to describe the intended meaning. In the Faux-Pas Test (Stone, Baron-Cohen, & Knight, 1998), the participants were asked if anyone said anything awkward or something that questioned an underlying motive. While these tests may appear useful, in my experience, many very high functioning adolescents and adults can pass the Faux-Pas and the Strange Stories tests but still manifest significant issues in vocational and leisure daily interactions. All this being said, the researchers continue to discuss the fact that we've yet to create the definitive test of ToM that captures the very real but subtle issues experienced in language-based relations by so many of the highest functioning individuals who have ASD-SCD.

Executive Function Skills (EF)

As discussed in Chapter 1, we use executive function skills (EF) to effectively multitask, plan, organize, and implement strategies to work toward a goal (Happé, Booth, Charlton, & Hughes, 2006). There are multiple types of executive function skills (Carlson, 2009). We use them in projects of a tangible, concrete nature (building block towers when we're very young to building bridges as a profession) and in those endeavors that are intangible, involving social, creative, analytical, or abstract mental processing. The ability to use cognitive organization to develop effective concrete or mental plans has been recognized as impaired in most persons with social cognitive learning challenges. Social interactions require active processing of multiple sources of information (sensory, thoughts and emotions of self or others, and contextual).

Individuals who see all the details yet can't organize or relate them to each other are easily overwhelmed. In response, they withdraw inward, retreat, or become highly anxious. Although the term "executive function skills" has mostly been used to discuss poor organizational skills, they're really comprehensive information-processing abilities that are integral to just about any physical or mental action

Executive functioning is the toolbox that allows us to effectively use split second, multisignal processing, planning, and responding.

we take. EF is emerging as a foundational cognitive concept for the development of the social mind. It's the toolbox that allows us to effectively use split second, multisignal processing, planning, and responding.

"Executive function skills" was first used to describe the multiple skills and functions executives need to perform to complete their job. It describes the fact that we're required to engage in many complex tasks to achieve higher level cognitive functioning. Activities ranging from tracking and responding to others' minds to the use of social communication and social pragmatics involve EF (Hill, 2004). Happé, Booth, Charlton, and Hughes (2006) found that EF deficits were characteristic of several clinical disorders including ASD and ADHD, with these EF learning challenges associated with specific aspects of social communication and social adaptation. Pellicano (2010) describes research demonstrating that early development of EF skills may lay the foundation for the development of ToM abilities.

Although the link between EF and CCT still needs to be explored, the theory suggests that the understanding of the big picture or the gist of social relatedness is tied to one's ability to structure thoughts or ideas into some coherent whole while considering many things at once. Think about how, in real life, we all don't really "maintain a topic" when talking with our peers. Communicative partners in spontaneous conversation track the concepts being discussed and make comments that connect back to any one of a number of ideas expressed. We maintain a connection to the central ideas put forth, but our goal is more about sharing our thoughts than staying on topic.For example, if I say, "I was in Washington D.C. visiting the Lincoln Memorial, and I was thinking about the current election," notice the lack of clear topic. My communicative partner could then respond by talking about her experience in Washington D.C. or even some other town she has recently visited; she could comment on the Lincoln Memorial or anything in history that reminds her of Lincoln or the Civil War, or she could talk about a memorial she visited, or she could possibly talk about the elections or something else she felt was in some way related to what I just said. As long as her comment or question is one that could be tracked back as related to the comment or question recently spoken or eluded to, the direction of the conversation has a free range.

Logically,this means that EF, ToM, and CCT are all integrating for us to maintain our connection with each other. However, this synergistic relationship is yet to be proved through research. What we do know is that it's very common for persons with ASD-SCD to have challenges in the sophisticated development of their ToM, CCT, and EF.

Emotional Processing/Emotional Regulation

Emotional processing/emotional regulation is the ability to recognize emotions within ourselves and others and to regulate our actions based on these perceived emotions (Attwood, 2003; Prizant, Wetherby, Rubin, Laurent, & Rydell, 2006). It's a social expectation that we relate to others based on how we feel and how we're making others feel. Like the other core concepts mentioned previously, emotional regulation is fundamental to effective social communicative skill development (Bronson, 2000). Social cognitive processing and the actions we make in response to this processing can't be considered outside of emotional regulation; social regulation is emotional regulation.

Individuals with ASD-SCD experience many challenges in emotional regulation, beginning at a very basic level with challenges in recognizing their own emotions. Many bright individuals with social learning challenges struggle to recognize, name, and gauge the intensity of their feelings or those exhibited by others. For some, their feelings may seem black and white, on or off, hot or cold, with no middle degrees of intensity until they learn better emotional recognition and regulation strategies. ToM is strongly linked to sophisticated emotional regulation; we have to be aware that people think and feel differently to consider what someone else is feeling and how this differs from our own emotional experience. High-functioning individuals with weak emotional regulation are often unable to establish self-calming and self-regulation strategies without being provided with cognitively-based emotional learning strategies.

Sensory Integration

Sensory integration is "the organization of sensation for use" (Ayres, 1979). We learn about our world through all our senses, not just through mental processing. Students with social learning challenges often have difficulty synthesizing sensory information. Any one or a combination of senses may be distorted. Individuals may be hypersensitive or hyposensitive (or both) and their sensory systems may fluctuate from day to day, even hour to hour. Sensory disintegration makes it difficult for the body and mind to process and respond efficiently, resulting in individuals feeling out of balance (Myles, Cook, Miller, Rinner, & Robbins, 2000). Sensory integration challenges potentially limit the information a person can absorb and process effectively, negatively impacting the person's ability to learn and behaviorally or emotionally cope with the complex world around him.

Development of the ILAUGH Model

Most professionals working directly with persons with ASD-SCD will agree that the weaknesses in the concepts described above are far easier to identify than they are to treat. Researchers continue to debate the similarities and differences among these concepts (Beaumont & Newcomb, 2006). Logically, it's easy to see how all of these concepts clearly overlap and work synergistically within the same individual. Isn't emotional regulation related to sensory processing as well as to an ability to consider another person's point of view? How does sensory regulation impact a person's ability to process the social cues required to develop ToM? Research, including

The take-home message is clear:
teaching social thinking and social skills requires that we take into consideration the whole child, rather than pick and choose social lessons and then assume they'll generalize across widely differing contexts.

studies by Pellicano and Happé and Frith previously mentioned, is actively emerging to show the connections among these core concepts that most parents and practitioners observe on a daily basis. Our programs must address all these core concepts and integrate them into a program that recognizes the complex social information-processing systems at work in individuals with social learning challenges, regardless of their diagnostic label. The question becomes—how do we do this?

As educators we look for teaching methods that can be replicated—methods that have a reasonable amount of structure to facilitate such replication and that provide us with ways to assess whether or not a strategy is working and to make appropriate changes if it's not. Within the realm of teaching social thinking and related social skills, this can be challenging. The abstract and not easily qualified nature of the core social concepts, coupled with their interdependent relationship, renders most professionals speechless when it comes to creating any type of organized, shared curriculum. We want standardized, logical, methodical teaching methods for a skill set that functions in a decidedly out-of-the-box realm of processing.

It was in the 1990s that I became aware of this lack of connection between what the research has taught us conceptually and cognitively about students with higher level language learning abilities with ASD-SCD and the predominantly behaviorally-based treatment programs established for these students. In response, in 2000, I created the ILAUGH Model of Social Cognition as a synergistic framework to help guide the development of a practical treatment methodology for both social and academic improvement.

The ILAUGH model explores a range of social learning issues and how these impact academic learning for many of our students. It addresses many conceptual-learning challenges described previously, providing the foundation knowledge and know-how to develop related treatment strategies for school-aged students and adults. Conceptually, the ILAUGH model is used as a guide by parents and professionals. It helps them to further understand their student's deeper learning strengths and challenges. It's not a curriculum model in and of itself or a step-by-step teaching outline. Every child with social learning challenges is different. The ILAUGH model gives us the framework and the tools upon which we create programs tailored to each child or adult while also helping us to describe with more depth what we routinely and casually refer to merely as a "social skills problem." The components of ILAUGH are described in the rest of this chapter.

I = Initiation of Communication

Initiation of communication is the ability to use verbal and nonverbal skills to establish social relations and to seek assistance or information from others (Rao, Beidel, & Murray, 2008). Many students with social learning challenges have significant problems initiating communication in stressful situations or when information isn't easily understood. Language retrieval is difficult in anything other than calm, secure situations. Even within the higher functioning population with ASD-SCD, the student's ability to talk about a favorite topic of interest or to attempt to crack a joke can exist in sharp contrast to how that student communicates when needing help or when attempting to gain social entry into peer groups. Yet, these two skills—asking for help and understanding how to join a group for functional or personal interaction—are paramount for any student's future social success.

By elementary school many students with ASD-SCD have significant social relational problems. The majority experience great difficulty initiating and maintaining friendships with same-aged peers.As our students get older, the ability to ask for help, anticipate looming problems, and communicate one's needs to clarify issues or assignments or to work through interpersonal conflict all require initiation of communication. Difficulty with initiation of communication spills over into the adult years as some of our clients continue to struggle with the skills to initiate communication to help establish friendship. They also struggle with asking for help or initiating discussions about dilemmas they confront in the workplace or in their personal lives.

L = Listening with Eyes and Brain

We're all familiar with the idea that you have to listen to learn in a classroom. Listening skills are usually thought to be related to the ability to process auditory information. There are basic tests to assess if a student can efficiently process auditory information to assure the student can understand what she is hearing in a timely manner. Students with ASD-SCD and related receptive language challenges are likely to have auditory processing challenges (DePape, Hall, Tillmann, & Trainor, 2012).

However, processing language in an interpersonal setting, where the listener is expected to also attend to the speaker by showing the speaker that the listener is paying attention, requires more than simply auditory processing. It also requires the ability to actively attend to the speaker with both one's eyes and brain. Simply put, the listener is responsible for gaining extra information about the speaker by listening and thinking with his eyes—this is true, even in very young children (Jones, Carr, & Klin, 2008; Prelock, 2006).

A core element of people's ability to listen or think with their eyes is the emergence of joint attention, as described earlier in this chapter. As children learn to track and respond to the joint-attention bids of others, they also begin to predict what may happen next or what someone is thinking or referring to (Mundy & Acra, 2006). Children with autism are most likely to have delays in their ability to engage in acts related to joint attention. They struggle to follow the gaze of others in social situations at two years of age, especially when trying to initiate joint attention bids (Chawarska, Klin, & Volkmar, 2003).

Klin, Jones, Schultz, and Volkmar (2003) demonstrated that eye-gaze patterns of persons with autism when examining a specific movie scene are unique when compared to their neurotypical peers, leading persons with ASD to formulate far different interpretations in the same social context.

From a social perspective, listening requires more than just taking in auditory information. It also requires the person to integrate information that's seen with what's heard, to understand the full meaning of the message being conveyed or to make an educated guess about what's being said when one can't clearly understand it. For example, classroom teachers expect students to listen with their eyes when they point to information that's part of the instruction. They also indicate to whom they're speaking in a class, not by calling the student's name but by looking at the student or moving closer. Students repeatedly relate to their peers through nonverbal cues, ranging from rolled eyes that signal boredom, to raised eyebrows that indicate questioning, to gazing at a particular item to direct a peer's attention.

Instruction in this essential and fundamental function of social interaction begins with teaching students that eyes share social information. Not all our students understand this concept, nor do they grasp that listening requires full attention to both verbal and nonverbal cues. Once this essential skill develops, instruction can expand to teaching students to relate to each other's thoughts through play and other activities of social relatedness, followed by extending the student's realm to attending to and processing increasingly complex cues that help students listen with their whole bodies.

A = Abstract and Inferential Language/ Communication

Most of the language we use isn't intended for literal interpretation (Kerbel & Grunwell, 1998; Westby, 2012). Our communication is peppered with idioms, metaphors, sarcasm, and inferences. Our society bestows literary awards to writers who are most creative with our English language. Each generation of teens creates its own slang. Kids who follow along are "cool"; those who don't aren't cool, suggesting to peers these weak learners of socially-based information lack the familiar collective social insights of their peer group. Ultimately they're less likely to be naturally included. The abstract and inferential component of communication is huge and constantly in flux. Overly literal interpretation of language is a hallmark characteristic of individuals with ASD and for some with SCD. Yet as educators we either miss this impairment entirely—thinking our smart, bright students must understand our nuanced communication—or it's addressed in the briefest of ways, with instruction dedicated only to explaining idioms and metaphors as part of English class.

Accurate comprehension of a communicative message depends first on the basic recognition that two codes of language exist: literal and figurative. It also involves recognizing and interpreting both the verbal words and the nonverbal cues that accompany them. It requires an individual to place the communication within the context of the social and cultural environment where it occurs. Furthermore, the listener must take into consideration any prior knowledge or history involved and the possible motives of the person initiating the message. Finally, emotional maturity and social development factor into how well a person interprets what's being said.

Active interpretation of the motives and intentions of others emerges in the first year of life and expands in complexity thereafter. Children quickly learn that their mom's tone of voice speaks volumes and that if they pay attention only to her words, they miss a huge portion of her message. As children grow developmentally, they understand that message interpretation depends heavily on one's ability to "make a smart guess" based on past experiences—what they know (or don't know) about the current person and situation and the available communication clues. Language users assume their communicative partners are trying to figure out their message. By third grade, neurotypical students understand that they're to infer meaning rather than expect it to be coded literally.

Abstract and inferential language comprehension appears to be directly tied to a person's ability to discern quickly and flexibly the different thoughts, perceptions, and motives of other people—in essence to "read the mind" of another from a social perspective. For example, when a 17-year-old teenager with high-functioning autism visited me at my house one day, I tried to strike up a conversation with him by saying, "I hear you're in the school choir." The teen responded with, "No, I'm in your house." This wasn't sarcasm, but literal language interpretation.

Students who fail to efficiently interpret the abstract, inferential meaning of language also struggle with academic tasks, such as reading comprehension, especially when required to interpret a character's thoughts and actions based on the context of the story and what one understands about the character's history and motives. Without the benefit of real-world experience, these students are unable to imagine how characters might think, feel, and act within the story.

Our students with social learning challenges are apt to have difficulty interpreting nuanced meanings carried through routine conversation, because they may become overwhelmed by the complex array of linguistic and nonverbal signals that may need to be processed and responded to simultaneously (Adams, Green, Gilchrist, & Cox, 2002; Saalasti et al., 2008). Many of our social learning challenged, verbal students demonstrate a significant discrepancy in their ability to infer language-based meanings (Norbury & Bishop, 2002). Idiomatic language, metaphors, irony, and innuendo as well as language based humor can also create interpretive challenges (Rapin & Dunn, 2003).

Brown and Yule (1983) explore in great detail the multifunctional nature of communication, even at the level of spoken language. There isn't one specific language utterance that's interpreted exactly the same way by all.

Knowledge of how to interpret and respond to communication doesn't only exist in interpersonal communication, it's also actively required in many aspects of our academic curriculum. Language arts curriculum requires the interpretation of literature in fiction or story books, all of which require a base understanding of social relationships and social language interpretation (Carnahan & Williamson, 2010; Tovani, 2000). Picture books actively require students to interpret and respond to nonverbal interpersonal and situational information to follow the socially related aspects of the story. As students grow older, they're required to read fiction as presented in novels. The social emotional mind of the reader is depended on to accurately interpret the information being presented. Our students who are highly literal interpreters of spoken communication will be highly literal interpreters of the required school readings, leading to serious and long-term challenges with reading comprehension.

Written expression also requires us to demonstrate a more sophisticated "voice" with each passing year of school. Teachers seek more than just correct grammar, spelling, penmanship, and punctuation as proof of good writing. They also want a student to use language indirectly, to go beyond exploring facts to supporting their ideas using emotion-laden content and persuasive and opinion-oriented essays. These expectations are mandated in the older student's core curriculum (National Governors Association Center for Best Practices & Council of Chief State School Officers, 2010).

Similar requirements to activate the social emotional mind to interpret and respond to core curriculum are also found in the analysis of lessons in history and social studies. Not only are students required to memorize the dates of battles or social conflicts, but by middle school they're also required to look at what persons in history were thinking and feeling. Doing this helps students interpret the decisions that were made that helped to shape history. To know the date of when the United States was founded isn't good enough; students are also expected to understand how the Pilgrims were escaping a lack of freedom in their choice of religion and expression of ideas. Understanding these issues helps the student gain insight into the basis of our country's constitution. A student then also has to relate the thoughts the Pilgrims had to the emotions they experienced as they felt compelled to leave their home country and then find the determination to build a new place to live absent from the conditions they'd previously experienced.

Abstracting and inferencing are core prerequisites for participating on the playground as early as our preschool years as well as in more formal classrooms during preschool, elementary school, and beyond. With each passing year the school aged student is expected to demonstrate rapid and comprehensive improvement in her ability to abstract and infer to stay abreast with the evolving demands of age-appropriate social interaction and active participation in academic programs.

U = Understanding Perspective

To understand the differing perspectives of others requires that one's ToM works quickly and efficiently utilizing executive functioning. As previously stated, between the ages of four and six, most neurotypical students acquire a solid foundation in verbally explaining concepts linked to what they know or don't know about how others may think. The ability to take perspective is key to participating in any type of group (social or academic) as well as interpreting information that requires an understanding of other people's minds, such as reading comprehension, history, social studies, and so on. Hale and Tager-Flusberg (2005) explore the relationship between discourse development and ToM. Our students who are slower to evolve in their understanding of basic ToM concepts are also slower to evolve in their ability to engage in discourse. Hale and Tager-Flusberg explain that discourse requires the use of pragmatic knowledge (understanding the social use of language) to organize information to be communicated in the most useful manner. This involves taking into account what the speaker knows about the listener, including knowledge, feelings, and other mental states.

> Perspective taking isn't one but many things that happen at once.

CCT also plays a role in perspective taking because one can only stay abreast of what's being communicated if he can focus on the central albeit frequently shifting gist of the message in conversational language. Social emotional tracking to attempt to determine how other people feel is critical for more highly attuned social participation, whether we're simply sharing space with others or actively participating in an interaction. Social emotional awareness of one's own emotions and related self-regulation goes hand in hand with emotional tracking of others' thoughts and feelings. These concepts are expected to steadily evolve throughout our preschool years and youth. Weakness in perspective taking is a significant characteristic of those with social learning challenges. However, like all other concepts explored in the ILAUGH model, one's ability to take perspective isn't a black or white matter. From my experience, in all likelihood there's a vast range of perspective taking skills across the autism spectrum and others with social learning challenges. In short, perspective taking isn't one but many things that happen at once, including CCT, EF, and ToM.

G = Gestalt Processing/Getting The Big Picture

Information is conveyed through concepts not just facts, as explored in our discussion of CCT. When involved in conversation, the participants intuitively determine the underlying concept being discussed (Loukusa et al., 2007). When reading, the purpose is to follow the overall meaning rather than just collect a series of facts (Myles et al., 2002). Conceptual processing is a key component to understanding social and academic information. Difficulty in developing organizational strategies can't be isolated from conceptual processing (Happé, 1997). Students with conceptual processing challenges often have difficulties with written expression, organizational skills, and time management. In addition, they tend to be overly tangential in their social relations (Van den Broek, Rapp & Kendeou, 2005).

H = Humor and Human Relatedness

Most of our clients have a very good sense of humor, but they feel anxious because they miss many of the subtle cues that help them understand how to participate successfully with others (Gutstein, 2001; Greenspan & Wieder, 2003; Prizant et al., 2006). It's important for educators and parents to work with them compassionately and with humor to help minimize the anxiety these children experience. At the same time, many of our clients use humor inappropriately; direct lessons about this topic are needed and relevant.

Human relatedness—the ability to bond emotionally with others—is at the heart of human social relationships and the fuller development of empathy and emotional regulation. (Human relatedness is also part of perspective taking.) Teaching students how to relate and respond to other people's emotions as well as their own, while also helping them feel the enjoyment that arises through mutual sharing, is critical to the development of all other aspects of social development that have been described.

ILAUGH Model Remodeled

At the time I published my first book, in which I introduced the ILAUGH Model of Social Cognition, a colleague sagely told me that once you've printed an idea, it's difficult to rescind it. Instead of rescinding the ILAUGH model, I now propose to revise it based on important new affirmations provided by research. The acronym

ILAUGH did well to support the multifaceted nature of social learning disabilities while also suggesting that we can use humor with our students. However, this acronym no longer lines up so cleanly.

More recently, in light of new and emerging research explored in this chapter, it makes sense to remodel the ILAUGH model to highlight understanding perspective taking and gestalt processing as key features in social processing that help to lead to all other aspects in the original ILAUGH model. Hence, if this set of information was announced to the public today, it would start by describing the research-related concepts that lead to the central and synergistic concepts referred to as *perspective taking* and *getting the gist* (gestalt). Abstracting/inferencing, initiating communication, listening with your eyes and brain, and humor and human relatedness would then be described as being part of these two domains. The figure below helps to demonstrate how the remodeling can be conceptualized:

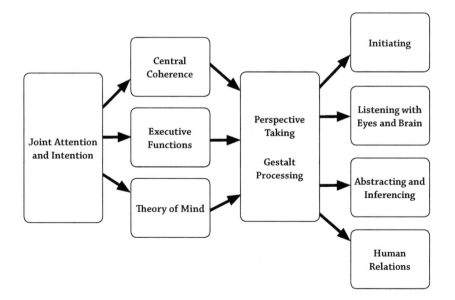

In reality, the ILAUGH model represents the multitude of concepts and skills children are supposed to acquire through normal childhood experiences from birth until the time they enter their school-age years. School administrative curriculum committees and K–12 classroom teachers alike teach the government-mandated educational standards, assuming these early developmental, conceptual building blocks are fully functioning in all students. It makes sense then that the child who doesn't naturally acquire these concepts can have much more difficulty learning the standards, a topic that's explored in the next chapter.

. . . .

Chapter 5

What Impact Do Weaknesses in Social Conceptual Information Have on Learning the Common Core State Standards?

With the passage of the No Child Left Behind Act (NCLB) in 2001, the U.S. Congress strongly encouraged public schools to teach students according to their state's educational standards. More recently, a set of educational standards, the Common Core State Standards, has been adopted by the vast majority of U.S. states to allow students across the country to be taught from the same set of educational expectations. In this way, school administrators could demonstrate their students were gaining specific academic knowledge and receiving a "good education." However, seemingly left out of the discussions about how to teach many of the standards is the reality that there are underlying social conceptual components that contribute heavily to a student's ability to participate in a standards-based education.

When a social conceptual, research-based learning model, such as the ILAUGH Model of Social Cognition, is used to explore the social cognitive processing required in our academic teachings, we begin to recognize the importance of teaching such concepts. They're central in creating the intellectual infrastructure for learning to master many of the educational standards that are taught to all students in the U.S. and even across the world.

Listed below in italics are selected examples of language-arts educational standards. The text in the third column indicates the social knowledge students must possess and be able to use fluently to be prepared to culminate their learning of the standard from the classroom or special education teacher.

Subject: Reading		
Grade of student expected to be proficient at the educational standard	**Description** of the educational standard	
	Educational standard	**Social Knowledge** related to this standard
K	*Determine the main idea of a text; recount the key details and explain how they support the main idea.*	It's expected that preschool children can intuitively sort out the main idea from the details that surround it in their play and communication.
1	*Compare and contrast the adventures and experiences of characters in stories.*	It's assumed children as young as toddlers are naturally learning to understand the different thoughts and experiences of different individuals.

2	*Acknowledge differences in the points of view of characters, including by speaking in different voice for each character when reading dialogue.*	By age four and a half, children are expected to be able to talk about how others think and feel as different from how they think and feel.
3	*Determine the meaning of words and phrases as they are used in the text, distinguishing literal from nonliteral language.*	It's assumed by age five that children are learning that words have multiple meanings and what people say isn't exactly what they mean.
4	*Compare and contrast a firsthand and secondhand account of the same event or topic; describe the differences in focus and the information provided.*	This requires basic perspective taking skills (ToM, CCT, and EF), which were expected to emerge prior to age five for the student to advance now to this level of social perspective taking.

Subject: Listening and collaborating		
5	*Engage effectively in a range of collaborative discussions (1:1, in groups, and teacher led) with diverse partners on grade 5 topics and texts, building on other's ideas and expressing their own ideas clearly.*	A form of this standard is written from kindergarten all the way through 12th grade with slightly more sophistication added to it each year. To meet this standard means children have intuitive social understanding related to verbally communicating with a range of partners. The seeds of this standard were expected to be planted from birth with evolving mutual engagement of the child with her caregivers during the first year of life and then expanded upon through the preschool years.
Subject: Writing		
6	*Draw evidence from literary or informational texts to support analysis, reflection and research.*	Incorporating different points of view and reflecting upon them to form one's own written response requires advanced perspective taking (ToM, CCT, and EF).

7	*Write narratives to develop real or imagined experiences or events using effective technique, relevant descriptive details, and well-structured event sequences.*	Standards for the creation of written narratives evolve in expectations each year from kindergarten through 12th grade. A narrative requires one to take perspective of others' thoughts and experiences to describe one's own thoughts/experiences in a manner that others can understand. Children are supposed to naturally acquire the basics to narrative language prior to entering kindergarten.
8	*Demonstrate understanding of figurative language, word relationships, and nuances of word meanings.*	Understanding figurative language and the nuance of language is acquired through finely-tuned perspective taking—we seek to determine each other's intentions as we decipher what's meant by what's said. This concept manifests in increasing sophistication throughout the elementary school years because teachers don't directly teach students to read each other's intentions. This and all other standards listed on this page increase in nuance and sophistication throughout the high school years.

As we explore how students learn to acquire information related to the standards associated with their age group, it becomes clear that teachers don't teach all the information associated with each of these standards. Clearly, if a student hasn't previously acquired the social thinking building blocks for the ninth to twelfth grade standards (not reviewed here), they'll be unable to benefit from the culminating lessons a teacher introduces to encourage more age-appropriate and elaborate social thinking.

Consider that for most of the conceptual language-arts standards, a teacher's role is one of facilitator, helping students gather, process, and respond to their social knowledge rather than directly teaching the social knowledge itself. For example, by fourth grade, students are expected to be able to "demonstrate understanding of figurative language, word relationships, and nuances in word meanings" (National Governors Association Center for Best Practices & Council of Chief State School Officers, 2010). The fourth grade teacher doesn't literally teach students what figurative language is. Instead, this is more of a vocabulary lesson introducing a new term to describe information the neurotypical students have previously acquired.

When exploring the developmental roots of learning figurative language, we must first begin to explore the emergence of abstract thinking. Symbolic play emerges at around 18 months as children begin to use one object to represent another (for example, using a banana to pretend it's a phone) (Piaget, 1962). Most of us have met a three-to-four-year old who is smitten with potty talk and becomes visibly excited when he realizes the word "but" has multiple meanings (but/butt). At this point we're observing the child acquire early intuitive learning in abstract language—realizing that words don't always mean the same thing.

Then in preschool and kindergarten most children find great joy in reading books, like the popular series *Amelia Bedelia* by Peggy Parish,which explore the concept of literal versus figurative language. In grasping the humor of this book, children must understand that Amelia gets into mishaps because she misinterprets her boss's instructions; she doesn't understand that language has figurative constructs. Yet our young neurotypical students are highly aware of this. (How many adults have stopped to consider that Amelia may be a young woman with autism or Asperger's Syndrome?) In fact our young students may not even know how to interpret accurately the figurative language Amelia is supposed to interpret. They simply understand that whatever she's doing isn't what was meant to be done. For example, when Amelia (the housekeeper) is instructed by the owner of the house to "dress the turkey," most children will laugh hysterically when they see Amelia put clothes on the turkey. While they don't know what "dress the turkey" means, they know it's not appropriate to put clothes on it!

Around this time, children can also be heard using idiomatic language (for example, "hold your horses," "liar, liar pants on fire," "ants in your pants") although they've yet to be taught about idioms or figurative language. While the social brain has been working toward learning about figurative language for many years, our school curricula wait until fourth grade to introduce this concept by providing a standard to "teach figurative language."

Following this line of evidence, it's ironic that national policy dictates that any highly qualified teacher should be able teach all students the grade standards because these standards are literally not taught by the teachers. Instead, the standards are a culmination of years of knowledge acquired and organized by the child based in large part on her capacity to learn this socially abstract information intuitively. So what's the teacher to do with the student with high-functioning autism in his class who, because of different brain wiring, has actually never noticed or considered that language has two codes, figurative and literal? His standard lessons are clearly not relevant to this student because these lessons assume prior social knowledge. What happens? The child is possibly referred to the special educator; or possibly her inability to keep up with the classroom teachings, which results in distracted, unfocused classroom behavior, is attributed to disinterest or noncooperation, and she's viewed as unwilling to learn and as a behavior problem.

As a whole, our educational system—the standards we teach by and the lessons we've used for decades—presuppose that the purpose of classroom education is to lay academic knowledge on top of a fully functional social brain. Education professionals from the federal level down to the classroom aide assume that four-to-five-year-old children come to school with a solid "social operating system." And therein lies the crux of the problem in teaching children with ASD-SCD. Even educators who are aware of this fundamental divide often fail to perceive the pervasiveness of their students' social learning challenges, especially when the students use language and have a reasonably strong non-socially-based academic intelligence—such as those who excel at learning facts, concepts related to science, math, and so on. Furthermore, these socially-based learning challenges may appear to increase in intensity as the lessons taught to students advance in social learning and critical-thinking complexity with each passing year. A student who may have done very well with the more concrete curriculum of first and second

> Education professionals from the federal level down to the classroom aide assume that children aged four to five come to school with a solid "social operating system."

grade may fall apart behaviorally when the more socially abstract critical-thinking curriculum overwhelms her by fourth or fifth grade.

We assume children know how to ask for help. We assume children have the skills to work as part of a large or small group in the classroom. We assume children are able to work independently. We assume children have the prerequisite skills to play on the playground with others. But these assumptions go even deeper—we assume children can attend in a group, that they learn by observing others, that they can imitate, that they know how to initiate communication, that they understand their own and others' basic emotions, and that they're motivated by social reinforcement. On an even more elemental level, we assume they understand that people have different minds, different thoughts, and different ideas. Many educators, parents, and counselors can't fathom that a child who has acquired some mastery over language concepts or who uses the vocabulary of a fifth grader while in kindergarten could be so lacking in the development of his social thinking and related social skills to make learning in the context of a kindergarten classroom problematic. Yet these students exist, and they're growing in number every year.

Given these often moderate to extreme social learning challenges, students with social cognitive learning challenges enter school needing education on two overlapping fronts, the academic curriculum as well as the social curriculum (Attwood, 2006). Therefore, we must ask ourselves this question: Is it realistic to teach both academics and social thinking within one environment, the "mainstream classroom," when the majority of other students in the class are developmentally on track from a social learning perspective? An equally challenging question is this: Are these other students as "on track" socially as we think they are, or are we overlooking needs that exist on a more widespread basis than we currently imagine?

Our treatment for students once recognized as having special learning needs often fails to get to the core of the learning issue. Instead of exploring needed core prerequisite knowledge, treatments often focus on having a student respond to the specific lesson being taught.

Consider the analogy of a tree for understanding how social learning advances in sophistication and complexity with the growth of the child. The root system for social learning is established by the child acquiring basic social understanding. This is presented through the evidence for ToM, central coherence, executive functions, cognition, language, and sensory processing. This root system enables the trunk of the tree to provide the stable support of the key aspects of intuitive learning related to the ILAUGH model. The branches grow, with each branch representing a different activity that children are expected to engage in through the implicit assistance of their social learning. There are branches to represent reading comprehension, written expression, playground play, working as part of a classroom group, and so on.

The leaves on each branch represent the range of skills we attempt to teach in pursuit of demonstrating that the student is acquiring more abilities to help make the branch stronger. Many of the leaves represent lessons that assume the social knowledge already exists. For example, if we focus on the branch representing playground play, the leaves we identify as necessary to help foster this concept include skills such as cooperating, taking turns, and being nice. When he attempts to teach a student to cooperate or take turns, the teacher will quickly find that many of our students don't have enough knowledge from the roots or trunk of the social learning tree for that child to demonstrate these more advanced social concepts.

Ironically, most treatment in our private and public teaching and therapeutic institutions targets treatment goals for skills that are lacking but doesn't explore more deeply the social learning that needed to previously occur for that skill set to emerge. Hence, the educators expect the student to develop core skills without the strength of a healthy root system and trunk to nurture further and more sophisticated development. Interestingly, when reviewing the progression of many of the Common Core State Standards, the reader can track how standards related to one of the anchor standards, such as listening and collaborating, evolve with each year of the child's education. If a child is way behind in his maturational development of information, which would prevent him from being able to "participate in collaborative conversations with diverse partners, etc." in kindergarten, focusing on leaf-based skills described in the progressively complex and related standards the following years in school will only place this child further and further behind in his growth toward reaching any part of the basic standard. However, if we start back at the beginning, even if the child is in fifth grade, and recognize that he isn't able to meet this kindergarten standard, we can look more at the developmental issues we need to tackle to encourage further learning for this child, even if it's not at grade level. This may also mean the child needs instruction away from the fully included classroom, where this level of basic instruction may not be appropriate within this peer group. At the end of the day, year, or childhood education, we want our students to learn information that helps them relate to others in increasingly abstract ways. For some of our students, this may require us to simplify our learning expectations to allow a student to learn from a point of strength rather than drown her in lessons that she can't make heads or tails of with well-meaning parents, teachers, or paraprofessionals doing the work for the student in the name of keeping this child on track with her peers of their age group in receiving a "standards-based" education.

This leads us to ask this question: How do we formulate teachings that impact root learning, to encourage the development of many different concept and skill abilities over time, even if the teaching isn't what the mainstream peers are being taught? The following chapters explore deeper cognitive teaching practices.

4. The leaves represent individual strategies/skills needed in executing that branch:

- The Reading Comprehension Branch may require students to:
  ○ Summarize what they read
  ○ Sort out details and facts
  ○ Understand a character's motives

- The Peer Play Branch may require:
  ○ Cooperation
  ○ Turn taking
  ○ Being friendly
  ○ Dealing with the changing rules, etc.

2. The trunk, dependent on growth of the roots, includes (in part) concepts related to the ILAUGH Model of Social Thinking:

I = Initiation of communication
L = Listening with eyes and brain
A = Abstracting and inferencing
U = Understanding perspective
G = Gestalt processing: getting the gist
H = Humor and human relatedness

3. Each branch represents one aspect of the diverse range of concepts/skills that emerge from the trunk's core conceptual development, for example:

- Reading and comprehension
- Playing with peers
- Written expression
- Conversational skills
- Working in a group

1. The roots of the social learning tree grow with neurological capacity:

- Joint Attention: Shared Intention and Attention
- Executive Functioning
- Central Coherence
- Theory of Mind
- Emotional recognition and reciprocity

Social
Thinking.com

. . . .

When Do We Use Social Thinking and Related Social Skills? How Do We Approach Teaching These Skills?

P erhaps the more fitting question is—when don't we use social thinking and related social skills? And the answer is, never! We use our social skills any time we're in the presence of people, regardless of whether or not we intend to communicate with them. We understand that we can't mow the lawn in the nude, that driving a car requires following certain rules of the road, and that committing certain crimes is against the law. When we're "alone"—not in the presence of others—we use social thinking skills for understanding characters in a book, movie, or TV program, in reflecting about past or present experiences, and when making future plans that may or may not involve others. Unless we live as a hermit in a cave, totally removed from society, we constantly use social thinking and social skills. They're naturally part of who we are as social beings. (Actually, that hermit would still be using social thinking skills. Think about it.)

The expectation that an individual will exhibit appropriate social skills when in the company of others begins as young as toddlerhood and is certainly active by the time a child goes to preschool. The reason many parents send their three- or four-year-olds to prekindergarten or attend Mommy and Me classes at age two is so their children can practice and begin to acquire—through social interaction—the prerequisite skills to ease their way into kindergarten. By then we assume that the young child will be able to understand there are social expectations and related social information to process and respond to when participating during circle time, lining up for a field trip, at meal time, and during group play. We expect that children can learn to not hit or bite others, to share toys, to understand turn-taking, and follow the teacher's directions. These social expectations widen and take on more complexity as children age. Subtle but significant shifts in social expectations take place with each year of school. More monumental shifts occur when a student moves into the more independent world of college and employment.

Typically developing children are neurologically primed for social development and are able to learn more about social expectations through observation of others. Children watch others and then think about what they observed and how it applies (or doesn't) to their own lives. This complex social information processing is the glue that ties together actions and environment and helps the child mature into a socially savvy adult. Without the connections that social thinking provides, children lack the ability to take the perspective of another, assess the social requirements of different contexts, and recognize that other people are information sources for their own learning. Generalization of learned actions is absent, and children are unable to apply social lessons from one setting to another.

This extends into academics, too. As discussed earlier, the appropriate use of social thinking is a prerequisite skill within academic subjects such as language arts, social studies, and history. Reading literature requires students to grasp the social emotional concepts being explored by the characters; social studies and history require social thought related to a person's motives, intentions, and personal experiences (Zunshine, 2012).

Interestingly, students who are overly distracted during group participation activities may be labeled a behavior problem. This is even though in all likelihood the students' self-distractions relate more to their inability to understand how to interpret and respond in the group or self-regulate their emotions or the surrounding sensory input. Instead of being due to a behavior problem, it's more likely a social thinking and/or sensory issue that leads to inappropriate behavior. Rather than focus on remediating the behavior, we need to identify the root of the problem and see if it relates to social thinking, then develop more effective teaching strategies.

What's missing is attention to the social thought process behind the action. We fail to identify the social knowledge underlying the social skill. As a result, we fail to teach the necessary social thinking that will result in the production of the specific social skill.

Our current emphasis on social behavioral responses (e.g., social skills) versus social thought can be especially confusing for very "bright" students who nonetheless endure social thinking challenges. We incorrectly assume that students who perform well on intelligence and academic testing also have equally advanced social

> When we teach social skills without relating them back to the core concept of social thinking, it's far more likely students will continue to fail to generalize what they're learning.

thinking skills. This is a truly dangerous assumption to make when teaching students with any type of learning challenge. We must probe deeper into assessing their social thinking skills. For example, a second grade student with an IQ of 150 loved talking about chemistry. In fact, he loved it so much he continued to talk about his beloved topic even when his listener got up from his chair and walked away from the student! The student continued to stare at the chair and talk, apparently unaware of how to adapt his language in the absence of a social partner. He may have been academically gifted, but he was socially clueless at a level that many teachers might find unimaginable. We don't regularly encounter people in our lives who don't understand that when a conversation partner gets up and walks away, we stop talking. This student didn't understand this very basic social concept. Imagine the nuances of social interaction he also missed!

Behaviorally-based, social skills teaching programs have achieved some success in helping children learn specific social skills. However, a common criticism of the behavioral-skill-based teachings is that this methodology is generally weak in encouraging students to transfer the use of a skill beyond the specific context in which the skill is taught. At the root of lack of generalization of a skill is usually a lack of poor concept development related to that skill. When we teach social skills without relating them back to the core concept of social thinking, it's far more likely students will continue to fail to generalize what they're learning (Crooke, Hendrix, & Rachman, 2008).

Proponents of a more behaviorally-based, social skills approach teach a skill as a set of behavioral adjustments and then wait until a certain level of skill mastery has been achieved before teaching the child to use the same skill in other settings. For some children, this type of regimented, repeated skill-based practice may be needed. Quite frankly, this may be all they really can learn given the more profound extent of their social learning disabilities as discussed further in Chapter 8. But it's important to keep in mind that a purely behaviorally-based, social skills teaching method, even one built on generalized skill practice, doesn't teach a student to relate the specific skill to underlying social knowledge. The student may leave the treatment room with a social skill, but not as a *social thinker* who can apply her social thought process across all environments. The student may learn to give compliments that make people feel good. But then the student uses compliments at the wrong time or in the wrong place. One example: A third-grade student interrupted the teacher's classroom instruction to tell the teacher her shirt looked pretty. The strength of behaviorally-based teaching methods for teaching sequenced information is that they excel in breaking down the information into a series of linear sequenced parts to help students learn isolated information that can then be chained together toward completion of a larger task. True applied behavioral analysis does an excellent job analyzing the elements of a task and teaching the elements to complete the task when thinking and problem solving aren't a part of the task to be completed. Using fluid social skills to perform a task, such as engaging in a conversation or knowing when not to blurt in a classroom, requires more than the sequenced performance of a chain of tasks. To be done in a manner that's considered "neurotypical," almost all social skills require social thought and problem solving. Once tasks require thinking and problem solving, we find behavioral teachings need to extend to more thought-based teachings, such as those provided through Social Thinking.

Consider how we traditionally teach the social concept of eye contact. We have one general set of instructions we use internationally to teach students to improve eye contact. We say, "Look at me." When the student looks, we reinforce him with a token, natural reinforcements, or both.

Stop for a minute and consider the fundamental role eye contact plays in social development. Eye contact is part of normal social neurodevelopment by a baby's second month of life. Babies intuitively learn to orient to a parent's face. They learn that this adult can better the baby's world through this shared experience, first by satisfying the child's needs and then, as a few more months pass, by supplying valuable information about the world. As new situations arise in their lives, babies make eye contact to get answers to questions, such as: Am I safe with this person? Did I really hurt myself when I fell down?

By 12 months old, neurotypical babies are neurologically primed to fully acquire joint attention, a social developmental milestone that enlarges their world, as discussed earlier. Joint attention is fundamentally the "joining" of our mutual attention for the purpose of mutual engagement or social problem solving. Students for whom eye contact is lacking don't just lack the skill itself. More importantly and more fundamental to social development, they lack the intuitive social cognitive connection to other people and their social emotional minds. These individuals don't understand that by making eye contact, important information can be learned about the world. An array of research demonstrates that once eye contact and joint attention are firmly established in the first year of life, a door is opened for increasingly abstract development of the social mind, allowing for more sophisticated use of body language (index finger pointing) as well as spoken language (Farroni, Csibra, Simion, & Johnson, 2002; Whalen, Schreibman, & Ingersoll, 2006).

Behaviorally-based social skills instruction may indeed increase eye contact in a student, but it may bring about little positive change in the child's understanding of why we make eye contact or the benefits of doing so.

Dennis was a nine-year-old boy with high functioning autism, with normal intelligence. He was fully included in a mainstream classroom, but because of his challenges in conceptualizing classroom activities, actively attending, and his very literal interpretations of instructions, Dennis had a full time paraprofessional for support. Dennis' Individualized Education Program (IEP) contained the goal to "use good eye contact," and professionals had been working with him on it for six consecutive years. However, even after all the instruction, when asked to "look at me," Dennis lifted his chin toward the speaker, but his eyes looked toward the floor. After conducting a social-communicative assessment, I determined that Dennis didn't realize that the iris of the eyes indicated gaze direction. He didn't realize that by looking at people's eyes, he gathered information about what people might be seeing or thinking about. Instead, when he was asked to guess what his mom was looking at, he made arbitrary guesses about anything in the environment. Clearly, teaching Dennis to simply "look at me" was ineffective; he didn't know what he should be looking at or the personal or social value in doing so.

As an alternative way of addressing eye contact, Dennis was taught social thinking and the related social skill pertaining to the use of his eyes. First he was taught, using concrete drawings and images, that the irises of the eye were like arrows—they point to something. He was advised to "make a guess about what people are looking at based on the direction you see the eyes looking." Once he improved significantly with this concept (in about three months), he was taught that people think about what they're looking at. His parents and paraprofessional were taught to teach Dennis to "think with his eyes" throughout his day to encourage him to think about what others are thinking about; for example, "He's looking at this sandwich on his plate—what do you think he's thinking about it?"

Over the course of the next two years, Dennis slowly started to look at people's faces and at the direction of their eyes. When his more challenged twin brother, who also had autism, came to the clinic one day, I observed Dennis talking to him in the waiting room. His twin brother was looking away, at which point Dennis took hold of his brother's face, turned it toward him and said, "You have to think about me when I am talking to you!"

Teaching Dennis to become a bit better at social thinking will take time while also requiring the treatment team to modify their expectations as to the ultimate treatment outcomes. For someone as challenged as Dennis at learning social information, it isn't realistic for his treatment team to expect that he'll master these concepts in the course of his childhood or even his adulthood.

It may seem a faster approach to teach a social skill rather than social thinking, but to what end? Dennis had to learn to recognize and consider social information, such as eye-gaze direction, before he could show an improvement in the social skill of eye contact. But it appears to be time well spent, because Dennis demonstrated he could take his social thinking into any environment, rather than only practice it in the therapy room. And he gained an understanding of why eye contact is important—as a pivotal skill that would open his world to other social lessons and social connections (Colombi et al., 2009; Murray et al., 2008).

It's also important to consider how delayed Dennis was at nine years old in acquiring this social knowledge and related skill. His neurologically-based inability to understand eye-gaze and its associated social thought meant he was more than eight years delayed in social development. As parents and educators who craft IEP goals for children with autism disorders, it behooves us to ask this vital question: When specific social thinking and related skills haven't developed for eight years, is it realistic to expect a student to learn these skills within the span of a year of IEP goal teaching? It's important that we teach students a deeper, more thoughtful approach to acquiring social information and producing the associated social skills. We must also respect the complexity of the social information they have to learn cognitively—information that typical students learn intuitively and usually much earlier in life.

Social scientists explain that teaching social actions over social thought can impede learning. Simmons-Mackie and Damico (2003) explore the need to research, assess, and provide qualitative treatment for social learning challenges by directly addressing one's social learning needs in context. They argue that social skills, when dissected into parts, lose their overall contribution toward creating social competence. Once the skills are taken out and treated as a skill, they're no longer working as part of a social framework. Looked at in this light, teaching students to produce specific social behavioral outputs without the associated deeper teachings about social thought and social context is unlikely to be the most effective approach in treatment when we expect these students to blend in using more nuanced, sophisticated social skills.

It's one thing to teach basic social rules to students who have obvious social impairments—there's a minimum level of social competency we all expect from others—and it's another thing to teach social behaviors to students whom we expect to mostly blend in with their peers. For example, there's a less sophisticated and a more sophisticated way to teach someone to produce a social greeting, such as saying "hi" to another person. The less sophisticated way can be taught through behavioral social skills, and the more sophisticated way would be taught through something like Social Thinking. Most parents and professionals easily recognize the child who doesn't acknowledge others he passes by. Everyone agrees the child needs to learn greetings. To teach this goal, a professional typically identifies one way in which we greet another person and teaches it to the student, such as, "Say hi when you pass another person or join other people." The student is then provided with a token reward or social recognition each time he uses this method to acknowledge another person. If the student uses this strategy most of the time, the professional may then report that he does this with 85% accuracy. The treatment team then celebrates how the student has met this goal, which implies he's now more socially competent. It sounds great, but let's explore the other side to this story.

This same student—let's call him Isaac—is fully included across his educational day. He's expected to fully interact with his peers in the classroom and on the playground. He's learned to greet others by saying "hi" to familiar people each time he sees them. He sees many of his classmates entering and exiting from the space he shares with them frequently. He now diligently greets them with each passing, which results in him saying "hi" to some of his classmates 15 to 20 times in a single day. He also greets them the exact same way each time he sees them—he looks at them, waves his right hand, and says "hi." His classmates giggle and talk to each other about the odd way in which Isaac greets them. His classmates may not be able to exactly describe what he's doing that makes them uncomfortable, but they know his frequent greetings keep them from wanting to relate to him in the same way they relate to their peers.

What went wrong? The professionals taught Isaac a general social rule—say "hi" to greet others—but they failed to teach the social nuance of that rule. They didn't teach him what to do once he's already said "hi" once to someone. Isaac should no longer be saying "hi" verbally after he's said it once to a person in a day. A more socially appropriate gesture the next time would be to make eye contact and give a brief, small smile, if that's the way that other students acknowledge each other. After third grade, many kids don't wave their hand or say "hi" to peers at all but reserve that type of greeting for adults. Instead, they acknowledge peers with momentary eye contact, a subtle lift of their chin, and say, "What's up?" The next time they see the same person, they glance briefly and just use the chin toss; the verbal greeting goes away. The type of peer-to-peer greeting used is culturally significant, and astute social thinkers will adapt their nonverbal and verbal skills based on that peer culture.

Cultures during a school day may include, but aren't limited to, the different peer groups that hang out during school breaks, the different classroom cultures, different home cultures, and so on. Cultural differences are alive and well on every campus but become quite obvious by middle and high school. Consider how a peer hangs out differently during classroom breaks with the jocks, the musicians, or the library kids, versus the kids who prefer computer gaming.

The ability to shift one's social skills to adapt to the many shifting social groups across a day requires more than learning social rules and being reinforced for abiding by those rules.

Social development is an intricate process, with concepts and skills interrelated and building upon each other. Helping students improve in this arena means we can't simply select random social skills to teach, one from column A and one from column B, and try to teach them unrelated to the larger whole of social connections and social adaptation in general. Parents and professionals have to be sensitive and have insight into the fact that for our students with social learning challenges, teaching these skills cognitively—when they're typically learned intuitively—is a cumbersome and slow process. To imply that social skills can be learned swiftly and seamlessly, when that's not the case, ultimately leaves parents, students, and other professionals with a sense of frustration and hopelessness. Although each treatment process has a type of client it serves well, each treatment also has a group of students its methodology doesn't suit. It's important to recognize which type of student needs which type of lessons to help them improve, based on their own social learning base.

....

How Can Cognitive Behavior Therapy Address Teaching Social Thinking and Related Social Skills?

Self-awareness of our own thoughts and emotions plays a critical role in the communicative process. This thought-based mechanism requires us to interpret the situation, be aware of how we perceive that others are interpreting the situation, and consider how each of us feels about this dynamic. When we're fairly accurate with our own awareness and interpretations, we often tend to produce what others may describe as "good social skills." But for our students who aren't as adept at understanding this social thinking process and who may have evolved into a negative mindset, we need to offer teachings in the development of this social cognitive process. Although ABA does well analyzing a linear task to create step-by-step teaching strategies to foster learning of that task, it falls short when attempting to teach synergistic concepts that are navigated by our own perceptions and thoughts. The teaching tools offered through classic ABA can be very helpful to our more rule-based linear thinkers who aren't achieving nuance-based social learning abilities. However, they fall short as a teaching technique when we encourage complex learners to engage in their own mental thought process to help them problem solve the subtle use of their own and others' social behavioral responses. The teaching tool that's demonstrating the most promise in this area is cognitive behavior therapy (CBT).

CBT is a form of psychotherapy that was first developed in the 1960s and continues to evolve in its application. In a nutshell, CBT is based on the idea that our thoughts—not the people, situations, and events in our environment—cause our feelings and behaviors, and that by changing the way we think, we can alter the way we behave. CBT is anchored by these three fundamental concepts (Dobson & Dozois, 2001):

1. Cognitive activity affects behavior.
2. Cognitive activity may be monitored and altered.
3. Desired behavior change may be influenced through CBT.

Professionals and researchers are beginning to demonstrate that CBT can be promising in the treatment of persons who function high on the autism spectrum and those with related social processing disabilities (Anderson & Morris, 2006; Beebe & Risi, 2003; Gaus, 2007; Kuusikko et al., 2008; Lopata, Thomeer, Volker, & Nida, 2006; Sofronoff, Attwood, & Hinton, 2005). CBT is often referred to as a form of "talk therapy" that focuses on the present, rather than delving into the past to understand the origins of behavior, as most forms of psychotherapy do. The tenets of CBT, while founded in psychotherapy, are now applied across a range of disciplines. Those who may benefit from CBT are language-based learners who can engage in the metacognitive process of thinking about thinking as a way to learn about their own learning. Marans, Rubin, and Laurent (2005) discuss CBT strategies (such as learning an "inner language") that help individuals cope with stressful events and the role they can play for persons with Asperger's Syndrome.

On the whole, cognitive interventions (as described by Simpson) attempt to shift the locus of control from the therapists, educators, and parents to the individual. Simpson (2005) explains that thought and other cognitive processes are generally assumed to mediate an individual's behavior and performance. Thus, changing these factors in a person is likely best accomplished by changing the individual's perceptions, self-understanding, and beliefs.

Many educators, occupational therapists, speech language pathologists, and other related service providers working with students with Asperger's Syndrome/high-functioning autism over the years have developed educational teaching strategies that, in retrospect, mirror the basic principles inherent in CBT clinical methodology. Examples of CBT-like treatment strategies developed by educators include Social Stories™ (Gray, 2010), Comic Strip Conversations (Gray, 1994), the Alert Program® (Williams & Shellenberger, 1996), The Incredible 5-Point Scale (Buron & Curtis, 2003), Social Behavior Mapping (Winner, 2007a), We Can Make It Better! (Delsandro, 2010), and The Zones of Regulation® (Kuypers, 2011). These professionals—all without formal training in CBT—have come to the common conclusion that their students need to be taught more about how their brain works and what information needs to be thought about. They need to be given strategies to regulate their own internal thoughts and external behaviors to function with increasing success in social environments. It's also become accepted that concepts of CBT can be incorporated into social learning/social skills groups to bring about positive change (Winner, 2005).

Carol Gray's Social Stories (2010) are a classic example of unknowingly applying CBT principles to help teach socially challenged students to cope with specific stressors. Social Stories are simple narratives that help students more fully grasp specific social scenarios, the related expectations and perspectives of others, and appropriate social behaviors to use. Social Stories are an efficient teaching tool, conceptualizing these ideas using the following three discrete types of statements:

1. Description (what's happening in the situation)
2. Perspectives (what others feel or think)
3. Directives (what to do)

Numerous single subject designed research studies have demonstrated positive results using this technique to help individuals manage more effectively in specific contexts (Reynhout & Carter, 2006; Toplis & Hadwin, 2006).

Comic Strip Conversations, another technique developed by Carol Gray (1994), uses visual supports to help explain how thoughts and behavior are interpreted by different people. The simple use of comic strip stick figures combined with cartoon thought and speaking bubbles allows students to concretely explore the chain reaction or social algebra at the heart of social interaction and to understand the origin of social conflict stemming from differing perceptions and thoughts. These comic strip techniques provide a visual model of appropriate social communication.

Two other therapy models, described in the books *The Incredible 5-Point Scale* (Buron & Curtis, 2003) and *A Five Is Against the Law!* (Buron, 2007), teach students to explore the different levels of their behavior using a simple five-point scale. On this scale, a "1" refers to the "best" type of behavior controls we use; a "5" refers to our worst behavior controls—being out of control. Students are taught to explore how the different levels of their emotions and behavior "look and feel" and what strategies can be employed to help them shift their behavior to a lower, calmer place on their own five-point scale.

Creating a visual map of expected and unexpected social emotional behavior reactions helps students learn the impact we all have on each other within social situations.

Social Behavior Mapping (SBM) explores the idea that all behaviors produced in a context shared by other people can be interpreted as social behaviors and influence our own and others' thoughts, feelings, and related actions (Winner, 2007a). In shared environments, how we act leads others to have emotional reactions, which lead to natural consequences. When the natural consequences are positive, the recipient feels good. When natural consequences are negative, the recipient feels bad. Creating a visual map of expected and unexpected social emotional behavior reactions helps students learn the impact we all have on each other within social situations.

CBT has been shown to be effective in teaching children in early elementary school when students are taught how to use their "social detective" skills to better observe a situation and learn how all people are expected to have thoughts and emotions about each other. Our set of lessons for second through fifth graders, *Superflex® ... a Superhero Social Thinking® Curriculum* (2008), has engaged children worldwide to help them to learn how to incorporate their social detective skills to use their own superflexible thought process to self-monitor their production of social skills (Winner & Crooke, 2010; Winner & Madrigal, 2010). They use these skills to defeat the "Team of Unthinkables" that may lurk in their minds.

In their own way, each of these programs supports the greater goal of CBT—to increase our clients' awareness of the impact of their behavior on others as well as on themselves (Briers, 2009).

....

Chapter 8

Do All Those with ASD-SCD Benefit from the Same Teachings? The Social Thinking-Social Communication Profile (ST-SCP)

T he saying goes, if you've met one person with Asperger's Syndrome you've met one person with Asperger's Syndrome. Those with ASD-SCD represent a heterogeneous population who vary in just about every imaginable way—personality; motivations; social, language, and cognitive abilities; learning preferences; hobbies; gender; coping strategies; desire to socialize; and so on. They're bound by the common trait of their struggle to attempt to communicate with others with ease. Yet even the way they struggle and how they learn strategies to help mitigate their struggle vary based on many factors. A primary factor is how much information they've naturally acquired related to interpreting social information (verbal and nonverbal).

We've found that if we can group students into treatment groups based on their social learning abilities and not their diagnostic labels, we're better able to design programs for them. What isn't as obvious in the research and writings about treatment of persons with ASD-SCD and what I've found in my clinical experience is that diagnostic labels aren't indicative of a student's social functioning level. The disorders described in the Diagnostic and Statistical Manual of Mental Disorders (DSM) don't directly account for the fact that ToM, central coherence, and executive functioning skills are all part of social development. Therefore, their presence or absence should be taken into account when labeling a student.

> Diagnostic labels aren't indicative of a student's social functioning level.

Professionals who specialize in working with students with Asperger's Syndrome, autism, PDD-NOS, nonverbal learning disability (NVLD), and ADHD find that different diagnostic professionals fail to agree on one of these labels, leading the student to receive many of the above-named labels as part of his diagnostic profile. When reviewing research in which the researchers sought to compare and contrast the functioning of students with NVLD to those with Asperger's Syndrome, I often wonder how they decided which participant was selected for each of these treatment groups given that a large number of people with Asperger's Syndrome also share the symptoms of NVLD. To date, researchers have assumed the diagnostic labels provided adequate information from which to group students into social skills treatment programs. This is likely one of the many reasons why the conclusions from the research on teaching social skills are so muddy.

Although Social Thinking or social skills treatment groups all focus on helping students develop stronger social relational abilities, the progress expected from a student is relative to the student's initial conceptual understanding and related social skill production. Some students with ASD have serious intellectual impairments that also result in limited language-learning abilities. These students often have significantly more challenges with understanding core concepts related to even the most basic social interactions while also experiencing highly dysregulating sensory systems. These lead them to display very weak social emotional self-regulation. The social learning needs and potential of this group of students are far different from those with ASD-SCD who have acquired language, have normal cognition, and can begin to infer basic information. This leads to the assumption that these different types of students need to be seen in different treatment groups, with each group provided instruction that relates to the group members' learning abilities.

How to begin and progress through that teaching depends strongly on the student's current social functioning abilities as well as the student's capacity for learning new information. Along this line of thinking, my colleagues Stephanie Madrigal, Dr. Pamela Crooke, and I have been exploring, from our clinical experience, how to best group our students to develop treatment programs that are relevant to each individual within the group while working to keep all members of a specific Social Thinking group actively engaged simultaneously. For those who have experience running social treatment groups, this is a tall order.

Over the years we discovered patterns related to our students' social, language, and cognitive learning abilities that help us predict how a student learns social emotional information. These patterns led us to form concepts related to grouping our students. This information encouraged us to create different lessons for the different levels of the social mind we developed. We found that students who function across the range of ASD-SCD could fall into any one of six different treatment groupings that are outlined in our Social Thinking-Social Communication Profile (ST-SCP). The ST-SCP was developed from clinical experience and hasn't yet been validated through a research study. Yet when the DSM-5 released its description of the three levels of ASD, these levels match up almost perfectly with the first three levels on our ST-SCP. However, we know that our students who may no longer be defined as having ASD using the DSM-5 and instead are referred to as SCD are also not a homogeneous population. The ST-SCP represents seven total levels of social functioning beginning with those we call "neurotypical."

Although the first purpose in creating the ST-SCP was to better define the social functioning level of each student to help us create a social skills/social thinking treatment plan, it also became apparent that we could use it to help advise parents as to more realistic outcomes to expect from our treatments. I've noticed that in treatment planning meetings, even with some of our most challenged social learners, treatment teams are often not comfortable sharing with parents the information that the children with more challenged social learning abilities will continue to have significant social learning challenges even after intensive educational and adjunct treatment programs are adhered to. This lack of clarity in the purpose and projected outcomes of a treatment program often leads parents to falsely assume their child will "recover" if not be "cured" from the treatment. Hence, families often create unrealistic treatment goals, which then lead to unrealistic transition planning for an adolescent student. Ultimately this means some students and their families aren't prepared for the child's limited ability to function in the adult world, leaving parents operating in crisis mode almost immediately upon high school graduation. To this end we also describe the projected outcome for that student, based on the category in which she functions on the ST-SCP, to better guide the treatment team, the education decision making, and transition planning.

However, we noticed that young children in preschool and early elementary school can make significant and sometimes remarkable social learning gains. Therefore, we don't want to predict how a young student will function throughout his life span. We did notice that by the time most of our students entered third grade, they were fairly set in their basic social functioning learning style through which they would then navigate the curriculum and interpret and respond to social information. For this reason, we only use the ST-SCP to create longer term decision-making for students eight years of age or older.

A key factor in developing astute social thinking and related social skills is the ability to observe social contexts and how people share space within these contexts, including the nuances of their social interactions. Observation requires awareness of one's surroundings and the people within them. In working with our students, we've noticed that they have different levels of awareness in their environment. Logically, a person has to be aware of her environment before being able to actively make increasingly sophisticated observations within it. In the more sophisticated social mind, our social observations lead to our social behavioral responses. When training fellow professionals, I'd describe some of our students as being "aloof," but fellow clinicians felt the concept of aloofness was too vague a description. I then started to use the term *social radar system* to better represent how we're expected to detect social signals to help us create related and expected social responses. Hence, neurotypical social communicators can be described as having a very active social radar system while our students' differing levels of social functioning represent, in part, different levels of social radar. The weaker the social radar, the more challenges in the person's social learning.

To help people further understand this concept, in one of my workshops, I show a YouTube clip of a "flashmob" called "Frozen Grand Central" (ImprovEverywhere, 2008). In this clip, at an appointed time, a group of more than a hundred people who have all come to New York City's Grand Central Terminal collectively stop in their tracks and freeze, regardless of what they'd been doing. They stay frozen in facial expressions and body position for about two minutes. Video captures the responses from others at the train station. After viewing the video clip, workshop audiences typically laugh as they watch the faces of people trying to figure out what's happening and why. This clip is a great example to describe how some individuals who have social learning challenges might simply walk through the train station at that moment and not understand that anyone was doing anything out of the ordinary, even when encouraged to notice those who are frozen. Another group of individuals might also walk through the station without noticing the frozen people until it was pointed out to them, and then they'd think it was really funny. Still another group of our students would immediately notice that the frozen people were doing behaviors that were unexpected for that context.

These groups represent a range of social radar, from weakness to strength, while also helping to explain why each group needs its own treatment strategy. The ST-SCP categories address these differences in students' social radar systems.

The profile also helps to predict a student's academic-learning challenges that are linked to social learning abilities. This information is critically important for making decisions that relate to what needs to be designated for treatment in the student's team meeting. These designated treatment items conform with the student's current functional abilities and also relate to her placement during the school day.

> The ST-SCP also helps to predict a student's academic-learning challenges that are linked to social learning abilities.

Additionally, the prognosis information included with each category in this profile describes what can be expected of these students once they become adults. Having this information can help families and professionals identify which types of educational lessons will most help a student in the transition to adulthood, remembering that the overall purpose of an education is to prepare a child to function in the adult world.

The original Perspective Taking Scale, as I previously developed, included three categories: Severely Impaired Perspective Taker (SIPT), Emerging Perspective Taker (EPT), and Impaired Interactive Perspective Taker (IIPT). This was only the beginning of a dynamic tool that my colleagues and I have continued to develop. Currently, six categories (including two subcategories) are represented in the ST-SCP, which has evolved thanks to help from my colleagues Stephanie Madrigal and Dr. Pamela Crooke; we're all practicing speech pathologists. The profile's categories and descriptions are summarized here. We hope over time to be able to elaborate further on this profile to see how the profile shifts with stages of development and maturity, and more specifically which lessons would be useful for students as it's recognized where they function on the profile. This profile (and related information) continues to be a work in progress. Our website, www.socialthinking.com, will provide information about any related updates as we create them.

The profile includes neurotypical functioning as an anchor on the scale. The other five categories represent differing levels of social functioning. The scale is designed to show abilities and issues that we've found that aren't specific to diagnostic labels. Hence, our profile isn't specific to autism spectrum disorders and instead explores the social functioning level of any person, regardless of diagnostic label. In this manner we can explore those with ADHD, nonverbal learning disability, emotional disturbance, and so on. This is because we've seen for years in our treatment groups that students are best taught when grouped by social functioning indicated by our profile, rather than by diagnostic label. The categories of social functioning (and subcategories) are:

1. Significantly Challenged Social Communicator (SCSC)
2. Challenged Social Communicator (CSC)
3. Emerging Social Communicator (ESC)
4. Nuance Challenged Social Communicator (NCSC)
   a. Weak Interactive Social Communicator (WISC)
   b. Socially Anxious Social Communicator (SASC)
5. Neurotypical Social Communicator (NSC)
6. Resistant Social Communicator (RSC): described as an alternative category in lieu of ESC or NCSC

In exploring each of these categories of social functioning, the profile takes into account different aspects of functioning related to the social mind, which include the following for each group:

- Understanding one's own and others' minds (including the use of social radar)
- Emotional coping (mental health challenges)
- Social problem solving
- Peer interaction including play
- Self-awareness
- Academic skills
- Bullying, tricks, mental manipulation
- Language and cognition

As you consider all this information, also keep in mind that there are only five levels that represent social functioning challenges to describe the lowest of low functioning to the highest of high functioning students who have social learning challenges. This means each category is still quite large in terms of the range of functioning it represents. For this reason, people may choose to describe a student as being at the high end or low end of one of the categories or as falling between two profile categories.

Uses of the Profile

Delineating the different social functioning levels allows us to describe, for example, why a particular student doesn't do well in his language arts class and will continue to struggle with mainstream classroom teachings as the coursework becomes more complex. This information also helps us to anticipate future success or needs. Logically, it makes sense that this same student will likely not succeed in a college level course and may need to explore vocational training as part of his high school experience.

This is not a profile of development nor is it "recovery-based." An individual isn't expected to move from one social functioning category to the next unless she started at the very high end of one category and then merged into the next category. Individuals who are best represented by one category at eight years of age are considered to be solidly within that category throughout their lives, although improvement within that particular category is to be expected.

This profile system is not a way for treatment professionals and parents to move individuals to the next "higher" profile category and should never be used as a measurement tool for determining progress in therapy or as a pre-or-post-treatment tool because that would imply that the scale is linear, which it's not.

The profile is also not designed for use with preschool children (modified play scales can be used for this age range) or with older adults (category descriptions don't fully describe their issues and needs).

The profile is appropriate for determining what type of treatment approach to use (for example, behavioral versus social cognitive or a combination), the trajectory of treatment, and the prognosis, which helps to guide us into discussions about transitioning into adulthood. It's also a crucial tool in determining which individuals should be grouped together for treatment.

ST-SCP Category Definitions

The following ST-SCP categories are described here along with related subcategories. For each level, first an overview of the group is provided, followed by the group's strengths, areas of noted relative weakness related to the categories being explored ("areas of concern"), suggested teaching and treatment strategies, and then the prognosis.

Traits from more than one group may seem to apply to one student. When this happens, it's best to determine which level includes the most traits related to that student.

Neurotypical Social Communicator (NSC)

For the most part, the individuals in this group are developmentally "on track" in their acquisition of milestones of social development beginning at birth. Although some may have an expressive-receptive language delay, their social abilities are a relative strength. They're reasonably flexible in working with a range of people and changing situations—in play-based, peer-based, and academic situations. While they do make social errors during their lives, these errors are considered within the bandwidth of "normal" social behavior and are just considered part of "being human." Individuals in this group continue to learn from their mistakes and become more adept socially throughout their lives. They've learned social thinking intuitively but benefit from some basic social communication reminders, particularly when they engage in social problem solving. The social world is too complicated for anyone to participate in without some support.

Strengths

This group has a strong social emotional connection to the world and an astute social radar system but can still become overwhelmed by social demands combined with the normal demands of stages of development; they may still face anxiety and depression, which are part of life.

Students in this group range in social functioning from people who appear "very cool" and who constantly adapt their social behavior to meet the expectations of the group (social chameleons), to those who tend to prefer to be in a smaller social circle and stick with a trusted friend, to those who are somewhat quiet in social situations. However, the individuals in this group are able to establish and maintain peer networks that allow them to feel connected within whatever community they choose while also maintaining employment as they age.

Effective Teaching Strategies

Some of these students may seek the help of counselors to navigate the complicated waters of social emotional relationships, work, and life pressures. Many seek the counsel of friends and family.

Prognosis

Neurotypical functioning implies that this group has good opportunities to succeed (and opportunities to fail) given the choices they make at achieving the job of their choice, maintaining their job, relationships, marriage, and so on.

Nuance Challenged Social Communicator (Includes SASC and WISC)

This category consists of two different groups: Socially Anxious Social Communicator (SASC) and Weak Interactive Social Communicator (WISC). Those in the WISC group appear to have solid social learning challenges as a cornerstone of their social skills weakness, but social anxiety often takes root as they get older and recognize that others perceive them as lacking in nuanced social skills. This pervasive social anxiety appears to be as problematic as their core social skills weaknesses, preventing them from easily accessing their social cognitive information. When this occurs, they appear to be more socially inept than they actually are. Though the SASC often appears to be much like the WISC, the SASC is able to work through issues related to social anxiety and social skills more quickly than the WISC once having acquired the tools to deal with his anxiety. However, because both groups benefit from the same teaching strategies, they're grouped in the same ST-SCP category, that of Nuanced Challenged Social Communicator.

Socially Anxious Social Communicator (SASC)

These are blenders and faders with anxiety. They try to blend in or subtly fade out and others are likely to describe them as shy or distant. They function "under the radar" and often try to appear to others as "fine" but avoid many social situations outside of their family.

Those identified as SASC have highly developed social radar; it's as if they interpret the information they receive through their social radar with exaggeration. Rather than recognize that people have thoughts about each other in mostly harmless ways, the SASC is often highly concerned about any thoughts another person is having, even while understanding that she also routinely has small thoughts about others when around people.

We hypothesize that this group is born neurologically to experience more anxiety and to intuitively doubt their social abilities. When comfortable or in their social element (usually around family and close friends), they appear much like a NSC. However, when their social anxiety emerges, it appears to diminish their access to their social cognition and they appear much more like a WISC (described next). The huge shift in their social behavior from appearing comfortable around others to appearing highly uncomfortable and disconnected from others marks the SASC. When feeling socially anxious, those who are in the SASC group over-focus on their feelings of anxiety and need to retreat from others, leading others to resist interacting with them. This then affirms the need of SASCs for their social anxiety: a Catch-22.

Areas of Concern

Many individuals are mistakenly thought to have behavior issues when they refuse to participate or don't participate as expected in activities that are anxiety provoking. Group work can be difficult throughout school and work, and many learn strategies to avoid social interactions, including isolating themselves through books, computer gaming, videos, and so on. Sensory integration and sensory processing issues need to be ruled out. It's reported that those with social anxiety, when compared to other types of anxiety, have the hardest time gaining and sustaining employment.

Strengths

This group has strengths in the areas of language and may have basic to advanced intelligence as well as the ability to achieve in a range of academic or nonacademic pursuits. Academically, this group can be quite solid as a whole. However, some tend to be anxious about their workload and may succumb to their anxiety, unable to complete their assignments.

Effective Teaching Strategies

The SASC benefits from a Social Thinking methodology combined with other cognitive behavior approaches for treating social anxiety. Social Thinking works best to help those in this group appreciate their own nuanced social competencies while also realizing how others interpret different aspects of their social functioning and how they can change what others think about them by shifting their social behavior. As they become more confident in this regard, they then can work at minimizing the presentation of their social anxiety. The competencies of these students can be explored and celebrated through guided practice, role play, and exposure before actively attempting to minimize their social anxiety. Mental health professionals should be actively involved in working with SASCs, especially if they can work on teaching and reteaching the core concepts of Social Thinking and related social skills as part of their social anxiety treatment.

The SASC can work well together with the WISC in a group.

Prognosis

Although they'll need to monitor their anxiety and continue to work to keep it within a level with which they can cope, if they can find their niche they have a good prognosis for living as successful adults with treatment. However, some fail to find their niche vocationally and socially, at which point they struggle to find professionals to help them with their social anxiety and the continued social learning they need to engage in now that the world is an even more complex social environment.

Weak Interactive Social Communicator (WISC)

The WISC may appear typical at first glance to adults and perhaps peers, but the sustained impression held by peers is that of a subtly awkward person.

These students demonstrate fairly well developed social radar in that they're highly aware that they have thoughts about people and people have thoughts about them and that each person has his own unique perspective and emotions related to that person's experiences. They're weaker at reading the social context to determine how to interpret meaning based on the situation. They may be neurologically less attuned in the actual moment of social interaction to interpreting a myriad of social stimuli simultaneously, such as others' facial expressions, body stance, tone of voice, semantics, and gestures, which limits the feedback they receive from others during social interactions. This is likely caused by a weakness in social executive functioning, making it difficult for them to process and respond to multiple sets of information in a timely manner (milliseconds to two seconds) to stay abreast of social interaction. One reason we believe they have these social executive functioning issues is that when they're shown a movie clip or asked to observe and interpret someone else's social interaction, they're often quite accurate in their interpretation. However, their social interpretations seem to decrease the more they're involved in the social interactions themselves. As the nuanced demands of social communication increase with age so does the discrepancy in how WISCs are perceived by their peer group. Peer rejection of WISCs is significant given their lack of nuanced ability to blend into a range of peer groups and show interest in their peers as effectively as the student would like.

This group often tends to have near normal to way above normal verbal language skills and cognition; most didn't have a serious language disorder when young. In elementary school, they're typically able to pay attention in a classroom but may be far more rigid than their peers and subtly more literal. Some are very bright (some in specific areas of interest and others in global areas of knowledge), but for many, their executive functioning challenges may also make written expression and organizational skills more difficult than would be expected given their academic intelligence. Hence, a number of WISCs are good at understanding the concepts assigned but relatively weak at getting the work done, papers written, and assignments turned in.

They attempt to work in groups but may have mixed success due to missing the subtle cues of how to relate with peers when the teacher isn't the leader. They clearly get along with some peers and in some situations better than others. This means they won't always stand out as pervasively making social errors but make enough errors for the peer group to single them out. They tend to prefer the attention of adults and may seek them out as often as possible to talk to, even during recess and school lunch breaks. Some of these students are very quiet and attempt to blend in by not talking to peers. Others who have more extroverted personalities may disrupt social interactions because they have difficulty gauging the nuance of expected responses—they may talk out of turn, talk too much, or try to be funny during a serious moment.

In peer-based social situations, as a way to survive the moment, they may focus more on their own thoughts and the expression of their own ideas rather than think about how people are thinking about them. The breakdown seems to be greatest when they need to demonstrate their social competencies in the middle of spontaneous social interactions. WISCs who were born with an extroverted personality can appear egocentric and monopolize the conversation. If more introverted, they tend to withdraw from group communication, implying to their peers that they aren't interested in being with others, even though they often crave others' acceptance. After the interaction, they recognize they've been rejected or are being treated poorly by their peers. As they move into upper elementary school and beyond, they can be keenly aware that they're doing something wrong socially but can't define what it is.

We think this group will pass the basic theory of mind tests (first order and second order false belief tasks) easily shortly after if not at the same time as neurotypical peers. They have a good sense of self and other as they've formed a better understanding of their own and others' thoughts and emotions than may be expected from persons diagnosed with more classical forms of "high-functioning" autism. This is so even if the WISC is weaker than expected at emotion regulation. They may struggle a bit with central coherence but not in the highly detailed over-focused manner of others with social learning challenges. As they transition into adolescence, the members of this group aren't typically as single-minded in their enjoyments, often having a range of interests across time or at any one time.

Many go on to develop professional careers or engage in more highly trained vocations as well as develop peer relations within a small community. Many also marry and raise a family. As they age, they may find the persistent social problems of their youth continue to emerge as they're expected to engage in highly nuanced social activity with their adult peers. This can cause them to seek counseling to sort out the complex challenges involved in establishing and maintaining social emotional relationships.

We believe this group is highly targeted by bullies because peers perceive WISCs to be somewhat neurotypical but just different enough to call them names, make fun of them, and so on. Their peers don't understand that they have a true social learning disability. To make matters worse, adults, particularly those outside of the home, see these students as charming and engaging with adults and "neurotypical enough," failing to see that the peer group wouldn't describe them in this way. Because WISCs may perform adequately to exceptionally on tests related to academics, teaching and counseling professionals may conclude that these students don't have any true social learning issues. This can happen especially because WISCs tend to pass most of our standardized social language and pragmatic tests. Parents often report that their children talk to them about feeling rejected and disconnected from their peer group. When they bring these issues to the professionals, their concerns may be dismissed because the adults find the student so easy to converse with. However, especially by middle school and beyond, no single adult monitors how a student functions throughout the school day.

Given how aware the WISCs are of how they're treated by their peers, they're at very high risk for developing social anxiety, obsessive-compulsive disorders (OCDs), and depression by upper elementary school and beyond. For many, by the time they're pre-teens and teens, mental health treatment is critical and needs to be blended with Social Thinking type treatments. As adults, WISCs often appear more paranoid because they easily recall being mistreated and feel that in general people won't be kind to them.

The WISC may have a more significant to subtle history of sensory-based challenges. As a WISC individual gets older, an occupational therapist should still assess her to rule out more pervasive sensory challenges that may limit the person from fully attending to learning, interacting in groups, or focusing on organizing her thoughts.

Assessment

WISCs are almost always able to explain the basic social rules ("talk the talk"), even when young, but they struggle to apply the rules in the moment with nuance and have issues with the social executive functioning of perspective taking ("walk the walk"). While able to pass theory of mind tasks, they may be weak empathizers right in the moment and relatively low in their understanding of how their intentions are being read by their peers during communication. They may also struggle to read communication nuances to intuit others' subtle communicative intentions.

These students should be assessed by observing them, when possible, with their peer group or through a series of informal dynamic

Social Thinking assessment tasks that explore how they respond in the moment.

Testing executive function skills is also recommended for this group because many have challenges in this area that may cause them to be less productive at completing schoolwork even if they're acquiring all the academic knowledge.

WISC students tend to be bright, but after they've completed standardized tests, they often fail to qualify for services, with their student study or IEP team saying their problems are too "mild." However, they aren't mild according to the students' peers but are only mild when compared to persons with more severe social learning challenges. As described below, those who have more obvious social skill challenges are more easily forgiven by their peers. The WISCs who we describe as having mild problems may find it very difficult to sustain a job or marriage as they become adults. This is because we're not nearly as forgiving of others' social errors or weak emotional reciprocity when we consider them to be neurotypical (even if in fact they're not).

Adaptive functioning can be a challenge for a significant percentage of WISCs. Weaknesses in areas such as hygiene, organizational skills to maintain their living environment, and poor organization of food for adequate meal preparation can all be issues for this group, even if they appear to "function well" superficially.

Strengths
This group tends to be solid to extremely good language users and

many have keen academic intelligence, scoring well to exceptionally well on tests. They may also demonstrate many other talents, such as in music, the arts, or even athletics. They can be voracious learners, specifically in the realm of science but also in literature, history, or any number of varied topics. They can have a good sense of humor and be willing learners of social information if it's presented to them in a more cognitive manner rather than simply telling them what to do socially. However, this group can be confused by subtle abstract language such as the language used when we communicate indirectly with each other.

Areas of Concern

Some students in this group do have academic issues, mostly related to feeling overwhelmed by the executive functioning load and inadequate social emotional coping mechanisms. Some may have what's described as dysgraphia (difficulty coordinating the physical act of writing) while also having simultaneous difficulty organizing ideas, sorting related details, or considering the reader's interpretation while at the same time focusing on grammar and punctuation. Yet when each area of written language is tested independently, these individuals can perform well. They may also have poor organizational skills and need more assistance to complete and turn in their homework. Some may have other learning disabilities that may or may not be related to their social learning challenges, such as dyslexia or difficulties learning abstract math concepts.

As previously mentioned, this is the group most at risk for persistent bullying, teasing, and trickery by peers, not only as children but into their adult years. Individuals in the WISC group may intentionally or unintentionally provoke or insult others. If they talk too much in class or in a meeting, they may be perceived as "know-it-alls" or "show offs." They may state their thoughts about another person without fully realizing how that person is feeling upon hearing this perceived criticism.

Anxiety and depression often plague the WISC. Their higher level social radar system unfortunately allows them to tune into the negative thoughts others may have of them without recognizing which social competencies they lack that contribute to the perception. This group is weak in fully understanding the depth and complexity of social emotional concepts, such as making and keeping friends, what it takes to maintain a marriage, and so on.

Effective Teaching Strategies

Especially for students who are 11 years old or older, strategies need to focus on the possibility of issues related to a combination of anxiety, depression, and weak social competencies.

Treatment should focus on exploring social emotional nuance and sophistication, including understanding how intentions are perceived by oneself and by others. WISC students require time to study and practice nuance-based social skills, which include dynamically adjusting social behavior based on the people and context involved. This group should be encouraged to realize they already know the social rules, but they need to work on exploring the social nuance.

The teachings of Social Thinking are recommended for this group, not exclusively through my work and the work of my colleagues but also that of other professionals who explore social learning and communication through a cognitive behavior format (for example, Tony Attwood, Carol Gray, and those involved in the SCERTS Model). Applied Behavioral Analysis (ABA) may be helpful when those in this group are very young to work through rigidities and inattentiveness in groups. However, it becomes less useful past elementary school and even inappropriate to use once the students are in high school and beyond.

Key areas for development across adolescence and into adulthood for WISCs are self-advocacy, assuming increased responsibility with regards to life skills, practice in the community, and accepting responsibility for their own learning.

With students who find it difficult to complete their schoolwork due to executive function challenges, even after strong attempts at remediation, it's best to be realistic about their potential for being able to do the coursework in a college or university program. It's important to help the students learn at whatever level they can learn how to manage their own assignments and how to advocate for themselves as they leave high school and enter into the university system. Cutting back on the number of academic classes during earlier school years can help these students focus on learning organizational skills for managing their workload. Those who haven't yet learned to effectively manage their workload would likely benefit from a transition to a college program that teaches academic self-management skills. Or, if the student has a strong history of rejecting the idea of completing classwork and homework, vocational training programs may be a way to help maximize his learning strengths in a more hands-on work environment. These same students may be able to participate in a university-type academic program after they gain further maturity and insight into how they learn best and self-organize to produce written assignments.

Prognosis

Prognosis for the WISC can be quite good but it can also be fragile. This group has one of the best prognoses for transitioning into the adult world and fulfilling their own expectations related to intellectual achievement, getting and maintaining a job, finding a life partner, and so on. However, this group also has the greatest risk of not having a safety net if unable to succeed. They're often achievement-oriented and bright but, as discussed, some may struggle to do their work independently because of organizational issues. It's not uncommon to see individuals in this group ill-prepared and overwhelmed by having to assume responsibility not only for work but also for their sleep schedule, hygiene, meal planning, budgeting, completing homework on time, developing peer relations, dating, and coping with their own sexual needs. Some may struggle to understand the extreme social nuances in the work environment and may struggle to maintain employment due to an inability to establish and maintain adequate work relationships.

Many who are perceived at one level as "successful" as adults ultimately seek counseling or are told they need counseling for their lack of nuance-based social emotional connection with others (spouse, friends, children, or at times even their workmates). Others have made choices in careers and partners that allow them a very stable, happy life but seek counseling to understand why they had so many problems as children or at other times in the past. We're also sure there are also many who have never sought counseling but are doing just fine, having emerged from the bumps and bruises of adolescence and young adulthood figuring out how to manage on their own.

Emerging Social Communicator (ESC)

The ESC group represents the largest range of individuals within the ST-SCP. The social presentation described here represents what people think of classically as high-functioning autism or Asperger's Syndrome, but many students diagnosed initially as ADHD or other categories that tend to involve social emotional regulation challenges also clearly fit this profile.

Note: Those who continue to present with strong symptoms beyond early childhood tend to be described as "weak emerging social communicators," and those that demonstrate many of these symptoms more subtly can be called "solid emerging social communicators." These aren't separate categories in this profile, however, because these students can be placed in the same group. It's important to note that when there are enough students to form different groups, then they can be grouped based on the "weak emerging" and "solid emerging" classifications.

Students in the ESC group have a weak social radar system and find it difficult to adapt to the social behavior of their peers without facilitation. They tend to stand out from the group as socially unusual, awkward, or aloof. They're weak at tracking what others are talking about and making related comments or asking questions as well as at reading situational and physical social cues (facial, gestural, tonal).

ESC individuals usually need extra time to process and respond to social information. Some have an unusual tone of voice and possibly a loud voice. Some have odd posture or rigid movements when communicating or sharing space with others.

ESCs exhibit a range of sensory integration issues (prominent when they're young), which may result in self-stimulatory behavior (flapping, toe walking, rocking, etc.), depending on the student.

Early strong characteristics are always present and observable in preschool or early elementary school and can be the reason for an earlier diagnosis for ESCs than for WISCs. In the early years, this group often lacks the natural development of joint attention and requires intervention to understand that others have thoughts that are different from their own.

However, the intensity of their symptoms and characteristics that define them as ESCs may gradually be minimized with therapeutic intervention combined with maturity, so that by middle or high school they may appear to have much "milder" symptoms. However, members of this group, while making progress in ridding themselves of more intense and maladaptive behaviors, face extra burdens as they get into upper elementary school and beyond because they're weak critical thinkers and social problem solvers.

The ESCs are sensory-seeking or less attentive when feeling overwhelmed or placed in large group environments. In school, their weak social radar systems prevent them from efficiently learning in "group think" situations. They're much better at concentrating and learning when only required to focus their social attention in a smaller group (for example, one to three other people). Ironically, because their measured IQ/learning ability may test as average or higher, we often place these students in large group learning environments assuming they're able to learn in a group. When they're unable to do so, a paraprofessional is assigned to assist. This means that the paraprofessional pays attention in the group context and then translates the information to the individual, who then attempts to complete the schoolwork. Some ESCs do learn to attend to the teacher in a classroom, especially when they sit in the front of the class but lack understanding of how to modulate their own behavior in a group. This results in instances of talking out of turn, talking for an extended length of time, and the inability to work well in peer-based groups.

Although clear social learning challenges exist, this group often enjoys being around others. Known to be off-topic, tangential, or perseverative in communication, they still enjoy communicating with a variety of listeners. They often have a very good sense of humor, and many actively seek social connection with one or two people. They often enjoy befriending others at school who function much like themselves and frequently seek out interactions with adults.

The ESC group is often celebrated early in development for their incredible honesty—not having flexible enough social minds to effectively manage mental manipulation (manipulating others and awareness that others may be manipulating them). As they get older (often by fourth or fifth grade), most are able to learn more about how this process works and may then participate in it but are quite delayed in this compared to their peer group. They may always be weak in discerning this type of information. For example, they may be able to lie on a basic social level when taught that not all facts should be stated aloud (for example, say something tastes good to make the cook feel okay).

Because of the weakness ESCs have in recognizing others' communication intentions, they tend to struggle with the concept of "stranger danger" when they're young and risk being easily tricked. They need to be taught that others have different thoughts or may try to manipulate their thoughts.

The ESCs have limited self-awareness of how they're being perceived; they also stand out among their peers as appearing more socially awkward or odd. Given that their peers can easily observe that ESCs were born to their social differences, the peers are far more forgiving of their out-of-step social behaviors than they are with the SASC and WISC groups. Friendship clubs and peer mentoring programs are usually ideally designed for the ESC. The NSC peer will much more readily volunteer to help with students who have more obvious social deficits, provided their own NSC peers recognize the peer mentor's actions as altruistic rather than an attempt to recruit the ESC to be in their own dynamic personal social circle.

The ESCs may not understand the social hierarchy of the play-ground and school, and they may want to be friends with the peer groups that aren't a natural fit for the ESC's social ability. ESCs may think they're being included when others laugh around them or make comments. Peer mentors can be helpful silencing the other students and also determining when an ESC may not be in the right situation at the right time.

Most persons in the ESC profile range have a significant history of a language-learning disability, and many have pronoun-learning challenges as part of their early language issues. Members of the ESC group aren't likely to pass the basic theory of mind tests early in development but will improve in basic theory of mind testing usually by upper elementary school or beyond. However, compared to NCSs, they still exhibit advanced theory of mind issues through-out their lives. Most motivated ESCs can learn the basic building blocks of social interaction by middle school or sooner even though they'll never be fluid or quick in their social and emotional process-ing. However, progress will be observed across the life span of the ESCs if they continue to work at learning social information as it's expected that all people do.

This group of students always has issues with being overly literal because they fail to read others' intentions efficiently or consider how situational cues help to interpret meaning. They process lan-guage as a surface structure without realizing that most language requires making social inferences to determine the intended mes-sage. An apparent lack of social processing paired with deficits in executive functioning and central coherence make it very difficult for the ESC to comprehend literature or the social nuances of the classroom. Many ESCs are described as having auditory processing deficits or central auditory processing deficits. Most struggle with sarcasm but enjoy a more slapstick form of humor. (Older ESC students begin to acquire more of a knack for irony and sarcasm.)

ESCs have very weak narrative language and many struggle to summarize their thoughts or write summary-based information such as book reviews. Some are skillful at conveying their thoughts in writing based on their own interests and perspective if they're able to create written work free from others' guidelines and expectations. For example, they may write a pretty good science fiction fantasy story but can't produce an essay on an assigned topic.

Most ESCs are highly disorganized; they tend to over-focus on details and lack conceptual thinking. They show perseveration in thoughts or interests and may have unusual interests compared to others of their age. They also have poor adaptive functioning skills (parents may call them "smart but clueless").

Most need extensive assistance to understand the variety of social and work expectations delivered each school day.

Most ESCs experience anxiety tied to the imperfections of how the world actually works compared to the way they think the world should work. Many struggle with transitions, with understanding what may be next on their schedule, or why their schedule may need to change on any given day. For example, they may become stressed if a class that's to end at 3:00 p.m. isn't actually dismissed until 3:03 p.m. They may also become easily confused in dynamic social environments, which may lead to emotional as well as sensory dysregulation. This group doesn't seem to have severe social anxiety because they don't have enough social awareness to be highly anxious about how they're perceived by others. However, they can be overwhelmed by the complexities of the world, especially when in preschool and elementary school. Their anxieties may calm a bit with age and maturity but can still be considered pronounced compared to their NSC peers.

ESCs are best when engaging in tasks where they work around others but aren't required to interact dynamically with others as part of their job description. Most struggle with jobs that require personal problem solving. Many are excellent scientists, computer programmers, horticulturists, animal scientists, or the many variations of those professions and similar occupational areas.

Strengths

Although some individuals within the ESC category are intellectually very gifted, others may have borderline verbal intelligence; hence, there's a range of academic learning abilities and language skills. It's not uncommon for academically gifted and talented ESCs to score very well on IQ and academic tests. Many have stronger visual learning skills than auditory processing ones. They may have strong scientific visual-learning strengths.

Many ESCs are excellent text decoders and can read (decode) early in development. They often do best academically in the early years of school when their attention to detail makes them strong rote learners. They can continue to excel in the areas related to their interests as they get older.

Many run into more complicated learning problems as they approach the curriculum of nine- and ten-year-olds (when critical thinking and problem solving are used to participate in the curriculum as well as with their peers). Reading comprehension of literature, fiction, and any material that requires social processing (for example, greeting cards or abstract humor in ads) will continue to be difficult for this group.

Many are quite motivated to do well when given behavioral systems and cognitive explanation. Some higher level or solid ESCs can become wonderful students because they're devoted to following routines, which include studying. If born to a tenacious temperament or encouraged to develop a pattern of engaging in hard work, the individual may become quite successful at meeting academic course requirements, even if unable to fully understand the coursework. Many high-level adult ESCs live most of their lives achieving different university degrees. They may be good at studying and absorbing information but not so able to apply it outside the classroom. When unable to find employment, they return to the university to seek another degree. This subgroup of ESCs can excel at learning in a structured environment. There are ESCs who become gifted professionals and excel in the high structure of a routine and scientific work environment, one that celebrates attention to scientific endeavor over social interaction. These ESCs can usually be celebrated for their strengths and be forgiven by neurotypical co-workers for their social awkwardness. Co-workers can see that the employee isn't being intentionally insensitive to the nuance-based expectations.

Assessment

The ESC is often one of the easier groups of students to formally assess because they have verbal language skills by the time they're in elementary school but are more likely to score poorly on tests of pragmatic language and problem-solving. Their social awkwardness is easier to document because they tend to lack chameleon-like behavior, tending to be more formal or polite in all social situations.

However, test results alone shouldn't be used to determine relevant treatment goals. It's important to observe this group in a variety of settings and develop treatment goals that help to establish core social thinking cause and effect, prediction, emotional development, reading comprehension, and so on.

Areas of Concern

Because they're more literal in their interpretation of language and nonverbal cues, ESCs will struggle to keep abreast of the growing problem-solving and critical-thinking demands of social interaction as well as academic topics that require social thinking—such as reading comprehension, written expression, and abstract ideas conveyed in middle and high school social studies lessons. Many will struggle when tackling grade level curriculum in middle and high school even if their test scores in a given subject (such as reading comprehension) indicate they're functioning at grade level.

This group also struggles to relate to their peers in a manner expected from their developmental age and measured IQ. Depending on their personality, some may struggle to figure out how to enter into peer groups and initiate social language and nonverbal communication to actively maintain interaction within the group. Others with more assertive personalities may barge into peer groups and dominate the conversation without realizing they're out of step with their peers. Due to a lack of understanding of others' motives, they may be more susceptible to being tricked or bullied without realizing this is happening to them.

It's not uncommon for ESCs to also experience challenges with adaptive functioning. Hygiene, clothing choices, bedroom or home organizational skills, creating meal plans, or paying bills in a timely manner can all be significant issues for the ESCs because these activities relate to their weak executive function skills.

Effective Teaching Strategies

ESCs will benefit from a variety of treatments over time and aren't well served by a single treatment method. When they're young, their treatment needs to be based on establishing or enhancing joint attention skills, sharing enjoyment with others, and helping to establish sensory regulation. In addition, expressive and receptive language skills are typically an area of continued focus. A blend of behavioral, relationship development, sensory integration, speech and language services, as well as the teachings of Social Thinking, will all be important. Often Social Thinking should be introduced only after establishing basic awareness of others as well as basic spontaneous expressive and receptive language skills.

Because of their lack of self-awareness and poor awareness of their own and others' social behavior, ESCs are far more likely to learn new Social Thinking and related social skills when directly mentored by peers or taught in lessons from educators or counselors than if they're simply included in activities where they're expected to model appropriate social behavior.

Young Children

For this age group, play ABA is often beneficial for establishing attention and basic skills with ESC students. Additionally, relationship-based interventions such as Floortime®, Relationship Development Intervention (RDI), and Integrated Play Groups® (IPG) are all needed for early social growth (Wolfberg, 2003). Addressing sensory regulation needs and visual tools to help structure the environment are also important (Buschbacher & Fox, 2003; Dettmer, Simpson, Myles & Ganz, 2000).

School-Age Plus

Appropriate models for this age group include the SCERTS model® (Prizant et al., 2006) and/or the Ziggurat model (Aspy & Grossman, 2007) combined with the Comprehensive Autism Planning System (CAPS) (Henry & Myles, 2007). Other relevant approaches based in cognitive behavior therapy include Social Stories® (Gray, 2010), Zones of Regulation (Kuypers, 2011), and basic concepts related to Social Thinking.

ESC individuals can work in a group of up to four individuals who are also ESC. Most enjoy the group process and usually consider the others in the group to be their friends. They tend to do well acknowledging others in the group but often don't know what to do to sustain the interaction or appreciate what others are thinking and feeling.

The ESC group benefits from continued learning about Social Thinking and related social skills at basic levels throughout their lives. Progression of lessons must start with first learning they have their own thoughts, others have thoughts, and finally how and why people manipulate those thoughts in increasingly complex contexts and across a range of people.

Transition to Adulthood

To determine the ESC's readiness or fitness for attending an academically-based college or university program after high school, it's critical to explore thoroughly each ESC person's ability to learn at the abstract and critical thinking levels and to independently manage her own unmodified homework assignments. If the student has a history of requiring intensive adult support to help her through academic coursework, the treatment team should encourage the student to participate in high school vocational training programs. Many ESCs are practical, hands-on learners, and vocational training provides them a more direct path to developing skills for independence.

Once employed, virtually all ESCs need some form of job coaching because they're not sensitive readers of subtle situational or social cues in complex environments.

Note: While not a preferred situation, at times a solid ESC is put into an intervention group with WISCs because of similar levels of cognition or language. In this situation, the solid ESC will lag behind others in the group in terms of speed and efficiency in understanding and using treatment information. Differences in social awareness and the fact that ESCs have a greater need for basic social lessons may frustrate the WISCs and impact their progression.

Prognosis

The characteristics of an ESC are likely to evolve into a less extreme presentation as the individual gets older. ESCs live with *guided independence* across their adult years. They're typically slow to leave the home. Many ultimately live independently but have a trusted team of adults to help when dealing with socially-based critical thinking and significant changes in their routine.

For most ESCs, it can be difficult to find employment without assistance, given their weak job interviewing skills. However, once in a job that fits their learning style, they can be highly productive and successful workers and are often likely to be employed for a long time. Their work peers will continue to notice their more obvious social, critical-thinking, and problem solving weaknesses and may provide them with some extra assistance or mentoring. In some ways, their more obvious lack of understanding may be helpful in a work and community setting because others are more likely to forgive social errors when they know the person can't help it.

Challenged Social Communicator (CSC)

Individuals in the CSC group are distracted in unstructured social situations but more capable in highly structured situations.

This group tends to be easily recognized by their obvious social learning challenges from a very early age and should be quick to have been labeled as having autism. They exhibit many if not all of the features of the ESC but with more extreme characteristics.

CSC individuals are usually overwhelmed in unstructured social contexts because of their very weak social radar system. They're detail focused, with weak ability to figure out relevant information (weak central coherence), so ultimately they miss the gist or gestalt. They have severe context blindness and although this is a significant weakness socially, it helps them attend more actively to scientific or minute details the NSC may not have noticed. They often are highly focused on their particular area of interest while having a limited social attention span. They're often observed to gaze around the room or at a specific object when more than one other person is communicating with them, and they have extremely limited attention in a classroom setting. Sometimes described as "aloof," individuals in this profile category still demonstrate interest in interacting with others but struggle to maintain attention to another when a person doesn't relate to them about topics they're interested in. Although we often state that students with autism need to participate in social skills groups, the CSC struggles tremendously to attend and learn in this overwhelming environment not only when very young; their difficulty with actively attending in a group spans their lifetime.

CSCs may be sensory-seeking when feeling overwhelmed because most have extensive sensory regulation challenges. Anxiety within this group is centered exclusively on changes in their world, including routines, people, and the environment. Given their lack of social awareness, they don't experience social anxiety.

CSCs have a history of expressive and receptive language challenges, challenges that are to some extent expected to continue throughout their lives. This is because they lack the ability to develop sophisticated linguistic structures or to comprehend complex abstract reasoning. For many, some form of echolalia may continue into adulthood.

The development of joint attention is markedly reduced for this group, with lessons related to this concept needed well into their elementary and eventually secondary school years. This group clearly fails the basic two theory of mind tests (first order thinking and second order thinking) at the time their NSC peers are passing the tests (at four to six years old). They'll persist in struggling tremendously with these concepts across their lives. For CSCs with near normal intelligence, the concept of mental manipulation (related to second order theory of mind testing) may be taught to them cognitively or conceptually to some extent with direct and intensive methods as they move into upper elementary and middle school. However, they'll still be extremely weak in applying this knowledge fluidly in less structured situations as they struggle to process multiple stimuli and intentions (within milliseconds to two seconds). This also means they'll have more severe weaknesses than others in recognizing stranger danger. They need to be taught explicit rules for avoiding potential hazards with strangers because they can't be expected to figure out who has good versus poor social intentions.

The lack of abstract language-based reasoning, combined with their tendency to over-focus on details, causes them to struggle tremendously with inference and prediction. As a result, they're very weak in socially-based critical thinking and problem solving.

It's not uncommon for the CSC to struggle to discern reality from fiction—this happens with most children (and many adolescents) in this profile category. They get cartoon or movie characters stuck in their heads and insist that these characters are real. They may maintain that things happen the way they do on TV and become frustrated when unable to replicate them. Given their lack of defining these boundaries, a student with CSC may state "my dad is buying a Rolls Royce," when the NSC would have stated, "I wish my dad was buying a Rolls Royce."

Basic theory of mind/perspective taking concepts need to be actively taught to this group, but it's a slow and long-term prospect to help them learn the absolute basics over time. The teacher should be aware she isn't teaching to proficiency but instead is teaching to help the student better understand the basic concepts that "my thoughts are different from your thoughts" and "we can possibly manipulate each other into believing something that isn't true." Even if the student remains clumsy in applying these concepts, the exposure to them builds awareness of others' minds and the idea that people may not always be honest in their interactions with the CSC.

Many individuals in this profile are good at decoding factual text and can also be good with math calculations; many excel at reading decoding and can quickly do basic math problems. However, this group commonly lacks the ability to comprehend inferential information such as that conveyed through reading literature or doing math word problems. As the curriculum becomes more inferentially based, CSC individuals struggle tremendously to be able to independently complete schoolwork. They'll continue to struggle to understand the assignments even when provided with a tutor or a paraprofessional. While CSCs may be delightful persons with many "normal" aspects to their IQ subtests, they'll most certainly struggle in the mainstream curriculum because it requires students to utilize more personal problem solving and critical thinking in their daily assignments. We explain to parents that the mainstream curriculum of language arts and possibly other subjects won't continue to be the friend of the CSC as he moves past third grade; each year will become progressively more difficult for this student.

Spoken and written expression are difficult for CSCs, compared to their same age NSC peers. They may struggle tremendously with narrative language. Peers and adults intuitively determine that individuals in this group have difficulties conveying a message accurately. Because of this, the NSC peer or adult will use 20 questions with the CSC to try and figure out what the individual is trying to communicate or what she needs if unable to state it succinctly. Their language is poorly organized. Related to this are their poor organizational skills for managing assignments without an adult helping to establish a system for them to understand expectations, what to do, and when to do it. CSCs will struggle to do their homework with any level of independence and won't remember to turn in their homework because that requires conceptual knowledge.

Awareness of the passage of time and a sense of urgency are often lacking in this group. When given tasks to do that don't capitalize on their strengths, they usually don't ask for help, may become anxious, and struggle to appear to others as if they're motivated to do the task. They approach a task slowly and often are unfocused as they move through it, if they're able to complete it at all.

The parents of CSCs often state that they're not accidental or incidental learners in that they don't absorb new learning from simply being exposed to new experiences. Instead, parents report that these students have to be explicitly taught concepts related to social learning and social skills, and they aren't capable of learning all complex concepts.

They're likely to have extremely limited self-awareness or none, which prevents them from perceiving what others might be thinking about them. The peer group is very quick to see that the CSC is socially atypical and is far more forgiving of their differences than they are for some of the other profiled groups. Trained peer mentors can be quite helpful in encouraging increased social interaction with CSCs, especially in one-on-one situations.

While individuals within this group may do well in a specific work environment, they often struggle throughout their lives with change. They can become very proficient with learning routine tasks, but when required to do the same task in a new environment they can struggle immensely. Given their weak central coherence, they typically learn by memorizing routines and not by conceptualizing the task. Hence, when asked to do the same type of task in a new location, they may become confused because they don't know how to do certain aspects of the task in a different place. For example, they may be able to continue to enter the same data on a computer as long as the log-in and data entry requirements are exactly the same. However, they probably won't figure out who to go to to ask for help or how to go about finding out what they need to know once the people in the situation have changed. This lack of conceptual thinking makes generalization of learning difficult. However, once employed in a *predictable routine* that has taught them not only to be accurate in their work and productive in the job, these individuals tend to keep it. This group tends to feel most comfortable adhering to a schedule. Once they're taught how to use a transportation system to move around their community, they're usually punctual and can learn (with direct instruction) to be more and more efficient in their productivity over time. However, the CSC group requires job coaching to help them learn the details of any new job.

The CSC lacks basic social problem solving skills, but as the NSC adults in the community become familiar with them, the NSCs realize this weakness intuitively and then often look out for the CSCs.

Almost all CSCs struggle to develop adaptive functioning skills commensurate with their factual learning skills. Behaviorally-based lessons—to help them develop skills for being in the community, organize their living environment, prepare reasonably healthy food choices, develop an awareness of time, develop more awareness of strangers—typically need to be incorporated into their treatment programs during the school day. It should be expected that they learn these skills with their family members and as part of any home programming.

Strengths

The CSC group is comprised of individuals with a range of intellectual functioning. Most individuals in this group commonly have "splinter skills" in the more comprehensive academic skills set, such as the ability to decode or remember and state factual information. Many also have scientific visual learning strengths over auditory processing but this isn't universally the case. Individuals in this group tend to be concrete thinkers who crave and need structure for their best performance. Because this group finds comfort in routine and predictability, they may do very well in jobs based in redundancy and routines.

While we're aware of the many learning challenges this group faces when expected to participate in the full inclusion type of educational experience, we should note that CSCs are often interesting, delightful personalities with their own unique preferences, not only in their participation in activities but also in terms of whom they choose to spend time with. They have a very interesting view of the world and frequently have an excellent, slapstick sense of humor.

Although the world can seem overwhelming to this group, once strong treatment programs are put in place, they can achieve success and feel proud of their accomplishments.

Assessment

The CSC will generally score poorly on most, if not all, social language tests and tests of problem solving. They'll usually also demonstrate expressive and receptive language learning issues on formalized tests. Tests of adaptive functioning typically show strong deficits in social and communication areas, if not in other areas as well. Qualifying these students for treatment isn't typically the problem. The more difficult consideration is to determine which treatments should be utilized at different times in their development to help them function as independently as possible. In our opinion, placing these students in a full-inclusion program—especially once they're in upper elementary, middle, and high school—in order to have them strictly learn the curriculum of their age group won't provide them with the functional adaptive skills they need for navigating adulthood. At the same time, they'll also be unable to learn many aspects of their curriculum due to its increased social critical thinking complexity even if they have a dedicated team of professionals providing learning assistance.

Areas of Concern

There are many areas of concern for this group; however, their lack of social understanding is immediately obvious to the peer group, which helps them to rally support from others. School-age peers and adults alike are likely to lend support without being told to do so.

From a learning perspective, this group over-focuses on facts; they're very, very literal. They all are considered to have expressive and receptive language weaknesses across their life, and we think that virtually all of these students began to acquire language in a disordered manner through echolalia. Further, their lack of conceptualizing about the world makes it much more difficult to teach them increasingly abstract concepts. Most neurotypical people take conceptual thinking for granted and struggle to provide the level of details this group needs to learn to succeed at tasks, and some complex reasoning tasks required in the curriculum are beyond the CSC's ability to learn. This can be a challenge in the classroom as teachers depend on a student's ability to predict and infer what's required to participate with others as well as how to engage in the curriculum beyond second grade.

The CSC group needs very explicit, direct teaching not only in school but in the community. They won't transfer the idea that the math lessons they participated in to learn how to count money have anything to do with using money in the community. Virtually all of these students need paraprofessionals, and later, job coaches to help them acquire basic understanding of how to participate in specific situations.

Effective Teaching Strategies

Similar to the ESC profile category, extensive and intensive therapies are important for establishing a shared intentional communication system for CSCs, including the following: joint attention skills, sharing enjoyment with others, helping to establish sensory regulation, and constant focus on expressive and receptive language. This group benefits from a variety of treatments over time and isn't well served by one type of intervention. This means that limiting treatment to only ABA or social relationship, sensory,

Social Thinking, or expressive/receptive language treatment will fail to address the myriad needs of the CSC.

This group requires individualized instruction for most concepts; when grouped with others, they're unable to sustain attention and therefore don't actively learn to be part of even a small group until they're in upper middle school or high school.

Highly structured programs that teach toward independence and problem solving, such as structured TEACCH (www.teacch.com), are tremendously helpful for this group. These individuals benefit greatly from structured teaching classrooms, and we strongly encourage the CSC children to be placed in this specialized classroom for most of the school day for any subject that isn't their own learning strength, thereby allowing them to learn how to use their own abilities to forge a sense of independence and success across their school years. When we're asked how to decide when to pull a child out of the mainstream classroom and into a specialized classroom, it's our opinion that students should be placed in more specialized learning environments like a structured TEACCH classroom when they can't do the majority of their schoolwork independently. This means if tutors, paraprofessionals, parents, and teachers are completing most of the assignments for the student, we feel that student needs to be placed in a more structured and slower paced learning environment to encourage him to learn adaptive skills to function more independently. For example, if the student can decode but not interpret socially based literature (language arts), work with the student to learn to use her decoding skills to interpret written instructions so she can learn to follow written routines without adult cues.

Treatment should be selected by exploring each CSC individual's unique strengths and weaknesses as a way to tap into eclectic treatment regimes. The appropriate intervention will depend on the cognitive, social cognitive, sensory, and language learning level of the individual within this profile and her age.

The CSC will strongly benefit from vocational training when in high school and transitional post-secondary programs. They won't do well post-high school in a more traditional academically-based college or university program. To our despair, we have observed some CSC persons get through their high school programs with reasonably good grades simply because adults have done their work for them. These students are then sent to community college classes that aren't designed to teach those with such literal learning skills beyond the classes that teach adaptive functioning (daily living skills) to young adults. We haven't yet seen a CSC individual graduate from a college or university program because that type of education requires students to take a range of courses about history, language arts, and science, many of which require conceptual knowledge beyond their ability.

Once the CSC is able to communicate spontaneously to discuss information that she perceives and has the basic sensory and behavioral regulation to attend in a one-to-one teaching format, Social Thinking treatment can be one of many tools used. Working on building the CSC's awareness and understanding of their own and others' social thoughts is critical. We have the following four major areas of basic social thinking that we work on with this group over all of their school age years, concepts about which they'll continue to learn more well into adulthood:

1. I have thoughts about myself.
2. I have thoughts about you so that I recognize that your thoughts are different from mine.
   a. I can identify what I know that's different from what you know.
   b. I can recognize who may be able to help me answer a specific question and why.
3. I can protect who knows my thoughts by learning to whisper or just keep a thought in my head.
4. I can manipulate your thoughts.
   a. I can hide information from you.
   b. I can lie.
   c. I can tell when someone may be lying to me.

Young Children

Functional ABA is often beneficial for establishing attention and basic skills in this profile group. Additionally, relationship-based interventions such as Floortime and IPG are all needed for early social growth. The use of visual schedules and emotion regulation is also important.

Prognosis

CSCs may require significant guidance throughout their adult years; the more successful CSCs can live with *guarded independence* during those years—meaning they may live in an apartment or as part of a group home and follow their routines independently, once learned. However, they need to be actively monitored because they may not realize when a problem may be developing. We also have found that this group becomes more able to actively learn about the social world all the way through adulthood. Hence with maturity, they may be able to grasp some basic social concepts that eluded them when they were younger.

CSCs are able to learn skills to become employed in a variety of highly structured and routine-based jobs. Most if not all individuals in this profile category don't benefit from or excel in university programs focused on academic performance. CSCs tend to be more hands-on learners because they don't easily apply information from one context to the next.

Significantly Challenged Social Communicator (SCSC)

SCSC students are inattentive and internally distracted. They appear to us to be singularly focused on internal thoughts and sensory input and conversely limited or at times unaware of the social and situational demands imposed by other people. Usually they're nonverbal or more likely minimally verbal without strong expressive language systems. However, many are a bit more adept at communicating through augmentative communication systems such as Picture Exchange Communication System (PECS) or computer-assisted programs.

The SCSC typically has at least four major areas in which they are challenged.

1. Significant cognitive impairment

2. Severe expressive and receptive language-learning challenges
3. Severe social relational issues
4. Serious sensory integration challenges

To account for the latter three areas of weakness, it's common that these individuals are diagnosed with classic autism. However, given the SCSCs uneven cognitive development that often measures in the intellectually impaired range, it's important to understand that autism alone doesn't fully describe this group's learning challenges because they also have a significant cognitive impairment.

Of all of the groups represented on the profile, members of the SCSC group can demonstrate a very uneven development profile. They may have a strong islet of intelligence related to music, art, or computers that's far more advanced than their ability to relate to others or communicate effectively using spontaneous language. However, this group is also one about which we understand the least given their inability to develop efficient, functional communication systems. The SCSC group hasn't been well studied due to their inability to communicate efficiently, and yet we can observe them to have personal preferences and emotional reactions not only related to objects but also people. It's unclear if for some in this group their sensory systems regulate sensory input so inefficiently that they can't begin to access their cognitive potential. For some, it's reported that through computer keyboarding they may develop the ability to express themselves in a manner that we did not expect. Therefore, it's best to assume we don't know enough about the actual working minds of the individuals we classify as part of this group. But as we observe them to learn about their desires and motivations, we can also provide treatments to try to help them function better in their surroundings and with other people. If they progress beyond our expectations, we shift our expectations!

Strengths

Some SCSC individuals have strong areas of intelligence—for example, talented artist, math calculation skills, ability to complete puzzles, navigational abilities on a computer that aren't predicted by their low adaptive behavior or communication or general cognitive skills. Individuals in this group learn best in a highly predictable environment and may learn core rote concepts related to their academic skills (math facts, reading decoding). Some are excellent text decoders and are able to follow written fact-based visual schedules into adulthood.

Many are considered to be friendly at times and enjoy the company of others, meaning they sit near others and stay calm while they engage in tasks of interest to them or routines they've been trained to complete.

A small percentage of those who are SCSC may have unusual areas of strengths and are referred to as "savants" given their other patterns of learning weaknesses. Some savant talents may include music or mathematical or science knowledge that's factually based.

Areas of Concern

This group could be described as having an extremely weak social radar system. They're not naturally attentive to those around them, particularly in a complex environment where many people are doing many different things all at once. Therefore, they won't benefit from educational environments where several students are placed together to learn in the group. They do their best learning in an uncluttered one-on-one environment with active sensory regulation treatments to help their brain and body learn to focus together.

All SCSCs have severe challenges with traditional learning approaches and working as part of a group (of any size). They struggle to self-regulate in a group. In fact, if a teacher talks (shifts attention) to another, the SCSC individual may become wholly inattentive or angry because of his lack of understanding of how and when to listen and learn alongside others.

These individuals will have severe language impairments that coexist with intellectual impairments. Many are nonverbal or minimally verbal. If language is developing, it almost always includes a high percentage of echoed speech and may have spontaneous communication at the word level; SCSCs have limited syntactical development.

The SCSC may have extreme sensory integration challenges. They tend to have intense demands for processing sensory information in specific ways, often engaging in repetitive patterns related to the sensory world (for example, flipping a string, flapping their arms, rocking their bodies, pacing back and forth).

All SCSCs have challenges in the development of their theory of mind, but it's thought that some may have more insight as they age than we can easily measure effectively. Although they may have strong preferences for who they want to be with and who they want to avoid, they lack the social knowledge and sophistication to initiate and sustain friendships or even basic politeness measures to relate to peers consistently (NSC peers or their own similar peer group). This group of students is virtually ignored by the school bullies because the SCSC is often too spaced out to even notice the negative intentions of the peer.

SCSCs are very, very literal with weak to severely weak auditory processing skills. Many are limited to being able to follow one-to-two step commands. Reading comprehension is limited to simple instructions or specified facts.

This group also tends to struggle greatly with written expression, although some can learn basic handwriting skills but have difficulty applying these skills to express more than basic wants, needs, or directions. As a whole, it's best to teach individuals in this group how to keyboard and skip handwriting altogether because they also have serious motor-planning difficulties.

SCSCs also appear disorganized in managing information from the greater environment; however, they can be very skilled at tuning into their own environment and routine. They can become distressed if their routine is modified or their organized materials are changed without their participation in the process. Some are quite self-injurious or prone to physical violence involving others.

They're much better learners in their areas of specific focus or interest while they struggle to learn information that isn't part of that focus or routine. They learn best when the activities they engage in are visual, concrete, and have a logical progression they can be taught to follow.

All SCSCs have poor awareness of adaptive functioning/life skills. A large part of their treatment programs, including those during the school day, should focus on developing functional routines and learning skills of daily living to help contribute to the individual forming some sense of functioning independently over time. Blending academic learning skills (math and reading) with daily functioning is ideal. They learn best when information presented to them is logical and serves a purpose.

Assessment

This is a difficult group to assess for their potential for abstract thought, such as theory of mind, because they have significant if not severe receptive and expressive language difficulties. It's difficult to use most formalized tests that require any aspect of back-and-forth social interaction (which is the test paradigm for most social language and language based testing) because the SCSC struggles to understand how to participate in these contexts. The best assessments are those that observe SCSCs participating in a series of functional tasks and determine what types of information help them to learn—for example, verbal, visual, physical cues, and so on.

Effective Teaching Strategies

The least restrictive learning environment for the SCSC is typically in a self-contained classroom based on their need for one-on-one instruction.

Students in this group need intensive and early intervention to assist with sensory regulation, joint attention, relationship development, development of functioning communication skills, organizational skills, and adaptive living skills. They also require blended treatments of sensory regulation and functional ABA to encourage the development of functional adaptive living and learning skills and functional communication skills.

Those in the SCSC group won't benefit from the core concepts of Social Thinking due to their lack of language development and associated metacognitive awareness. This is a group that benefits from highly integrated treatment models such as the SCERTS® model, the Ziggurat model, or CAPs.

The TEACCH model is a critical program for this group, helping them learn through routine and structure.

Prognosis

Most SCSCs will continue to learn, albeit very slowly, throughout their lives and will make gains when compared to their own level and rate of learning. The SCSC is a person who is highly dependent on adult support and will remain dependent on caregivers to help with decision-making, emotional regulation, management, and changes in routines. All individuals who are best described by this profile should be legally conserved by a responsible adult as they enter into adulthood.

Resistant Social Communicator (RSC)
(An alternative category on the ST-SCP)

Note: This is a subgroup of students who were often thought to be ESCs or WISCs but didn't benefit from group learning experiences. This group falls between the ESC and the WISC with regard to social knowledge level.

The reason this is an alternative category and not a solid category on the profile is that many of our students in adolescence who function as a high level ESC—when given lessons in social thinking and maturation—evolve into WISCs and don't progress through the RSC category. Thus, RSC is a separate and distinct alternative category on this profile.

RSCs are insisters and arguers. They may say they aren't interested in others but they're class clowns or they seek out people to complain to about how no one understands them. In short, they're attention seekers who get people to attend to their inappropriate actions but then act like they didn't want the attention.

These individuals don't blend well into a group because they make the group be "all about them," and some may take great silent delight when receiving the full attention of the group (negative or positive). When encouraged to work at blending into the group, they tend to argue and resist, making offensive statements to adults and peers alike and often say, "I don't care how I make people think and feel!"

Interestingly, when RSCs have individual treatment, it often becomes apparent that their understanding of social thinking and related social skills is significantly delayed, with a lack of understanding of some basic social concepts. Therefore, their attempts to take over the group may be due to a lack of understanding of group dynamics that they've refused to acknowledge until the therapist establishes a safe one-on-one working relationship with them. However, like all of us, they want social validation, needing to be acknowledged by others even if they don't want to admit it. Therefore, they do want some level of attention from others but don't know how to achieve it in a manner we would describe as socially appropriate most of the time.

Individuals in the RSC group have a fair social radar system in that they're aware of who's around them and that there are group expectations. However, they aren't well tuned in to how people feel about them or how to meet the expectations of the group, although they won't admit it. Instead, they tend to think in more black-and-white terms ("that person likes me" or "that person doesn't like me") without understanding the subtleties of the mind or the shifting impression we can make on people in a day that builds into our social emotional memory.

This group doesn't efficiently make the connection between the fact that how they behaved yesterday impacts how people treat them today or tomorrow. Instead, they understand how they want to be perceived and therefore think they *are* perceived this way. The RSC often perceives herself to be bright and greatly misunderstood.

This group can be openly defiant and often demeaning to others who don't agree with their line of thinking. However, when they do connect positively with another, they can be very sweet to the other person for at least a short period of time. They may also have a good sense of humor with regard to what they find funny and believe that everyone else enjoys the same jokes or comments as them. Many tend to become more exuberant with their humor but don't easily understand that people may not be laughing with them.

RSCs are often more literal than their peers in their interpretations of social situations, reading comprehension, and so on. They're often incredibly rigid in their thinking, insisting that people follow the rules they believe should be the rules. When they don't follow their own rules, they shrug it off as their weakness. For example, they may insist on pure honesty from others but then are often caught lying themselves.

Many RSCs have other learning disabilities but often measure intellectually as solid if not bright in their overall full scale IQ. Younger children in this group are likely to be somewhat slower to pass basic theory of mind tasks (first order thinking, second order false belief testing, and so on), and some may have a specific language learning disability (SLI). They often state that they understand you have a different opinion than they have; they just think you're an idiot for not following their line of thinking. By the time they're in middle school they can be quite manipulative. They can be very good at lying, but they have difficulty understanding when others lie to them. They can be naïve without realizing it and so easily taken advantage of by their peers. They may do things to try and fit into a desired social group without realizing they're being used by their peers. Most of their friendships aren't deep. They may have one or two childhood friends who have stuck by them into adolescence; as they age, most don't form new friendships that aren't cyberspace-based.

It's not uncommon to see the RSC diagnosed as behaviorally or emotionally disturbed. It's very common that they're well known in the office of the school disciplinarian; some become school phobic as they age into upper middle school or high school. By high school at the latest, virtually all have commingled anxieties or depression as they often face peer rejection and have difficult relationships with their parents. Yet, when counseling help is offered, they may seek isolation and avoid working on relationships stating, "I don't care." Only a persistent counselor that focuses on relationship-building as the first priority will break through.

It's not clear to us why one person becomes a RSC and another person with similar social cognitive functioning doesn't. We assume that one's temperament or personality plays heavily into this. These students are also extremely hard to parent, and if the parent gives into their demanding nature, it can exacerbate the problem.

Assessment
Why is this group so difficult to assess to determine their social learning disability? To begin with, we're all just human. Most of us are driven to work with students who tend to make us feel good about our work and our efforts as parents and professionals. The RSCs use a strategy that doesn't serve them well in the long run

but does provide them with the perceived power they seek in the moment—they try to make people (including professionals who work with them) feel like fools when in their presence. Once they've offended us, at times deeply, it's relatively easy for the professional to minimize the conclusion that these students have a learning disability and maximize the idea that they must have emotional disorders because they're seen as trying to hurt people who are attempting to help.

Strengths

Many RSCs have normal to way above normal verbal intelligence and may score average to above average on academic tests. They're often very good at fact-based learning and frequently have talents in the arts, in using computers, or even in sports (but they have difficulty being team players). Their ability to use humor can be quite clever, when infused at the right time and place.

Areas of Concern

While some RSCs may be diagnosed with a language-learning weakness, most are perceived as good language users and are especially skilled at arguing as they approach their teens. However, they may not perceive themselves as argumentative and instead appear to think that if they just keep explaining something, the other person will eventually get it.

From a mental health perspective, they can become depressed, which can manifest itself in lashing out at others in a blaming and condescending tone. This group tends to wear out not only their teachers but their parents and siblings. Most don't appear to have a lot of social anxiety (they tend to be oblivious to how they're impacting others) because that would require a more tuned social radar system. However, they do face serious mental health challenges because they face so much rejection. This is a group characterized by weak flexible thinking, relatively weak abstracting, poor problem solving, and they're often highly disorganized. Over time, they may (or may not) receive a diagnosis of a learning disability related to these core characteristics.

From an emotional processing point of view, RSCs appear to be somewhat sluggish or limited in their understanding of the nuanced fine lines that define our different emotions. They tend to be more black-and-white thinkers with regards to reading or interpreting others' emotions. Therefore, they don't project others' emotions effectively nor do they effectively regulate their own emotions to stay emotionally in step with others. They're often seen as highly emotional and reactive and may be diagnosed with Opposition Defiant Disorder (ODD) if not as bipolar.

It's likely many have undiagnosed sensory integration challenges; an occupational therapist should be consulted to rule out these conditions and address any other diagnostic issues.

Given that they're an "alternative category," RSCs will also experience the same learning challenges as ESCs or WISCs, depending on which group they best align with in their core learning skills. We often see our RSCs function right on the borderlands of the ESC and WISC.

Effective Teaching Strategies

This group benefits most from intensive individual therapy during their most resistant periods. However, treatment won't progress if the RSC hasn't yet established a solid, trusting relationship with an educator or counselor who is spearheading their program; it takes time to develop these relationships. Even if the RSC does form this relationship with a professional, the professional should still count on the RSC being surly at times, testing the boundaries of the relationship.

RSCs tend to prefer people who have direct treatment styles, giving them clear information about what they're doing well. As they begin to respect a professional, they can begin to receive feedback based on what they need to work on to learn more about the social emotional process.

Unlike more traditional social learning programs where we teach students about what others expect from them and then help students learn to adapt their thinking and behaviors to meet the needs of others, treatment for the RSC needs to begin by helping them to see what they expect from others to help keep them comfortable. They often need to begin with what we describe as "inside-out treatment" for them to anchor socially through recognition of their own social value system. By studying who they like and don't like and why, they realize they're forming their own social impressions and reacting to what they think and feel based on how others treat them. It will take some time (maybe years) to help RSCs to appreciate that if they require others to act and respond emotionally in certain ways in order for the RSC to like them, it eventually makes some sense that others likely have those same social expectations for them.

Unfortunately, individuals within this group have received a lot of attention for not participating well in groups. Yet, as treatment professionals and parents we erroneously begin treatment by insisting they should modify their social behavior so they can blend into the group when they don't understand the value of blending. After all, they get so much valued attention for standing out. When we begin treatment by presenting them with social expectations that others have for them and asking them to work to meet those expectations (what we call "outside-in treatment"), we don't find this to be a successful approach!

It's important to recognize how much the RSC needs to learn about social information. Some RSC students need to begin with early intensive lessons related to "thinking with their eyes" and eventually move on to learning how we use a "brain filter" and the "social fake" to survive social times when we may want to blend into the group and not do or say things that make people have "weird thoughts" about us. This same type of treatment is needed for adults who are considered to be RSCs.

Deep Social Thinking lessons and cognitive behavior therapy are ultimately the treatment tools for this group, but during the early years of development (young childhood and adolescence), ABA and reward-based systems are needed to motivate them to participate in treatment that they find to be nothing but hard work. A real problem with RSCs and behavioral management systems is that they try to figure out how to manipulate the system or the people who have created the system. They make a game of trying to find the holes in the behavior plans.

The RSC is often a logical, practical thinker who benefits from vocational training programs when in high school. They're more prone to struggle in classroom learning environments given their challenges with working in groups and staying organized. Some really dislike having to go along with another person's expectations, including the teacher's expectation for the homework that needs to be done to meet the class requirements.

Prognosis

If RSCs receive treatment before adulthood (when young adults and before) and acknowledge that they have a social emotional learning disability and need to learn to adjust their behaviors and emotional responses based on others' expectations, they can shift back onto the original ST-SCP categories. Their prognosis then is more in line with the high level ESC or low level WISC. Still, many RSCs need extra guidance into their adult years with critical thinking and understanding others' complex motives (much like the ESC).

If not actively treated as children and adolescents, this challenging group can become very dysfunctional adults filled with anger and blame. We think our prisons hold many RSCs. They also tend to end up on the doorstep of the psychiatric community, who may not know what to do with them because medication alone doesn't soften their edges when relating and responding to others. Many adult RSCs are unemployed and may be rejected from their families.

Concluding with an Uncomfortable Observation

In later adolescence and middle school, most NSCs don't want to assist or be the peer-mentor to the "solid" ESC, RSC, or WISC because the larger peer group can't as easily define these students' social thinking differences. To be frank, the peers think this higher functioning group of students with social learning challenges looks "too normal" to have special compensations made for them. At this point in their own social development, the NSC peers don't want to be aligned with students who are socially different in more subtle ways. Most NSCs of this age are struggling to make their own place in their school's social system, and they become less agreeable to work with or mentor these higher level students who appear to be so "normal looking." They fear this relationship may lower their status among their own peers. In fact, it's this higher level group that tends to be more bullied by NSCs, but individuals in this higher level group can also be guilty of actively bullying others.

Ironically, those students who function in the lower categories of the ST-SCP get the most peer assistance. From our observation, peer-based mentor-training programs tend to be the most successful when the NSC is assigned to work with more awkward ESCs, CSCs, and SCSCs. As they volunteer to help the more obviously challenged students, NSCs may actually gain social status among their NSC peers. However, we strongly encourage school-based programs to work with NSC mentors to develop more awareness of the social learning needs of all students, even those who appear more nuance-challenged. We also encourage school districts to incorporate bully-management strategies that encourage all students on a campus to become more active bystanders who help to advocate for students when they see them being bullied. Learn more about this topic at www.teachsafeschools.org.

Surprisingly little is known in our educational and mental-health treatment communities about how we use social communication concepts and skills to form societies from a normal developmental perspective (Winner, 2007a). The importance of this statement can't be underestimated. If we base treatment decisions on a person's outward social skill production (symptoms) and not on the core concepts related to how that person processes and responds to his own and another person's social mind, our treatments will always lack depth. Further, if we place individuals together in treatment groups in which they share relatively few social learning strengths and weaknesses and emotional coping mechanisms, but do share a diagnosis, we usually fail to provide good use of the treatment sessions or best practices.

Chapter 9

....

Who Is Responsible for Creating and Teaching Social Thinking and Related Social Skills? Is the Same Set of Teaching Techniques Relevant for All Persons with ASD and Related Social Learning Challenges?

The quick answer to the first question, of course, is *everyone*! On a more practical level, it's impossible to identify one professional or care provider as singly responsible for teaching students or clients who need to learn more about social thinking. The many professionals who need to teach social thinking include pediatricians, psychiatrists, clinical psychologists, counselors, social workers, regular and special education teachers, speech language pathologists, educational psychologists, board certified behavior analysts, and occupational therapists. Not one of these professions consistently devotes even a part of its program to the early and ongoing social development of the mind and how this mental construct fosters related development of social skills, reading comprehension, and so on. As the founder of Social Thinking, I've been invited to provide grand rounds or workshops to a wide range of professionals on the previous list, and the feedback is consistent—no one profession has been routinely trained in this type of development and learning. In fact, when I was asked to speak at grand rounds to a team of well-respected psychiatrists who worked for a large urban hospital, I was told, "Be nice, be careful with these folks; they're afraid of autism."

Until that situation changes, the educators, doctors, and counselors are left on their own to seek information to further their own awareness and learning.

Speech language pathologists are taught to be aware of social pragmatics and the "use" of communication (primarily social verbal language), but few graduate school programs delve into the complexity of social learning. When treatments are recommended, they're mostly more behaviorally based, social skills-based teaching methodology (for example, pick an observed deficient social skill and teach them a different skill such as topic maintenance or turn-taking). Psychologists and mental health counselors are skilled at exploring the social emotional complexities of the mind for persons with reasonable perspective taking abilities, but their teaching programs generally fail to consider how to teach social emotional information to persons who can't efficiently understand their own and another's perspective simultaneously. Occupational therapists can help prepare the body and mind for learning but aren't taught specific strategies related to the social executive-functioning challenges of this population. Teachers and behaviorists learn to teach students specific skills and develop or carry out behavior plans to attempt to increase the consistency of desired behaviors and decrease the consistency of undesired behaviors through tangible reward systems. However, they're not instructed in how to define the broader social landscape in ways that are meaningful to our higher functioning students with social thinking challenges. Parents responsible for teaching social skills to their children in their homes and communities aren't prepared for the challenges of children who don't actively and intuitively learn social thinking and related skills in their early years of life as a by-product of coexisting with others.

However, more than any professional, parents avail themselves of the Internet to learn about ways to help their children, and many parents are exposed to ideas related to teaching Social Thinking before professionals are. For this reason, I've found that many parents of kids with social learning problems have learned more about Social Thinking than many professionals. When I provide trainings, I encourage parents and professionals to learn together because this is relatively new information for all groups.

While it's true that a wider range of professionals is expressing far more interest in ASD-SCD than at any time in our history, developing treatment strategies for those with social learning-related conditions is still a nebulous black hole for many. In fact, because "autism" originally referred to students who demonstrated significant cognitive and language-based learning challenges (many were nonverbal), the early and general agreement was that the counseling-related professionals wouldn't treat persons with autism. That was left to the professional educators. The core diagnosis of autism shifted into what's now known as "autism spectrum disorders" (ASD) a few years after Asperger's Syndrome was recognized in the DSM-IV in 1994. As mentioned in Chapter 1, how we diagnose those with ASD-SCD is changing again with the DSM-5. However, the counseling-based mental health professionals haven't fully sorted out their role in the treatment process for those with different social abilities across the ASD-SCD spectrum of functioning.

Counseling professions didn't have a method for determining who on the autism spectrum could benefit from counseling. Professionals and educators struggled (and continue to struggle) with how to qualify students who were more proficient with language and intellectual skills but who presented as having social behavior problems. Although we've improved greatly since 1994 in diagnosing those with social learning problems as ASD, SCD, ADHD, or with related other labels, our professional organizations haven't been as well organized in taking on the role of educating their members about treatment for those with ASD-SCD at the level of the university curriculum. This is due, in large part, to the fact that while we can observe and diagnose the problem, the research is lacking in how to define the range of problems observed that negatively impact our ability to develop treatment plans. For example, a growing community of professionals recognize that social learning challenges co-mingle with anxiety. This co-mingling of issues creates a unique set of challenges that need to be further defined and explained to develop a refined treatment plan. This also requires us to explore how we can unite our fields of study because mental health has typically managed anxiety treatments, and speech language pathologists and behaviorists have managed social learning challenges. Perhaps through refining the lens through which researchers explore the different levels of the social mind, as suggested in our ST-SCP and the DSM-5 descriptions of ASD and SCD, more refined treatments will emerge. Without solid research to prove the clinical relevance of developing different treatment strategies for those with different levels of social abilities, it's difficult to introduce ideas into a profession at the university level. Yet for those of us who are clinicians—working with our clients with social learning challenges on a daily basis—the fact is we need to adapt much more quickly than will the research or the university curriculum.

There's a growing movement of professionals across different domains who recognize the central, overriding role Social Thinking has in helping to further educate many of our individuals with ASD-SCD and related disabilities. These professionals are making headway in this area of teaching and learning. In many cases, the speech language pathologist or the school psychologist tends to be viewed as the "lead" profession in school districts to help tackle the curriculum development in the area of social thinking and related social skills. Some professionals embrace this role and others aren't comfortable with it, given their lack of training and the paucity of related published research.

So How Do We Move Forward?

In reality, we who work together with our families and students take it one student at a time. The input from each of the professions previously mentioned contributes to a better understanding of the sensory, cognitive processes, and learning styles of our students. Furthermore, the personal insight into a student offered by his parents, and possibly by the student himself, is invaluable in establishing a strong treatment team. While a large team won't necessarily be working with each student, it's important for professionals to always consider themselves interdisciplinary—meaning they learn about and embrace treatments of all different professions to use in their own clinical setting. For example, it's less effective to work with a student with social learning challenges if any one professional isn't somewhat educated in sensory sensitivities, a basic understanding of counseling principles, basic learning principles, and a developmental understanding of social communication. Working with a range of professionals allows us to share different professional insights, helping to develop a larger set of effective treatments.

The team "attitude" is as important as the range of professionals who make up the team. Any attempt to discuss and define social thinking requires group members who respect the range of challenges these students present and who can, without judgment, put aside preconceived notions of social competence. These professionals should also be willing to think outside the box of their professional training and be comfortable with doing this. Not everyone can do this. Consequently, the best person to take the lead role on a team is the person who is most curious and actively interested in learning about the student, willing to embark on an unbiased exploration into her social, sensory, and communication strengths and weaknesses, and is motivated and organized enough to then coordinate lessons with other professionals and the parents. At times this person is the speech language pathologist or school psychologist, but it can also be the behaviorist or special education teacher. I've even worked with paraprofessionals who have become the "social thinking specialist" in a district for students with ASD. Parents are concerned with helping their children now, with finding people who are willing to take charge and find a way to give these students lessons in social thinking and sensory regulation and also who can develop a greater awareness of each student's mental health. With this knowledge, students can be provided with strategies to learn to cope and to learn new information that will help them have greater success both now and in the future.

At the same time, professional fields of study must acknowledge and respond to this urgent call to action to begin teaching concepts relevant to social understanding, social thinking, and related social skills. University programs need to start addressing within their curriculums the varied and complex nature of social relations for all disciplines related to the diagnosis and treatment of autism spectrum disorders and persons with related disabilities (ADHD, NLD). Perhaps the development of Social Thinking treatments helps to be the harbinger of a new field, one of the "social cognitive specialist"—a professional who has core training in a range of different but related professions, who understands the interrelatedness of challenges faced by people with ASD as well as other diagnostic labels, and has working knowledge of core treatment strategies in areas such as occupational therapy, speech language communication, behavior, social skills and social thinking, academic education, and counseling.

One key function of a treatment team is to determine how the student learns social information, where he functions on the ST-SCP scale, and how treatment will align with what the team has learned about him.

It's our premise, developed from our clinical experience in a range of settings as well as from working with families and treatment teams, that by exploring and clarifying our students' social learning levels, we can make far more insightful clinical decisions about which types of treatments may best serve the client or student. We can also determine where to begin in the treatment process and who best to group the student with—and if she'll benefit from a group learning experience to acquire more social information. As discussed in the previous chapter, our ST-SCP framework to explore a student's level of functioning also allows us to see more specifically how a student may function academically in different aspects of his curriculum, helping us to understand the student's needs across the day.

Social cognitive teaching is best suited for those students who were born to or who have emerged into solid language and cognitive skills, even if they had early developmental challenges in this area. This teaching methodology is generally thought of as being the most helpful for students in preschool or older, with a verbal IQ of 70 and above, who also possess a systematic, functional, expressive communication system that enables them to communicate beyond the level of basic wants and needs. Cognitive behavior strategies require metacognition, or the ability to think about thinking. These strategies are less effective and may be completely ineffective with students with strong cognitive impairments and those who lack the ability to process and respond to sophisticated language-based descriptors. The educational team may also find that Social Thinking can be introduced as one of many treatments when our solid-language-using children are in preschool and early elementary school, and that Social Thinking becomes increasingly effective as children move into upper elementary school, middle school, high school, and beyond. Developmental age is also important for making socially based treatment decisions, given that maturity helps our students to slowly develop more self-awareness and self-monitoring skills.

> Social cognitive teaching is best suited for those students who function at the higher end of the autism spectrum or those diagnosed with Asperger's Syndrome.

At the end of the day, even if we as an educational community haven't spent much time exploring how to teach social skills, a lot of money is spent attempting to teach these skills to students in schools as well as in private clinics. In reality, a lot of money is spent poorly when parents and professionals approach social learning as a haphazard set of social skills instructional techniques without developmental methodologies based on concepts taught to us through research and theory-driven practices that are more finely attuned to a student's specific social learning strengths and weaknesses.

Also critical in this discussion is the exploration of how to place students into effective treatment groups. We've consistently found that students grouped by their social functioning levels (discovered through ST-SCP) learn more effectively in these groups. Emerging Social Communicators learn most efficiently and effectively when grouped with other ESCs. Nuance Challenged Social Communicators learn and relate more effectively when grouped with other NCSCs. Significantly Challenged and Challenged Social Communicators struggle to be effectively taught in the context of a social treatment group because they benefit more from one-on-one treatment. Those who function in the category of our NCSCs typically have more self-awareness than those who function as ESCs. Thus our NCSCs, when grouped with ESCs and when they're in upper elementary school or older, may explain that they don't like the social group they're in because there are other students in it that they feel they could teach social skills to, and they don't want to be in the same learning group as "them" (the ESCs).

It's important to keep in mind that our students who have more awareness also have more self-esteem attached to how they're perceived by adults and peers. Our NCSCs have expressed to us that they worry when they're placed in a group with "lower functioning kids" (when compared to themselves) because they feel adults see them as functioning at that level. A university student in a graduate program summarized it well when he said, "If they did not move that other man out of our group, I was going to have to discontinue my participation in the group because we had very different treatment needs." At the same time, we're very familiar with the concern professionals have that they don't have enough students of one functioning level to group into a program in their school or that they *have* to group all the students to be seen at the same time of day. Our response to these real concerns is that when treatment is provided poorly, it's a waste of money and resources. It may also be counterproductive in teaching students what they need to learn. If a student could benefit from Social Thinking but has been grouped with students who are far more advanced, the curriculum won't be taught in a sufficiently explicit way for that student to learn. At the same time, if a student with a higher ST-SCP profile is grouped with students who have lower ST-SCP profiles, that student might refuse to continue to engage in the lessons and instead become a behavior problem as a way to try and escape lesson plans that aren't sophisticated enough to meet her needs.

As work in the field of social cognition evolves, it will become increasingly important for parents, educators, administrators, and politicians to recognize that students with various diagnostic labels (ASD, SCD, social anxiety, and so on) not only have a range of social learning challenges but also a range of sensory regulation challenges, differences in temperament, and so on, that also have to be considered in the treatment process. There's no one treatment program that is or will be applicable to every person with an ASD-SCD diagnosis. We currently stress that each individual is unique and that the characteristics of those with social learning challenges can manifest in students with an infinite number of permutations. At the same time, there are some common social learning traits that help us to learn about different types of social learners in a more systematic manner. Learning to create systems for teaching social concepts to different levels of social learners across a range of professionals and parents is ultimately our goal. While these treatment ideas were incubated while I worked as an SLP in the public schools, our private practice clinic has been employing and evolving this more sophisticated type of treatment for years, with strong approval from our families and the professionals we train. Yet we also recognize that we have a long way to go to help our community create a systematic approach to social learning that can be organized in a manner that's conducive to clinical research. We share these concepts and ideas with the hope that our university students, professionals, and parents continue to explore them to help us generate the systems that are needed to create more efficient and effective treatment practices.

The following email was received from an SLP who has been studying how to apply Social Thinking in her community for a few years. It's been slightly modified to allow this group to remain anonymous.

> I wanted to share some positive and exciting news. I was given the opportunity to help with a very difficult to manage first grade class from January to May of this year. The students were of course not inherently bad, but the mix was toxic at times, and traditional behavior management tools were not working. Perhaps in desperation and in an attempt to save the teacher and the students, I was asked if I would introduce Social Thinking and Superflex to the class. I have used this approach with my spectrum kiddos and other students since my training with you in 12/08, but it had never gotten any schoolwide or administrative support through the years. The benefits of this approach

were certainly respected, as was I, but it was not viewed as something that could/should be implemented with all students to increase a positive social environment within the school setting. I was unsure how it would be received, as this particular teacher was very seasoned and in my opinion, was going to be a "hard sell."

The results were amazing. The Social Thinking tools reshaped this class and allowed the teacher to "teach." She admittedly said that she was convinced now more than ever that the social arena had to come first. Creating a classroom environment where students became "thinking about others" kids, and where Superflex strategies were taught and reinforced on a daily basis, provided a positive learning environment. Social Thinking was tied into the classroom management, and the overall classroom environment was transformed from a negative "nothing is going to work with this bunch" to a positive, enjoyable group of first graders. The parent response was striking, and many comments were made in our end-of-the-year parent survey.

As a result of this successful implementation, my principal is supporting the implementation of Social Thinking across the first and second grade classes at our school in the coming school year. She has always been a data-driven, RTI, all-about-curriculum administrator and like most educators viewed the academic piece as most important. Now, however, she is seeing that the social needs of our students must be met as well, and in doing so we allow the students to be academically successful and provide a thoughtful, safe school environment. I am also a member of our school's Positive Behavior Intervention Support (PBIS) committee, and we're planning to incorporate Social Thinking into our schoolwide PBIS system next year.

Needless to say, I am so thrilled and pleased to have my colleagues and school community finally embrace the possibilities of Social Thinking for all students. As we're faced with an increasingly egocentric, fast-paced, disposable world, Social Thinking reminds us that thinking about others can make the world a better place, and decrease bullying and unkind treatment of others.

Here's a comment from an SLP working in a public school system setting:

Our behavior specialist and I have worked closely together as members of our county's autism team and in coming up with behavior plans for our emotionally challenged students. She has seen the huge benefits of Social Thinking in our work together over the years, as well as the work done with the first grade class this year, as her son was a student in this class. She'll be helping me implement Social Thinking at my school this fall. We're also trying to write a grant to implement Social Thinking across our county.

Please receive this as one more confirmation that you are indeed making a difference in the lives of many students, with and without disabilities, and teachers too! Thank you!

Chapter 10

What Is a Framework for Teaching Social Thinking and Related Social Skills?

T eaching social thinking requires us all to become more active thinkers about the social learning process. One of the more daunting problems associated with this realm of learning challenges is the absence of a common vocabulary to observe and describe social expectations. While we have a way to define and prescribe treatment for more traditional learning disabilities, such as reading, decoding, and math calculations, we haven't yet developed an explicit vocabulary for teaching social concepts in a straightforward manner. Previous chapters have explored the multidimensional and dynamic nature of social problem solving and social behavioral expectations. Although to some degree we can call our social interpretations subjective, we tend to have collective agreement related to which social behaviors our peers produce that make us feel comfortable and which make us feel uncomfortable. This is true with preschool- and school-age children as well as adults. Yet in most cultures we (the peers) don't typically directly address a social skills behavior problem by discussing it with the person who has caused the discomfort. Instead we feel more comfortable talking about the person's troublesome behaviors with another peer rather than with the person who actually engaged in the errant behavior.

Our societal reluctance to discuss these concepts spills into our discussions related to how to develop a treatment program for our students with social learning challenges. It's a topic we avoid. When we state that someone has social skill problems, what we really mean is that his behaviors make others uncomfortable. In meetings, a student's social behavior appears to be far more difficult to discuss than if the same student had math- or reading-related learning disabilities. Social issues affect how we personally think and feel; therefore, talking about the issues we observe may embarrass or offend others in attendance at the meeting. It becomes easier to assign broad, impersonal judgments—"he's just eccentric," "he doesn't want to have friends," or "but she's so smart"—than to roll up our sleeves and pick apart the dysfunction everyone senses but fails to address.

It's no surprise that it's even more difficult to develop effective treatment strategies based on these elusive, subjective descriptors. More commonly, as discussed previously, our students with social thinking impairments are lumped together under the umbrella description of "behavior problems." We then create a behavior plan for a student, assuming an intact social brain. The plan most likely fails because we don't teach a student cognitively why her behavior is interpreted as problematic.

We often teach based on the assumption that our students understand that they aren't cooperating, aren't respectful, or are impolite.

For example, we tell a child he has to change her behavior because it's "rude" or "inappropriate." (How so? To whom? In what situation?) If understanding behavior was that simple, wouldn't our smart students with Asperger's Syndrome/ASD-SCD understand these concepts easily? *That's exactly what we think!* So we keep teaching the same way, expecting them to "get it," and we attribute all sorts of negative qualities to these students when they don't learn. Perhaps it's we professionals and parents who need to change, we who need to learn about the very real, brain-based social thinking challenges that these students experience. We may cognitively understand that our students have social problems because they have a diagnosis of ASD or a related social learning disorder. But these diagnostic labels don't provide us with information about what each of these diagnosed students needs to learn socially. For example, persons with Asperger's Syndrome or similar social thinking disabilities can't grasp the very idea that others perceive them to be rude. Or that a natural way of information processing for neurotypicals may not be seen as "normal" for the person with social challenges. We assume our students understand the underlying, implied, and related social message of our behavioral teachings and then wonder why our students "fail to learn."

To help mitigate this recurring spiral of unmet expectations, I began a social anthropological exploration of the normal developmental evolution of social relatedness. This resulted in the creation of a treatment methodology now described as Social Thinking Concepts and Vocabulary. One idea behind teaching social thinking is for us neurotypical educators (parents, professionals, student mentors) to acquire a better sense of what it is we do intuitively—how we actually think in social terms—to be able to teach it more explicitly. Even a teacher with good social skills may not be able to teach social thinking well. That's because what she does socially was learned without self-awareness of how she acquired the information and that her thinking and skills would continue to evolve with age. As educators, we also have to explore the methods and mechanisms by which students with social learning challenges cognitively learn information that isn't acquired through the normal developmental process.

To this end, Baron-Cohen (2009), who originally elaborated upon ToM, has presented his newest ideas in what he calls the empathizing-systemizing (E-S) theory. In his earlier work, Baron-Cohen (1995) defined and discussed ToM as a way in which we explore our own and others' mental states and how this aspect of the social mind is more limited in development in students with ASD. In Baron-Cohen's E-S theory, he compares the diversity of thinking abilities in neurotypicals to those with ASD. In a nutshell, neurotypicals represent a group of people who demonstrate a range of functioning abilities, from those with highly evolved systems of understanding core scientific concepts (systemizers) to those people who are highly sensitive to what people are thinking and feeling (empathizers). Not surprisingly, he found that in general neurotypical males tend to be stronger systemizers, and neurotypical women tend to be stronger empathizers. He postulates that everyone functions on a scale of empathizing and systemizing (although plenty of men and women fall between the two types of thinking). Baron-Cohen then goes on to describe how his research demonstrates that persons with ASD tend to represent a group of people who have more extreme systematizing abilities and are far less able-minded in their empathizing abilities.

Baron-Cohen's research states that most individuals on the autism spectrum represent different degrees of an extreme male brain (systemizing) and have far less ability to empathize.

Baron-Cohen points out that we can capitalize on our ASD clients' strengths—namely, systemizing—to help nurture their weakness in empathizing. He recommends treatment programs based on teaching in a structured manner the more abstract social requirements, such as how another person is thinking and feeling (empathizing). Developing frameworks to help explain abstract information in more systematic, concrete terms is at the core of Social Thinking treatment ideas.

As we seek to break down information into more systematic parts to teach social thinking, we need to better observe the many and varied lenses through which we function socially. Providing socially grounded information to our students requires us to step back and explore the social process through which we function. Learned from years of intervention experience with this population, two fundamental social, cognitive-behavioral frameworks have arisen: the Four Steps of Perspective Taking and the Four Steps of Communication (Winner, 2005). These frameworks effectively help students to consider the basic synergistic and multi-stepped processes supporting social thinking and resulting in the more astute production of social skills. Rather than develop static instructional curriculums, frameworks were devised to encourage our professionals, parents, and their clients or students to better explore how we can consider a load of information across a range of situations.

The four-step frameworks also provide paradigms through which parents and professionals can more systematically observe the social dilemmas faced by our students to teach them more detailed information about social thought and related expectations. Our educators can better observe their clients to develop more astute social learning lessons for individuals of differing ages and differing developmental levels of social thinking. These scaffolds also provide a set of concepts that can be shared with students to help them refine their own skills in observing the social world. The key in helping our students is in recognizing their need to develop better skills related to observing people in context as a first step in acquiring a more solid social thinking footing or root system upon which they can explore more advanced or nuanced concepts.

The Four Steps of Perspective Taking explain that social behavior is based on social thought. It's only after we consider those around us—and what they may be thinking and feeling—that we adapt our behavior according to these thoughts. These four steps occur naturally in nanoseconds of time in neurotypicals, often without conscious thought. Furthermore, it's an underlying social expectation of being human that all people engage in perspective taking any time they're with others, even if there's no direct interaction.

It's an underlying social expectation of being human that all people engage in perspective taking.

The Four Steps of Perspective Taking

As soon as I share space with you—

1. I have a thought about you; you have a thought about me.

2. I try to determine why you're near me, what you may want from me (motive/intent). You wonder why I'm near you, what I may want from you.

3. Given that I know you're having a thought about me, I wonder what you're thinking about me. You know I'm having a thought about you, and you consider what I'm thinking about you.

4. I monitor and possibly modify my behavior to keep you thinking about me in the way I want you to think about me. You monitor and possibly modify your behavior to keep me thinking about you in the manner you'd hoped for.

We teach that virtually all of our time spent in the presence of other people requires active perspective taking and that students exist on a continuum of perspective taking abilities (as described in Chapter 9). Every aspect of communication and sharing—inside and outside the classroom—comes back to these four steps and involves taking into consideration not only our own thoughts, but the thoughts of other people in specific contexts. This becomes one of the first steps in teaching students with social thinking challenges: I think about you, you think about me, and we act in consort with these thoughts we hold.

The Four Steps of Communication help define the synergistic and dynamic process we call face-to-face communication. When a student doesn't communicate well, we often teach him to use his language better. However, these four steps illustrate that a significant amount of our communication is also dependent upon how we use our social mind, body, and eyes.

The Four Steps of Communication

1. Think about others and the situation. I think about my possible communication partner(s). I consider what I know about them, the situation, as well as what they know about me.

2. Establish physical presence. This includes how close or far away our bodies should be (an arm's length from each other), how we orient our bodies (turn our shoulders, head, hips, and feet) and how we use gestures. Our language allows us to share specific information verbally; our bodies are an additional source of information. If our bodies are overly rigid or overly relaxed as we communicate with others, this can be interpreted positively or negatively, depending on the context.

3. Use your eyes to think about others. We use our eyes and notice how other people use their eyes as part of the communicative process. Our eyes help us to determine the context, think about others' thoughts and feelings, and send clear communicative signals about whether we're interested in what they're saying, and which people we do or don't want to communicate with.

4. Use language to relate to others. It's usually expected that we use our language to demonstrate interest in those we're communicating with. People in communication with each other want their partner to be interested in them.

Take note of how much time we spend teaching students the fourth step of communication without giving great importance to the initial three steps. We assume our students already intuitively know them. Yet consider this—a student can successfully hang out in a group of peers using the first three steps only, but a student can't successfully hang out with others using only the fourth step while disregarding the other three. By teaching that communication is a much larger concept than just using appropriate language, we begin to ameliorate many other aspects of social functioning.

The book *Think Social!* (2005) includes many additional lessons, which have become known as a body of teaching tools referred to as Social Thinking Vocabulary and concepts. These are designed to help professionals and families explain Social Thinking concepts using more specific terms and impart valuable social information related to the Four Steps of Communication and the Four Steps of Perspective Taking.

By using this common vocabulary, parents and professionals can speak the same language with students to help them "crack open" presumed social concepts. Students and their various caregivers can speak more consistently and explicitly about the social process. This vocabulary also aids with creating concrete strategies to use with a range of students and across different age groups. Some examples of Social Thinking Vocabulary and related ideas and terms are described in Table 1.

Table 1

Social thinking: The ability to consider your own and others' thoughts, emotions, beliefs, intentions, knowledge, etc., to help interpret and respond to the information in your mind and possibly through your social behavioral interactions.

Social skills: The ability to adapt your behavior effectively based on the situation and what you know about the people in the situation for them to react and respond to you in the manner you'd hoped.

Why do we use social skills? To impact how we make people feel, which then impacts how they feel about us.

Sharing space: Refers to a person coexisting with one or more people in a situation without the intent to directly interact with these other people. When sitting together in a classroom, students are more likely to "share space" rather than to directly and consistently "interact," yet we all are expected to think about people and what they may thinking or expecting, even when we're simply sharing space with them.

Perspective taking: Thinking about others' thoughts and emotions and considering what they think and feel about you. Helping students understand that they and others have thoughts, emotions, intentions, motives, belief systems, prior knowledge, experience, and personalities that need to be interpreted in light of the social situation in which they're sharing space with others.

Being a Thinking of You (thinking about others) person; or Being a Just Me (thinking about yourself and only what you want to do) person: These are terms to define the difference between what people expect from you when you're part of a group versus what you can do differently when you're not sharing space with others.

Thinking with your eyes: Using your eyes to interpret a situation and the nonverbal messages others are sending through their facial expression, gestures, and stance as well as to show others that you're thinking about them.

Flexible thinking or flexible brain: Using mental flexibility to interpret verbal and nonverbal information based on different points of view or different contexts. This is the opposite of having a rigid or "rock brain," where one follows a rule all the time or can't interpret subtly different meanings in language or expression.

Keeping your body and brain in the group: Understanding that to participate effectively within a group, our bodies need to be situated in a manner that shows we're interested and connected to the group, and our brains need to keep thinking about what the group is thinking.

Your body rolled out of the group: A student's body is turned away from or physically removed from the group. Others notice that the student isn't working as part of the group.

Your brain rolled out of the group: A student's brain (and thoughts) are distracted from what the group is doing or talking about. Other people in the group notice that the individual doesn't appear to be working as part of the group, even if her body is in the group.

Blue thoughts (good), red thoughts (uncomfortable/weird thoughts): Refer to how our actions, words, and even physical dress or hygiene create good thoughts and weird thoughts in others' brains (the impressions that we make). All people create good thoughts/feelings and occasionally weird thoughts/feelings in others across a day. People remember the thoughts/feelings they have about others. If the student primarily implants good thoughts/feelings in others' minds, that's how the student is remembered. If a person produces behaviors that contribute to others having mostly weird thoughts/feelings, that's what these others mostly remember. Behaving really well after producing a significant amount of weird/uncomfortable thought/feelings behaviors still leaves people remembering uncomfortable thoughts. Our weird-thought memories appear to be more powerful than our memories of good thoughts about people. However, as professionals seek to teach this lesson, emphasize that these good and weird thoughts are simply thoughts. We're not teaching that people as a whole are good or weird! We're teaching that each of us produces behaviors that will be interpreted by others and then remembered by others on a range from positive to negative memories. In general, we seek to relate to people for whom we've formed positive memories.

Whole Body Listening: The idea that the whole body (eyes, ears, mouth, hands, feet, bottom, and brain) needs to be focused on another person or the group to listen and show you're listening (Truesdale, 1990).

Following hidden rules: Rules that aren't clearly announced are considered the hidden rules. These are largely social nuances people intuit through observation and experience. If you're not sure of the hidden rules, you can ask someone. For example, a hidden rule at school is that you're usually supposed to keep your shoes on, even if you take them off at home.

Social observation: Teaching students to think with their eyes to consider the situation and the people within it to determine the hidden rules.

Doing what's "expected": Once we've figured out the hidden rules, we're expected to abide by the hidden rules by doing the expected behaviors associated with those rules. For example, if the hidden rule is stay quiet while the teacher is talking, it's then an expected behavior to keep your voice quiet while the teacher is talking. People tend to feel calm about others who do what's expected in specific situations. We prefer to use the words "expected" and "unexpected" to describe students' behavior rather than "appropriate" and "inappropriate" as we seek to move away from an emotional judgement call and prefer to teach students to better observe a situation to figure out what's expected.

Doing what's "unexpected": Failing to follow the set of expected rules, hidden or stated, in a situation. When we do what's unexpected, we often make others feel frustrated or stressed, leading them to treat us more harshly.

Make a "smart guess": Taking information you already know or have been taught and making an educated guess with the information. We use the term "smart guess" rather than "educated guess" because younger children can understand the concept of "smart" before they can understand the concept of "educated." Most social and classroom interactions require smart guesses.

A "wacky guess" is making a guess when you have absolutely no information to help guide your thought processes. In school we rarely ask for (or expect) this type of guess unless students are playing a game based on luck.

People files: A visually concrete way to teach that we all are continually learning information about others and filing it in an organized way in our brain. We seek to recall this information later when we see or interact with that person again.

Social Wondering (wondering about others): A concept that helps students begin to explore the idea that we're expected to have a social curiosity about others because we can never know everything there is to know about someone. Social Wondering means you have a thought about someone's experience, emotions, or beliefs, and then you ask a question to gather more information about that person's thoughts.

Asking questions to people about these other people: Demonstrating interest in others by asking them questions focused on their particular interests or thoughts, rather than just on what the speaker would like to talk about.

Sharing an imagination: Refers to students who can imagine the creative ideas and intentions of others in order to collaborate with these others by sharing how their own creative ideas can connect with others. Shared imagination is at the basis of group imaginative play. It's believed that those who have strong shared imaginations are better able to participate in conversational language as they get older, given that conversations require a shared imagination.

Singular imagination: Refers to students who have their own solid or creative imagination but who struggle to imagine what others may be thinking or feeling, making it difficult for our students with a singular imagination to collaborate or even cooperate with others during play. It's believed that those with stronger singular imaginations struggle to learn to relate through conversation, given their intuitive lack of ability to imagine others' experiences and feelings.

"Baiting" or "Bridging" questions: Questions you ask people to try and get them to talk about what you want to talk about (for example, "Did anyone go to Hawaii this summer?").

Add a thought: When talking to others, we consider how their experiences relate to our experiences. We then add our own thoughts to help connect our lives to their lives. This is one of the most popular forms of commenting. When we talk to others, we use different types of questions and comments to sustain and expand social relations.

Figuring out other people's plans: Determining what people are planning to do next based on observing their physical actions. We can also start to figure out what people are planning to do by interpreting the subtle meaning in their language, which is a higher level skill. This is a more basic way to describe what it takes to read others' intentions or motives.

Doing the Social Fake: To demonstrate interest in someone else's topic that you don't find inherently fascinating.

Doing what's expected during the boring moment: A set of socially acceptable/expected behaviors one uses when he isn't interested in what the group is doing at that moment.

Whopping Topic Change: When a comment is made, and the listener can't determine the thread of information that connects this comment to what was previously said.

Tiny problem versus big (earthquake) problem: Helping the student put personal problems in perspective; understanding that problems differ in severity and our reactions need to match accordingly. For example, a student who breaks her pencil lead is expected to be less emotionally distressed than a student who has broken her arm on the playground.

The rules change with age: Teaching students that the social rules they acquired when they were younger may have evolved in complexity and sophistication as the child ages. For example:

- **Apologizing:** You're expected to say you're sorry to a peer you've bumped into or shoved in kindergarten, and this simple language-based apology will be accepted by your peers. However, by the time you're in upper elementary school, you're expected to demonstrate some remorse in addition to simply saying you're sorry.

- **Hugging your parents:** This is totally acceptable in young elementary school and completely unacceptable by upper elementary school and beyond. By these older ages it's expected for a student to greet his parent just by saying "hi," and he doesn't need to look enthusiastic during this greeting.

Chapter **11**

· · · · · · · · · · · ·

What Are Some Guidelines for Teaching Social Thinking and Related Skills to Groups of Students?

Best-Practice Teaching Guidelines for Social Thinking

As more and more educators and professionals have sought to learn this methodology, a number of common best-practice instructional guidelines have arisen. Effective Social Thinking treatment programs seem to share the several principles discussed in this chapter.

Evaluate the client's level of social thinking, and start as basic as is necessary.

It stands to reason that we'll continue to make significant social assumptions until we have a better picture of a student's level of social thinking, perspective taking, and social communication strategies as outlined in Chapter 8 about the Social Thinking-Social Communication Profile. Our evaluation should be based on some level of objective analysis, rather than our own socially oriented perceptions of what the student does and doesn't understand. Take note—neither chronological age, intelligence test scores, nor diagnostic labels are indicators of a student's level of social thinking; nor is expressive verbal ability. We must evaluate to what extent our students possess pivotal social thinking strategies and start wherever we need to start. Given the difficulty creating standardized tests to measure socially complex, synergistic tasks, informal dynamic assessment tasks can be helpful in defining core social thinking challenges.

Tailor teaching to the client.

Explore, test, and probe to learn the student's individual strengths and weaknesses, then design the treatment based on the student's individual needs. This is in direct contrast to creating a program based on a student's diagnosis. As discussed earlier in this book, social thinking abilities of our students will vary greatly, even within the same diagnostic label. Good programs take an individualized approach; beware of prescriptive programs based on a label.

Provide multisensory learning opportunities.

Learning is a sensory experience facilitated through multiple input channels. Verbal communication is only one teaching modality and may be the weakest channel in many students on the autism spectrum, even those who are highly verbal. It's difficult to gauge how much our students are attending to extended verbal directions or explanations unless they're actively participating in a related discussion. Use visual tools such as Comic Strip Conversations (Gray, 1994), Social Thinking worksheets (Winner, 2007c; Winner, 2011), or videotaped sessions to supplement teaching and learning.

Teach without assumptions of prior social knowledge.

If we teach social skills by encouraging students to do what's "polite" or to "show respect," they likely don't understand intrinsically what these concepts mean or how others interpret them. Our lessons should serve to make the implicit explicit. For example, we assume school-age children understand what it means to be learning as part of a group. We don't usually think to stop and evaluate

> Chronological age isn't an indication of a student's level of social thinking, nor is expressive verbal ability.

whether or not a child understands group learning or whether she has functional social skills that will allow her to be successful in a group situation. Children with social thinking learning challenges often come to school without these critical skills. For example, a third-grade "bright" boy with Asperger's Syndrome raised his hand, eager to answer the math problem the teacher posed. When the teacher called on another student sitting next to him, the boy with AS angrily hit the other student because he "stole my answer." Even though the boy with AS sits in the classroom and is very bright academically, he doesn't easily grasp the concept of "group think" and related social skill concepts that allow his peers to seem to work so easily as part of a group. For our students with social learning challenges, our initial goals aren't to move them forward in their social behavior, but instead to move their thinking backwards to find where they're lacking in their social knowledge and provide a deeper source of information to help them understand why we use selected social skills to function in a classroom. The use of Social Thinking Concepts and Vocabulary is a helpful tool for this type of teaching for both children and adults.

Teach flexible thinking.

We can never expect our students to grasp and become proficient with the changing landscape of social communication and social thinking if we teach within a structured, regimented, unchanging format. The program must be able to adapt quickly to the needs of the student, in each situation, in real time, rather than making the student adapt to artificially contrived, teacher-led and teacher-controlled social lessons. This means teachers are best when they're comfortable with "thinking on their feet," quickly adapting lessons and grabbing every opportunity that presents itself to teach and naturally reinforce social thinking. (These situations are everywhere!) Hence, it helps for the educator to have a strong grasp of the basic Social Thinking frameworks (Four Steps of Communication and Four Steps of Perspective Taking) as well as Social Thinking Concepts and Vocabulary. "Perfection" isn't our goal in teaching social thinking and related social skills. It's more about helping students make progress in learning about their social thinking and related social skills, and viewing that as a path to move them forward along a continuum of social learning. The truth is that social learning evolves in all of us, challenged or not, throughout our lives.

Use a team oriented approach to treatment, with all teachers and parents "on board."

Our social world is confusing enough without the adults responsible for teaching our students making it worse through inconsistent teaching methods. Social thinking instruction requires at least a multidisciplinary, but preferably an interdisciplinary team approach. The team should establish a consistent philosophy that all participants adhere to and use to problem solve in the moment and teach consistent lessons across different people and settings. This includes at home, at school, and in the community.

A number of treatment models have recently been published that encourage integrated, school-based teaching that can be tailored around a student's needs. The most comprehensive educational approach is the SCERTS® model (referred to in Chapter 8), developed over the last two decades through the ongoing work of Prizant, Wetherby, Rubin, Laurent, and Rydell (2006). The SCERTS model is a synthesis of developmental, relationship-based and skill-based approaches that provides a framework to bring about progress in three areas: social communication, emotional regulation, and transactional support. In 2006, the SCERTS team released a two-volume manual that guides parents and educators in consistently and effectively implementing the model.

Other treatment frameworks, although more simplistic in nature, serve the same goal—to encourage teams to work together to facilitate teaching common social goals. These include The Comprehensive Autism Planning System (CAPS) (Henry & Myles, 2007) and The Ziggurat Model (Aspy & Grossman, 2007). These related frameworks provide practical lessons that can be applied easily in an educational setting, helping to supplement information presented through the SCERTS model.

Hold all people accountable, including the student.

An important aspect of any Social Thinking treatment program is holding people accountable to their active participation with these teachings. In and of itself, this is a critical concept, one that should be actively reinforced in the student and the adults governing the program. What good is it to spend time creating individual programs if we don't make the student responsible for implementing the strategies he's taught? Parents, counselors, and educators equally share this responsibility. They're accountable to each other and to the student to do their best to understand how to present social challenges from a deeper perspective and analyze which lessons and strategies need to be explored, reinforced, and/or modified to assure that the student is gaining the ability to learn and use the concepts. The student then needs to be actively held accountable to act on the information he's learning. Being accountable for applying lessons learned in real time is critical for adolescents who are preparing to transition into the adult world where each person is expected to be accountable for himself.

Ensure that the program is meaningful to the student.

Not all students with social learning challenges feel the same level of intrinsic need to connect with the rest of the world at different points in their own maturation. In addition to teaching how, we need to help these students find meaning in the why of social connections. We must explore their social interests and devise non-judgmental ways to motivate these students—in other words, to help them find "what's in it for them." Social learning is difficult and often laborious, sometimes requiring years of patient involvement. Students must understand how this knowledge will benefit them and be applied across a range of situations in their daily lives. The best way to start to do this is to encourage our students to recognize how much they care about how people treat them before they're expected to care about how others feel based on how they're treated by our student. Without our spending time, sometimes a significant amount of time, to help our low motivation students recognize the social expectations they hold for others, it's difficult for them to understand that other people have social expectations for how they like to be treated by our student.

Teach the neurotypical students Social Thinking Vocabulary to help them learn to mentor, but still provide small, dedicated social learning opportunities for our students.

To a greater or lesser extent, we can all benefit from social instruction. Demystify the social challenges these students face by extending instruction to all students on campus. In this way, everyone develops a greater appreciation for the fact that social learning isn't intuitive to all and that each of us sits on a different spot in the vast spectrum of social abilities. At the same time, avoid thinking that core Social Thinking lessons can be deeply taught in an environment where the student is surrounded by her neurotypical peers (the mainstream setting). Our students need a time and place where they can explore issues at a deeper and slower pace than their neurotypical peers. It's of great benefit to train peer mentors in Social Thinking, and this training no doubt helps the peers develop further self-awareness of their own social thinking. However, our students benefit greatly from having a time when they can explore these concepts away from having to "perform" them in the moment. Neurotypical educators and peers are mistaken when they think that if our students can explain a concept or nod in agreement to indicate they understand it, they should be able to perform the related behaviors accurately and with nuance. Like all of us, our students learn deeper lessons first by exploring them cognitively before they can alter their behavior to align with their new thinking. Here's one way you can gain further perspective on this concept of learning to think through something first before being able to do the corresponding behavioral action. Consider how many times you've explored cognitively why you should exercise more, eat more healthily, or drive more slowly but are unable to sufficiently modify your behavior to align with your alternative way of thinking.

Teach that social thinking goes beyond teaching "friendship skills."

Quality Social Thinking programs recognize and teach that life involves learning to effectively navigate positive and negative social experiences as well as learning to better analyze social situations to more fully comprehend information presented to us in the form of literature, social studies, and history lessons. It also involves learning to be able to fully interpret movies and TV shows. Social thinking involves developing improved critical-thinking and problem-solving skills. At the heart of problem-solving and negotiation skills is learning to interact with people you don't like as well as people you do like, so that all people will continue to seek out interactions with you in the manner you desire. In the past I described and provided instructions for students to keep "friendship files" in their mind to remember information about their friends. Actually, we should teach students we keep "people files" in our brain to remind ourselves of information about whomever we encounter on a regular basis, whether we like that person or not!

Teach a definition of "social thinking and social skills."

Being social is a nebulous concept for most of our counselors, parents, students, and educators. Many equate it to social times that are expected to be filled with fun (e.g., recess, parties, weekends). It's important that we make it more concrete by clearly defining the social experience. The social experience, as discussed earlier, has three parts: 1) social thinking, 2) social skills production, and 3) emotional evaluation during and possibly after the sharing of space.

Using good social skills then can be described as being able to adapt your behaviors effectively based on different situations and what you know or don't know about the people in those situations. We also teach our students about the core conceptual frameworks of the Four Steps of Communication and the Four Steps of Perspective Taking to encourage them to explore the many and varied aspects of the social mind.

> Good social skills is being able to adapt your behaviors effectively based on different situations and what you know or don't know about the people in those situations.

The art of teaching involves how we engage students with different Social Thinking lessons across their ages of development. Given that social rules and nuance evolve with age, there's new information to add to the core curriculum each year of a student's life. As students get older, they're also required to assume more responsibility for caring about how others feel and self-motivation for acquiring skills needed to transition out of the traditional school years.

Hence, although the definition of social thinking and social skills remains static, the way to teach our foundational information changes over the years of a student's development. The early years may focus on teaching students basic lessons in social awareness and learning as part of a group. Our middle school students usually require us to attend to their increasing angst and anxiety as they, like everyone else, long to be part of a peer group whether they're comfortable admitting it or not. During the high school years, our students are learning more strategies for coping with anxiety and depression while also continuing to learn more refined strategies for sharing space with others, interacting, and possibly even flirting. Different lessons continue into and throughout the adult years depending on stages of life to better understand the hidden rules of the social emotional community they're now immersed in. Even our clients who choose to spend their time with other people with social learning challenges still have to learn to cope with each other in increasingly sophisticated ways!

Unfortunately, many of our students have attended "social skills groups" that focused on playing board games to teach turn-taking or explored learning about topic maintenance in conversations.

After a while, they felt like they weren't learning anything new. Ultimately this experience makes them think they already know everything there is to learn about social skills. By more broadly defining social thinking and related social skills along with core learning frameworks, we enable them to open their mind to a different view of learning and participating in a group social learning experience. Because so many educators and students have experienced social skills groups for which there was insufficient planning and social discovery, we prefer to call our groups "Social Thinking groups." This encourages people to recognize this isn't the traditional form of behaviorally-based social skills teaching. It's equally important to stress that acquiring social competencies involves actively learning throughout our lives not only about our own and others' thoughts but also about the increasingly complicated emotional aspects of relationships (personal or professional). This continued exploration requires motivation and dedication to the goal of helping ourselves be appreciated by others in the manner we desire, in large part to ward off depression or other mental health challenges.

Teach the concept that friendship takes work!

While the focus of Social Thinking isn't solely on making and keeping friends, this is a motivating factor for many (but not all) of our students. Whether we actively seek friendship or not, we all seek social validation. Friendship and social inclusion are flags that one is being accepted by others, thus being validated socially and emotionally. Yet many of our students don't recognize that friendship and social inclusion take effort on their part. To be sought after as a person others want to be with means you have to make an effort to think about other people while monitoring and possibly modifying your social behavior so they continue to feel comfortable around you and possibly with you. More advanced friendship involves connecting with peers and friends outside of the environment in which they met (e.g., asking a friend a student met at school to come over to their house or meet at the mall). We've observed our students desperately wanting friends but then refusing to contact anyone as soon as they go home, even if we've explored strategies they feel comfortable using from home. These strategies can include using Facebook, emailing, or texting (if they aren't comfortable talking to someone on the phone). We actively teach our older students (middle, high school, and older) that social learning takes work. As part of this lesson, we teach that friendship isn't always fun. It involves boring moments, at times faking you're interested in what someone else is talking about or playing a game that isn't your favorite. Yet the reward for tolerating the discomfort is that you have someone to appreciate and someone who desires to be with you over time.

Appreciate the complexity and allow your lessons to progress slowly.

The reason Social Thinking was developed was to acknowledge that social learning is complex and multifaceted. Here are some of the many areas we all need to learn about and explore in order to provide lessons that respect the complex nature of our students' learning disability:

- Our students' developmental phases
- The abstract demands of the curriculum
- The related mental health challenges that emerge from our students with social learning challenges

- The fact that the demands of the social world continue to evolve as students get older
- The demands placed on them by other aspects of the community (family, religious ceremonies, sports, etc.)
- The nature of the student's existing peer relationships (i.e., if she's mostly accepted, ignored, or rejected by her peers and teachers)

For many of our students, appreciating the complexity of their learning and emotional issues is the first step toward respecting how difficult all of this is for them to learn and adapt to, especially in a quick and efficient manner. Learning social thinking and related social skills is a slow process. Attempting to speed up the learning by writing overly optimistic 12-month treatment goals can accidentally discourage the student and his educational team. This might happen especially if the team members aren't entirely honest about the student's social abilities and needs both in his social relationships and classroom group learning abilities.

Educators — keep on learning!

At times the mere thought of the many different, subjective aspects of social thinking and social education can overwhelm an educator, and inertia can easily set in. Start slowly and build. Realize that this is a learning process for you as well as for the student. As you both become more proficient, you'll make mistakes and the early learning stages may feel uncomfortable. As you become more capable as a teacher or mentor, rest assured you'll continue to make mistakes! Navigating our own social lives is tricky at best; teaching others how to help navigate their own is fraught with complications!

Don't give up! The progress you see in students will encourage you to incorporate more and more social instruction into your daily teaching. Use the social tools and encourage Social Thinking Vocabulary and related instruction frameworks to teach yourself, your students, and their caregivers to speak more specifically about social concepts. As you explore these concepts, add your own ideas to the material. Being able to define the problem is the first step to helping mitigate it.

Although the field of instruction in Social Thinking and related social skills is still in its infancy, many clinical professionals are jumping on board to address the needs of this growing population. With our creative thought and professional backgrounds, especially in the understanding of the different thinking and emotional patterns of individuals with ASD and related social learning challenges, we're slowly expanding treatment methodology to help students learn more about social relationships, social understanding, social emotional regulation, and appropriate social skills. The real gain in our understanding has been in moving beyond the idea of teaching individual social skills to generalizing this understanding. By doing this, students learn skills that can be adapted across contexts, not for just a 12-week semester or school year, but over the long term, gaining knowledge they can use and build upon into adulthood.

Chapter 12

....

How Does Social Teaching Fit into What We Typically Call "Education"?

As readers have come to appreciate by this point, social thinking and related social skills are used throughout the school day—whether a student is working independently, is part of small-group or large-group instruction in the classroom, is moving from class to class, is present during lunch and recess, or is participating in extracurricular, school-based activities. Social thinking skills enable a student to make sense of the academic curriculum, understand characters and events in current-day and historical accounts, and acquire the prerequisite knowledge upon which future class assignments are predicated. There's no place or situation within the school environment where social thinking and related skills aren't used.

Therefore, a natural conclusion is that these skills are so germane to any student's education that social teachings should take their rightful place as vital classroom curriculum and no longer be relegated to only helping children navigate social aspects of the playground or lunchroom. Instruction about social participation needs to be focused more explicitly in the classroom. The Council for

Exceptional Children (CEC) studied teachers' perceptions of their neurotypical students' social skills in the education classroom. Their conclusion was that social teachings need to be made more explicit across all grade levels for all children, not just children with social relational challenges (Lane, Wehby, & Cooley, 2006).

This may reflect popular thought, but administrators continue to take a limited perspective toward social learning during classroom time. Query different teachers and school administrators about practices relating to the teaching of social skills, and the majority will respond that social skills should be taught during recess. Although recess is certainly a setting not structured by adults that requires on-the-spot social thinking and related skills, it's only one of many contexts in which we need to teach important Social Thinking concepts. Given the short amount of time students spend in recess, it can be argued that perhaps this is one of the least productive environments within which to focus social skills teaching. The student spends far more time within the classroom setting, in small and larger group learning, on a daily basis. This is where the presence or absence of social thinking skills will most affect student success overall. Furthermore, a child who isn't socially adapting well in the classroom isn't often picked by her peers for playground play, making it more difficult to teach her social skills during recess time.

From a social perspective, it's our students' ability to adapt to a variety of social contexts that best prepares them for independence and adulthood and increases their chances for success in our society at large. This is the general message of a book entitled *Self-Regulation in Early Childhood* (Bronson, 2000). In a very literal sense, education encompasses far more than academics alone. Developing an increasing concept of self-control to enhance self-reflection can transform the manner in which students learn. Helping children to reflect on a task in an age-appropriate manner can promote learning not only by enhancing task performance but also by promoting higher order cognitive operations, such as changing the way in which a stimulus is presented in memory and accessed during cognitive tasks (Sodian & Frith, 1992). Durlak, Weissberg, Dynicki, Taylor, and Schellinger (2011) investigated the possible benefits of teaching kindergartners a universal social and emotional learning (SEL) program. When compared to the control group, the SEL participants demonstrated "significantly improved social and emotional skills, attitudes, behavior and academic performance that reflected an eleven percentile point gain in achievement."

Despite a widespread acknowledgement that education goes beyond traditional academics, parents, teachers, and schools often butt heads in coming to terms with just what constitutes

> Social teachings need to be made more explicit across all grade levels for all children, not just children with social-relational challenges.

an "education" during the school day. For instance, many students with significant social cognitive challenges are academically gifted. They have good verbal expressive abilities and strong IQ scores, and they rarely qualify for special education services because of this. They sail through certain subjects, while struggling or failing other subjects that require critical social thinking concepts and related skills. At age 15, they may be able to devise brilliant mathematical equations with thinking more typically demonstrated by university students, but they can't summarize a simple seventh-grade reading passage. They find it difficult to organize their time and their assignments, turning in outstanding content but days late or off-topic because of poor time-management and weak executive functioning skills. Parents of these "bright" students frequently listen as the education team members acknowledge that the student has a medical diagnosis of ASD-SCD, but in the same breath explain that this same student doesn't qualify for individualized educational services because his test scores reveal "no academic problems in spite of the fact his portfolio assessments show a lack of completed work."

Congress passed the No Child Left Behind Act (NCLB) in an effort to develop a more rigorous education for children in the United States. However, missing from this important piece of legislation was a definition of "education" that might guide how we teach our children and achieve "success." I had the opportunity to pose questions to the panel that helped develop NCLB, and I asked the group—"What's the definition of an education that supports the foundation of NCLB?" They responded by saying that no definition of an education had been developed, and this exercise was up to each state to take on individually. Going back to my home state of California, and perusing the California Department of Education website, I could find no definition of what an education is or should be. There was only the statement that we educate students using good teaching practices and highly qualified teachers.

We need to create a clear definition of what an education is, based on the research that studies how children learn, what's important for them to learn, and based on what's needed for them to be successful in the adult world. How do school personnel really know how to develop and implement educational curriculum without a definition of what an education should represent? How do educational teams assess if a child is being properly educated if we have no universal definition of an education?

We assume children are receiving a good education if they have high test scores, yet our tests scores fail to explore a student's adaptive functioning, executive functioning, self-regulation, and social emotional self awareness—all of which are critical skills for achieving increased success as an adult (Saulnier & Klin, 2007).

The Individuals with Disabilities Education Act (IDEA 2004) regulations state that a "local education authority must provide a free and appropriate public education (FAPE) to a special education student even though the child has not failed or been retained in a course and is passing from grade to grade." In writing this regulation, Congress recognized that education was to be defined in a broader sense than just academics, and that despite their academic success, some students may still need special services. The law outlines a two-pronged test to qualify for special education services based on this criteria:

- Does the student have an identified disability?
- Does the student require specialized instruction to address any areas of suspected disability and resulting deficits?

Notice the law doesn't say "to succeed academically." This is good news for our students with social cognitive deficits. It means if students have deficits in nonacademic areas (including social and functional performance) as noted on an assessment protocol, such as an Adaptive Behavior Scale, their areas of weakness should be addressed within an IEP that contains specific goals and services, regardless of whether they're progressing in the academic curriculum and achieving passing grades.

For years this legal avenue to help our students with social thinking challenges has been available to us. The trouble is that few education professionals use it, in large part because NCLB has forced educators to become test-centric. This means teachers in many school districts have been pushed, much to their chagrin, to solely focus on helping their students improve their test scores. If a teacher observes a student not relating well with her peers but that student does well on tests, it's current thinking that this means the student is "well-educated" and has no further "educational" problems.

The fact that federal special education law supports educating students throughout the entire school day, even if they have adequate test scores, may be enlightening to some parents and educators.

However, significant challenges still remain in getting appropriate services for students with social cognitive challenges. Helping students learn the vital life lessons that spur them on to adulthood isn't nearly as simple as implied in our public policy.

One way in which we can help to qualify students for special education who test as "bright" but who are obviously lacking in social emotional competencies or executive functioning skills is to look for institutional guidance through a school district's mission statement. For instance, the mission statement for one school district in California states that their students should be "lifelong learners who are effective communicators, informed thinkers, self-directed learners, collaborative workers, responsible members of society and information processors." As the education team meets to discuss whether a student qualifies for an IEP and it's stated that the assessment revealed the student has difficulty with social interaction or emotional regulation but fails to qualify for services because she has no "educational need,"ask the administrative representative attending the meeting to see their district's or state's definition of an "education." It's only at that point that they'll likely realize they don't have a definition!

We also can explore how executive functioning, social learning, and emotional regulation can be addressed through districts that are adopting the national recommendation of using Response to Intervention (RTI) approaches across school campuses. This approach can explore the teaching of Social Thinking at the first, second, and third levels of RTI (Hawken, Vincent, & Shumann, 2008) in tandem with Positive Behavior Supports (PBS). This combination (of Social

Thinking and PBS) appears to be a promising practice, as a number of administrators are beginning to report increased success with both academic and social emotional development, though formal research on this intervention has yet to be done. This practice can help all or select students gain or enhance skills critical to their success.

So we come back full circle to the issue that started this section— how does social teaching fit into our current definitions of "education"? It's a question with no easy answer. However, with an understanding of the current research on learning and developing effective skills for living as an adult, we can make headway in serving our students with social cognitive challenges. Collectively and individually, educators, service providers, and parents must begin to question what they think they know about the world of education. They need to stop assuming that we as a public educational system understand what it means to "educate" our students. We need to encourage our IEP team members to discuss what an education means and also think about other commonly used terms or concepts we assume imply good practices. Among these are "full inclusion for all students all of the time," "peer modeling to teach appropriate social behavior," and "teaching social skills." While these assumptions may have their own merits, they all have their own pitfalls. It behooves those of us who work in the field of education to continually question and evaluate our practices, recognize the strengths and weaknesses of the routines we have in place, and stir up the pot from time to time. By expanding our discussions and treatment ideas, we can be sure that our students are achieving the success in learning new ideas and concepts that will contribute to their life in a meaningful way, once they graduate from high school.

Chapter 13

· · · · · · · · · · · · · ·

What Are Evidence-Based Practices? How Do They Apply to Teaching Social Thinking and Related Social Skills?

Professionals who set standards for public education and parents alike want our students to grow and learn within an effective, economical, and safe environment. We want to know that students are being taught using a meaningful curriculum and teaching models based on best practices in the field of education, which includes in its definition social emotional learning. An emphasis on children receiving a "quality education" has been present for centuries. However, with the passage of NCLB in the early 21st century, Congress reaffirmed this basic tenet of education, enacting specific requirements within the law that call for practices that—to the maximum extent possible—arise from scientifically based research (SBR). "Evidence-based practices" is the terminology widely used now to describe a teaching methodology that's based on research.

This focus on teaching practices backed by evidence of successful outcomes is an important step toward advancing our knowledge and understanding of the learning styles of persons across the autism spectrum. The sometimes elusive challenges of this group have spawned a wide variety of treatment programs marketed to parents and educators, often described in slick advertising lingo, promising near-miraculous levels of improvement. Some even promise that the child will be "cured" of his autism. Some of these programs have merit; others are questionable at best. They range from more traditional behavior-based programs to more eclectic music and movement therapies, from language and communication strategies, to video modeling, to swimming with dolphins or wearing bronze bracelets. A host of biomedical and homeopathic remedies are now touted as effective in repairing the biophysical challenges associated with ASD, while various forms of psychotherapies and intensive forms of both behavioral and social cognitive treatments have been created and are being widely advertised within the autism community. While many students are learning more using one or a combination of therapies, there's little SBR that adheres to scientific protocols that supports most of these approaches. Rather what "data" exists is often the result of single subject studies (considered a lesser research model) or from the anecdotal accounts of parents and educators.

This question therefore stands: In a field as young as ours, and within a population that manifests symptoms on a vast spectrum of ability, how do we adhere to the federal requirement to use evidence-based practices when little if any SBR evidence exists?

SBR means that a single treatment method has been subjected to broad research and extensive evaluation, with studies following specific scientific procedures, in much the same way medications are tested by pharmaceutical companies and the FDA to assess their effectiveness for a group of patients with similar symptoms. And therein lies the crux of the problem when considering SBR for the treatment of individuals with ASD. By their very nature, persons with autism spectrum disorders aren't a homogenous group but are inherently heterogeneous. There are no neat, research-defined groups or subgroups with common characteristics that manifest in similar ways upon which further research of these various treatments can be studied to meet the standard of what's considered SBR. Despite the common characteristics—such as a language impairment, social deficits, odd or repetitive behavior—that define a diagnosis on the spectrum, the ways these challenges manifest from child to child are distinct and are considered unique to the individual. Simpson argues that our public educational policy needs to loosen its definition of what's described as "evidence" if we're ever to have more realistic measures for varying treatments across the autism spectrum (Simpson, 2006).

Zosia Zaks, a parent and a person who is herself on the spectrum, probes into this conundrum of aligning SBR with autism treatments. She explores this topic in the first segment of a six-part article on intervention strategies, which appeared in the January-February, 2008 *Autism Asperger's Digest,* a national magazine on ASD. In her discussion about research, she points our attention to several important issues, including the ethics involved in even conducting such analysis:

A major problem is the structure and nature of scientific research itself. For example, how can we standardize entry requirements into a program, a necessity for accurate efficacy rates? We can't say with surety that all children entering a certain intervention program have the same levels of challenge or even the same types of challenges. It would be next to impossible to find fifty-eight children with exactly 22 percent speech delay, 37 percent social delay and 16 percent repetitive behavior—and then administer treatment X in a standard way for one year, resulting in improvements that can then be tallied like ticks on a yardstick. Furthermore, the "power" of a study is largely determined by the number of participants. Is it realistic to generalize the results of a study with only twelve participants, however positive or negative they may be, to the rest of the autism population?

Secondly, defining the categories of behavior that a research project will track is complex as well. Is a child who can't talk but is able to communicate using pictures or signs still considered linguistically challenged? What about a child who hugs his parents and responds to their questions but simultaneously does not engage with anyone else? What set of behaviors or skills should researchers focus on? How can they measure an amount of deficit or improvement for behaviors that are defined in subjective terms?

A third problem involves the types of studies we could conduct. If we want to compare treatments using scientific protocols, technically we would need a control group of autistic children who received no interventions. This would be unethical.

Given the pressures educators and administrators face to use evidence-based research in selecting treatments for students with ASD, where and how do social thinking and related social skills fit—when they themselves are highly subjective and open to individual interpretation? Is it even possible to produce "research" substantiating an area of skill development that exists, to date, without common agreement as to its definition, form, and function within this population? And yet we need to keep in mind that even when educating neurotypical children, the ways in which policy makers and administrators adhere to the SBR in creating curriculum and teaching practices is inconsistent. For example, there's no SBR to support that five-year-olds learn well when seated in a classroom doing academically-based paper and pencil tasks. In fact the research for preschoolers and kindergartners counters this mandate and instead strongly encourages that we need to teach children emotional awareness, perspective taking, problem-solving, and self-regulation to help them better prepare for academic study and classroom participation as they get older. Numerous books have documented the research supporting what's considered effective teaching for our early learners (Bronson, 2000; Gopnik et al., 1999).

Therefore, it comes as no surprise that relatively little research to date has been undertaken in the area of social skills treatment for individuals with ASD.

Nonetheless, professionals working with students with social learning challenges are attempting to explore various treatment methodologies in formal and less formal ways, looking for any patterns of obvious success or failure that might be applicable to this population. One of the very real challenges is figuring out which segment of the population benefits best from which type of treatment model. When one study compares and contrasts the findings of several other research studies it's called a "meta-analysis" of the research. Within scientific circles this is considered a high form of independent research. But even these studies can be fraught with problems that render the "scientific" findings questionable, especially when they're comparing studies that aren't necessarily working with the same level of student challenges or may be using very different treatment paradigms.

In 2007, Bellini, Peters, Benner, and Hopf conducted a meta-analysis of the effectiveness of social skills programs within school settings. The definition of "social skills programs" was very broad—the authors included in their analysis 55 single-subject research studies that attempted to teach any form of social skills to persons with ASD. These studies encompassed students of various functioning levels from kindergarten through twelfth grade, using different treatment methodologies that lasted for different lengths of time. Naturally, the results were largely inconclusive given the wide disparity of individuals, skill levels, age, time spent in treatment, skills taught, how they were taught, and by whom. Yet in its opening summary, the study drew this one singular and powerful conclusion: "The results suggest that social skills interventions in schools have been minimally effective for children with ASD," implying we can't teach social skills effectively in schools. Quite a broad pronouncement for a meta-analysis that compared apples to oranges.

The paper also offered some general conclusions that appear to be counterintuitive to those of us who have worked in schools with students across a range of ages, including these assertions:

- High school students are more apt to learn from social skills treatments than are preschool students.
- The best place to teach social skills is in the classroom environment, rather than through more individualized pullout services.

In the conclusion of this meta-analysis, the authors postulated that our best treatments are those that are individually rather than group-designed. At least this one point seems to be on track.

To the woe of many professionals dedicated to helping this population gain functional social learning and related social skills, a press release written by persons other than the study's authors accompanied the public release of their article. The press release led with this damaging and highly inaccurate title: "Study: Social skills programs for children with autism are largely ineffective." The press release overgeneralized the article's findings, and then media outlets, as they often do, immediately circulated this and other equally damaging headlines in print and on the Internet to suggest that school's autism programs were getting a failing grade and that social skill programs were largely ineffective.

Unfortunately, educators, parents, service providers, and lay people saw these headlines, and by all accounts, considered them "fact." Any school administrator who wants a quick reason not to support social skills teachings in her school was handed the very ammunition she needed—a "research study" disproving the effectiveness of social skills treatment programs. Despite follow-up articles and statements that corrected the inaccurate headlines and more accurately explained the research findings, the damage was done. The lesson is this: While the emphasis may be on practices grounded in SBR, not all SBR can be taken at face value.

It's paramount in a world where media headlines are often meant to attract attention and produce sales or website hits that we continually keep in mind that not all research is "good" research. Study findings should never be blindly accepted without further investigation of the data and the methods used and a careful reading that analyzes whether or not the data supports the conclusions. It's no longer enough that a research study appears in a peer-reviewed professional journal for professionals and parents to consider it "gospel." Even highly respected journals have acknowledged misprints and post-publication findings of data tampering and misstatements by study authors.

We must begin to ask more sensitive questions when evaluating research being done with this population, questions that acknowledge these factors:

- The diverse range of functioning within individuals with ASD-SCD

- A definition of "social skills" that are in the process of being taught and a clearly described treatment methodology
- Age of the student
- Related mental health challenges the student may exhibit
- Emerging professional wisdom that different treatment methodologies are likely best applied to different segments of the autism spectrum and those with related social learning challenges

The Bellini article has taught us that if we ask a question that isn't sensitive to the differences across ASD-SCD, our results will also be insensitive and inconclusive. We also need to acknowledge that it's difficult to research a concept that's so poorly defined, such as the general idea of "social skills teachings." Furthermore, whether we like it or not, media's interest in issues related to ASD-SCD grows on a daily basis. Reporters and writers inexperienced with this population are prevalent and are taking the lead in information sharing. Their reporting can just as easily hurt as help the dissemination of accurate information. In the end, the responsibility lies with each of us to fully investigate rather than blindly accept what we read, because the media's interpretation of research gets the widest readership of all.

How do we do this? How does a teacher, a parent, a school administrator, or a speech therapist assess treatment efficacy, given the different levels and varying profiles of individuals with social learning challenges? We can start by keeping in mind these points:

1. We're just beginning to explore ways in which we can "sub-type" those with social learning challenges. To date there's not a general consensus. While the DSM-5 has proposed three levels of functioning associated with ASD, many professionals fail to agree with the conclusions of the DSM-5 committee. In this book, we have suggested the use of the Social Thinking-Social Communication Profile (ST-SCP), but to date it hasn't begun to be formally researched. This tool has been shared openly with parents and professionals internationally, and the preponderant feedback is that it serves a purpose in creating functioning treatment classifications and cuts through the confusion of the many different diagnostic label options representing those with social learning challenges. However, it understandably can't be accepted as a valid approach until researched. This is why we provide the profile for free on our website (www.socialthinking.com) to encourage researchers to validate through research what our clinical experience has taught us for years. Until this is done, it's more widely accepted that researchers

> Instead of assessing treatments across the spectrum, we need to focus on analyzing them within the spectrum.

and treatment professionals look to adaptive functioning of an individual as being more important even than a student's language levels or cognitive functioning as possible profile markers to determine the level of functioning. What this means is that at this point in our understanding of ASD-SCD, we're not able to reach agreement on standard definitions of who has different variants of social learning challenges, which makes it difficult to research best treatment options when we've yet to define how we treat different groups of social learners.

2. Treatments for our students shouldn't only be sensitive to the type of social learning, self-regulatory, sensory, and adaptive-functioning characteristics manifested, but also to the age of the person exhibiting the disability. Thus, in our analysis and the decisions we make, we must take into consideration that preschool learners will respond differently than will school-age students or young adults. Instead of assessing treatments across the spectrum of social functioning, we need to focus on analyzing them within the spectrum of persons with social learning challenges and focus on what makes sense to teach at differing ages of development. Common sense (and yes, we should rely upon this in the absence of SBR) tells us that the physical, social, and emotional development

of a four-year-old will be substantially different than that of a seventeen-year-old; four-year-olds are expected to learn basic social rules and seventeen-year-olds are expected to be learning social nuance to align with the social expectations of their peers. And while we don't have SBR to support our methodological development of this type of curriculum, we do have strong developmental research from a variety of fields (anthropology, psychology, sociology, speech and language, and education). This research provides a strong compass for developing specialized treatments that align with normal developmental models of learning that we can utilize to create what we consider to be "best practices based on the research."

3. If we accept that the core nature of ASD-SCD is a social emotional learning disability (and most experts in the field agree with this), we must also acknowledge that persons with social challenges experience mental-health issues that affect their functioning in other areas—particularly individuals with an awareness of what other people think of them (Green & Ben-Sasson, 2010; Pine, Guyer, Goldwin, Towbin, & Leibenluft, 2008). Therefore, despite our desire to group individuals into categories or profiles of ability, effective treatment will always be based on the social emotional needs of each student. To do any less vastly increases the behavior problems

exhibited by our students, from the lowest to the highest functioning. As we attempt to define different treatment methodologies for different levels of the social learning spectrum, this overriding principle needs to take center stage. A program will only be considered good treatment if it's flexible enough to cater to the presenting student's personal social emotional needs. Programs without this component are doomed before they even start.

4. Treatment for persons with social learning challenges can last a lifetime, given the nuance and sophistication of the ever-changing social world and the complexities we encounter as we get older. We use faulty logic from the onset if we assume we can measure comprehensive shifts in a student's social skills behavior within the short time periods that characterize most research studies. Not coincidentally, most research is designed to span eight to twelve weeks, the length of a school semester, to allow university students to design and carry out studies. Is it realistic to think we can measure change in a student's social learning and social skills abilities after only eight weeks of treatment? Of course, the answer is no.

5. Furthermore, social skills behavior is fragile and highly dependent on a person's social emotional coping mechanisms at any point in time. From

years of experience working with this population, it's been noted that students may regress at times, even though they're learning valuable new social information and social skills. This "regression" happens not because they aren't "improving." It often takes place because as their social thinking and perspective taking abilities grow, an overwhelming amount of information starts to "make sense," bringing about a certain level of confusion and anxiety until it can be sorted through and thought about. At times, depression can set in as they begin to understand how different they are from their peers. As students become more socially aware in the realms of school, academics, self-advocacy, friendship, and problem-solving, they experience far more increasingly complex issues. Progress may not always take an even, upward path. Do we pronounce a program as ineffective because, during the time period of the study, regression occurs? There are too many issues at play for simple judgments like this to occur. We should never underestimate the amount of work it takes our students to learn to think socially, nor should we fail to recognize the pervasive levels of stress they live within on a daily basis.

6. Treatment should take into account these factors that affect a student's social abilities: temperament, level of social learning challenges,

level of cognitive impairment, language development, sensory processing, adaptive functioning,
self-regulatory abilities, mental-health challenges,
and developmental age. Without differentiating
for these variables, we reach conclusions that are
at best inconclusive.

7. As our students progress in their own development
of social thinking and related social skills, their neurotypical peers continue to march ahead with their
own intrinsic and more advanced development of
these concepts. It's a mistake to think a goal for our
students is to catch up to their peers. Social learning is one of the few areas for which all people will
continue to engage in learning throughout their
lifetimes whether they're aware of it or not.

Through the preceding discussion, it's relatively easy to consider
that, in actuality, requiring SBR treatment programs to teach social
thinking and related social skills is an impossible quest at present.
How can we assess an area—social thinking and social skills—that's
never been clearly defined, in a population of individuals—those
with ASD and related disabilities—that has no common grouping
upon which research can be based? We have put the proverbial cart
before the horse in being asked to provide scientifically rigorous
evidence for an area that remains highly subjective and open to
interpretation in every facet of its application! Nevertheless, many
of us continue to pursue the development of treatment methodologies that can be shown to be effective through research methods

developed for more individualized instruction, such as Single Subject Designs.

Bigger questions loom overhead, questions that aren't typically discussed at IEP meetings or among those who steer public education and special education laws:

- How do we define "social skills" in terms that can be measured and controlled?
- What specific skills are to be called "social skills"?
- What short-term and long-term outcomes do we seek in teaching these skills?
- Can we teach any level of refined social skills in the absence of social thinking?
- What's the goal of social skills treatment? Are we expecting to "cure" students with ASD-SCD and related social learning challenges or to help students improve their ability to process and respond to social information, compared to their baseline abilities?
- How do we define "mastery" of skills that change and evolve as children age and mature?

The time is now to address these questions and others if we expect to make any headway in providing education to our students. Never before has the incidence of ASD and related social learning challenges been higher; it grows with each passing year in proportions that approach a national emergency. In 2012, U.S. Centers for Disease Control and Prevention (CDC) released its latest autism figures. The CDC report, which analyzed data from 2008, indicates that every 1 in 88 children are diagnosed with ASD. This is a 23 percent rise in diagnoses of ASDs over a two-year period. The study reports that on average 1 in 54 boys was diagnosed with autism, compared to 1 in 252 girls (CDC, 2008). While these statistics have been widely circulated, what we should also consider is that these are figures generated as a result of data taken in 2008, *and the data are now considered "old."* In all likelihood, social learning problems impact far more children than we're even considering (for example, students who are considered "emotionally disturbed" or diagnosed as having "oppositional defiant disorder").

When we pair this explosive need for education and services with a more intensely defined national educational policy focused on SBR, we find public agencies stymied, unable to act because there's no clear indication of where to go or how to get there. Many administrators draw this line in the sand: unless there's evidence to support the teaching of social skills, there will be no social skills teaching programs in the school. They neglect to undertake an investigation into the issue to determine if this mandate is even possible. In fact, I was motivated to write this book due to the growing number of special-education directors calling, all asking the same question: "What evidence-based social skills teaching programs are available to use in our school?" The interest in providing students with programs to address their social challenges is alive within our community. What remains unattended to are the questions that must be asked—and answered—before strong evidence-based practices can be created to meet these needs in an efficient, cost-effective manner.

Until these more global discussions take place, as a community of parents and educators, we must use caution when deciding best practices for teaching individual students social thinking and related social skills. As we do so, let's ensure we're not making educational decisions for each student based on a political educational policy (PEP) rather than on an individual education plan (IEP) that respects the unique and diverse needs of this population as a whole.

Rethinking and Reframing Evidence-Based Teachings

Virtually all professionals will attest that teaching social thinking and related social skills is virgin territory within the larger community of individuals responsible for the education and care of individuals with ASD-SCD and other social thinking challenges. As mentioned earlier in this book, professionals who have spent the most time exploring the concept of social functioning have done so in fields unrelated to ASD—for example, cultural and evolutionary anthropology, cultural linguistics, and sociology.

Those of us within the ASD-SCD community with an interest in exploring these questions related to social thinking and social skills are still feeling our way around in largely uncharted territory, stepping into the role of pioneers in mapping out a new world for understanding of ASD and related disabilities.

The good news is that explorers have gone before us, leaving a bumpy trail that offers some direction. There are professionals in various areas of expertise who have already considered what it means to use evidence-based teaching methods. They don't all concur on one formal definition. In fact, what constitutes evidence-based practices varies among different arms of treatment professionals.

Behaviorists tend to adhere to a definition of evidence-based practices as those arising from "scientifically rigorous" research completed according to formal research protocols, even if the content of their queries isn't based in a developmental understanding of social thinking and social skills. On the other hand, allied health professionals (psychologists, counselors, occupational therapists, and speech language pathologists) define evidence-based practices as those that "recognize the needs, abilities, values, preferences, and interests of individuals and families to whom they provide clinical services, and integrate those factors along with best current research evidence and their clinical expertise in making clinical decisions" (ASHA, 2005). Behaviorists want to see hard data that supports a teaching methodology, even if the methodology itself lacks generalization of those methods beyond the environment in which the skills were taught. Allied health professionals seem to take into consideration that not all aspects of functioning can be objectively defined, tested, and measured, and that success depends on many internal and external variables, all working in concert with each other. This disparity in defining evidence-based practice only goes to reinforce the fact that we're in the fledgling stages of understanding and reaching consensus on this term and how it should be applied within our education system. Clearly further discussion is warranted.

Within the realm of teaching students with social learning challenges, it's the allied health professionals' definition that gives us a fighting chance to discover how different practices can be used successfully. Social thinking instruction involves treatment that explores not only social communication but complex social emotional responses. If our goal is to determine the best or most promising practices, we need to consider more than the best scientific evidence. Social skills play out in the real world, one that involves family and client values, cultural differences and economic backgrounds, not to mention the clinician's experience in the field itself, any preconceptions and perceptions that clinician brings to the experience, the mood of the client and treatment chosen, and the people the client may or may not be grouped with to receive the treatment.

A Starting Point for Treatment

This is in large part why Social Thinking was created—there was no clear treatment pathway for acknowledging that students with higher language and intellectual skills could learn information differently and more comprehensively than those with lower language and academic-learning skills. I had an early interest in autism when "autism" was thought of and mostly viewed in the classic sense. I had strong developmental, pragmatic, and behavioral training as well as clinical experience, and I'd spent years working with classically autistic students. So when I began to work with clients who were intellectually more astute, I recognized the need for more detailed and specific social cognitive teachings. In developing the teachings of Social Thinking, I also reviewed research and found that my teaching model largely aligned with what the researchers were discovering about social cognition and learning differences. Thus, while the methodology of Social Thinking isn't SBR, it's based strongly on developmental and social cognitive research, clinical experience, and input from families.

Even though we've yet to discuss and reach a consensus on the global treatment questions related to teaching social thinking and related social skills, there do exist professionally developed teaching methods that can be used with students who have social learning challenges, who are higher functioning, and who have some demonstrated level of social communication skills. These best practices use cognitive-behavioral techniques steeped in developmental knowledge coupled with behavioral teaching practices based on research evidence. These practices are applied in concert within a context that takes into account the individual strengths and weaknesses of the specific student with social learning disabilities. When treatment is approached in this way, we begin to notice that a methodology does exist that supports our goal to teach students social thinking and related social skills. Effective strategies arise from several sources—such as naturalistic behavioral treatment techniques, social emotional strategies as part of the SCERTS model, relational therapies, Social Stories (Gray, McAndrews, & White, 2002), Social Behavior Mapping (SBM), and other social thinking and related social skills methodologies. Which strategies we use and in what combination is highly dependent on the profile of the student, her age, and family preferences, while also accounting for the student's unique needs in her current educational context.

The overall concept of teaching social thinking and related social skills isn't uniquely tied to the work I've done in this field. Many professionals whose work spills over into this area understand the pivotal role social thinking and social skills play in the overall success of the individuals with social learning challenges. The philosophy and basic treatment tenets mentioned here are shared by many other pioneering treatment professionals in the field of ASD-SCD (Arwood & Kaulitz, 2007; Myles, Trautman, & Schelvan, 2004). However, my primary work for over two decades has been solely in the field of developing Social Thinking strategies and related social skills. It's encouraging that this work is beginning to attract the attention of independent researchers internationally. Crooke, Hendrix, and Rachman (2008) demonstrated positive treatment and generalization effects with a small-group, single-subject design exploring Social Thinking treatment. Elementary-aged boys were taught Social Thinking concepts such as "expected/unexpected," "think with your eyes," and "listen with your whole body" in a small group therapeutic setting. Robust gains in both skills and generalization of skills were demonstrated when the boys were placed in a new setting—a pizza party. This research supports the theory that if we teach students to think socially, they can use their thinking and use it effectively outside the therapy room (Crooke, Hendrix, & Rachman, 2008).

> The success of any treatment method is largely dependent on the quality of the person offering the treatment.

The Role of the Teacher

No discussion of evidence-based practice is complete without considering the role the teacher plays in the outcome of any educational program. Behavior doesn't occur within a vacuum, and it's common knowledge that behavior arises from the interaction of a person and his environment. That environment encompasses the people in it, including the teacher.

Currently, the SBR evidence-based practice movement curiously omits the role of the professional and paraprofessional and even the parent as critical components in any successful treatment program. Scientific data can be compelling, but doesn't necessarily provide evidence of good teaching when students learn through social interaction with teachers. In a nutshell—the success of any treatment or educational method is largely dependent on the quality of the person offering the treatment.

Many articles have been penned to date about the "art and science" of teaching (Justice & Fey, 2004; Kent, 2006; Ratner, 2006). Effective education does more than teach "facts" to students. The role of the teacher is to instill a quest for learning in students, providing them with concepts and skills to successfully navigate the social environment of the classroom as well as to allow them to continue to learn outside the classroom. Test scores are only a small part of what it means to receive an education. Therefore, the value of an experienced parent or professional—one who can take advantage of teachable moments or recognize when learning is at a standstill and shift gears as needed—isn't to be underestimated or omitted from our discussions of SBR methods. Certainly parents, educators, and education administrators recognize that a good teacher trumps scientific data any day. SBR alone will never assure success in teaching students to become successful adults.

What qualities distinguish an educator who is most apt to achieve success in teaching children with challenges in social thinking and related social skills? In 2007, I had the opportunity to lead a team discussion in Orange County, California with school-based professionals who work with students with Asperger's Syndrome and like disabilities. The goal was to explore best teachings in light of the art and science of teaching. The group defined the "art" as teaching dynamically by doing the following:

- Being flexible in responding to the student's needs
- Choosing goals that meet and support the needs of the student and the team's focus
- Taking advantage of teachable moments
- Being able to monitor the "macro" and "micro" aspects of education
- Teaching at the student's pace
- Developing social emotional rapport with the student
- Understanding how to group kids to foster maximum learning
- Applying calm, consistent discipline based on positive behavioral supports
- Earning the trust of the student
- Considering the student's and family's values

Student and family values are often overlooked and underappreciated in assessing the various treatment methods. Yet they're a basic component of program development and contribute significantly to program success or failure. Furthermore, teachers and counselors aren't with a student 24 hours a day, and the need to practice these skills doesn't stop once the student leaves school.

Therefore, parents play a critical role in treatment success. How they view the program, and whether they feel skilled at encouraging continued social learning and the related IEP goals and objectives at home or in the community can motivate or deter them from supporting the lessons of the professionals. And the motivation of the student to expend the huge effort that social understanding and related social behavioral adaptations requires is paramount to success. A student who doesn't enjoy this learning or can't perceive the value it may have for him, will likely be uninterested in doing the necessary work, either in school or outside of school.

The Social Thinking approach described in this book has been actively taught at the clinic I founded in California and by other treatment providers around the country since 1998. As part of the measures to gauge treatment success, parents are regularly surveyed. While this method of gathering data obviously doesn't formally meet the definition of SBR, it does provide anecdotal evidence about the treatment methods utilized with the students and their parents. In 2006, 40 parents responded to a survey of services; 100 percent reported positive results for their children. A very high percentage of parents mentioned the helpfulness of the Social Thinking Vocabulary concepts, which gave parents a tool to teach their child to self-monitor behavior at home and opened up opportunities for family discussions about social processing and social expectations. The parents of a 45-year-old woman with high-functioning autism and a history of behavior problems wrote to say the program has given them "hope that her life can improve . . . for the first time our daughter has started to modify her own behavior. She is more controlled, less hostile and makes more of an effort to express an interest in other people's activities."

Social Thinking lessons encourage students to observe more actively and consider and process social information in context as a prerequisite to forming a social (skills) response—to think socially before acting socially. At times, students are asked to make journal entries to explain how their Social Thinking program has helped them cope in their communities. Two teenaged boys in a Social Thinking high-school program in an eastern state wrote journal entries six months into their treatment programs to answer this prompted question: "How do you use Social Thinking in other places or times outside of the Social Thinking Center?" A sample of their responses follows:

> At home, at parties, in all sorts of places. I look around and see what others are doing, and then if I'm doing something unexpected or different, I'll try to stop doing that behavior and then I'll ask them to do something with me.

And another response—

> Anywhere when I am trying to understand people when they're being confusing . . . whenever people are being confusing, which unfortunately is kinda often.

A twelve-year-old boy who has worked with me for three years summarized what he learned this year at our clinic:

I finally got it that people think about me all the time whether I want them to or not, so I have to monitor my behavior all the time whether I want to or not."

Most recently a 35-year-old, highly educated woman with AS acknowledged how upset she often became when experiencing other's negative behavior. She felt people treated her badly in spite of her good intentions. However, after studying the concept of reading others' intentions prior to responding to them, she came to our session enthusiastically describing how she took the time to read someone's intentions and realized they weren't trying to be mean to her. In fact, they'd wanted to just converse with her! She relayed how well the conversation went once she recognized the person wasn't asking her a question to try and put her down. She then went on to comment that she thought this may have been the first time in her life she'd stopped to consider the intentions of another before responding.

Chapter **14**

· · · · · · · · · · · · ·

Summary: We End at the Beginning

The superficially conceived concept of simply teaching social skills misrepresents the dynamic and complex process that's at the heart of social skill production. Before we can act socially, we need to be able to think socially. Professionals in fields such as evolutionary anthropology, cultural linguistics, and sociology have spent generations studying the complex nature of social development in human beings and society. However, this is an area of new exploration within the realm of educators and clinicians.

Our education system is built upon certain assumptions about the social development of children. Educators assume that children enter school-aged programs with an intact "social operating system" that's been progressively teaching the child through mostly intuitive means since birth. School-based lessons are predicated on the assumption that by the time the child enters public school, certain basic social skills are ingrained—skills that allow children to attend, learn, gain access to groups, and blend in from a social behavioral perspective with their peers. However, students with social learning challenges, often diagnosed with ASD, SCD, or ADHD, have developed neurological differences that preclude the natural social operating system from functioning, to greater or lesser degrees. These individuals need to learn cognitively social information their peers have gleaned intuitively, social information that to date hasn't been woven into our current definition of education or the standards that support it.

Special education law as enunciated in the Individuals with Disabilities Education Act (IDEA 2004) stipulates that students need to learn social as well as academic information as part of their educational programs to help them improve in their skill base when compared to their own baseline functioning. Public education policy, specifically, the No Child Left Behind Act (NCLB), mandates that children will improve

Before we can act socially, we need to be able to think socially.

when compared to their peer group. This has ushered in a new focus on using scientifically-based research(SBR) in choosing specific teaching methodologies that will help children perform on a par with their peers in content driven by our educational standards. This includes children with neurologically-based learning challenges. Our special education mandate (IDEA) documents progress by comparing the student's progress to the student's baseline abilities whereas NCLB documents progress by comparing each student to all other students of the same age. This presents us with two distinct educational policies that coexist in every school district but aren't on the same philosophical train track. The disparate nature of these two mandates has resulted in confusion within the ranks of teachers and administrators everywhere.

These questions loom large and go largely unanswered: "What evidence exists to support teaching social skills programs?" "Which program models are backed with SBR?" "How do we define social skills in light of evidence-based practices?" "What if a student fails to make progress commensurate with his peers—is his progress still relevant?"

The answers to these questions are complex and we're in our infancy in exploring them. To date, education professionals have responded to the call for social skills instruction by using concrete behavioral techniques. While this has proven relatively effective for our "lower functioning" or "intellectually challenged" student population, this type of instruction is grossly insufficient for addressing the more cognitive-behavioral learning needs of students who demonstrate a range of social issues—ranging from not understanding social rules to lacking the social nuances—yet have near normal to above normal intelligence and verbal expressive skills. These bright but socially inept students need to be taught to think socially as a precursor to learning more subtle and expected social actions that help them relate better to each other and their mainstream peers.

This exploration into social thinking and social skills poses 12 critical questions that explore the dynamic nature of the social behavioral response we describe as "social skills" as well as the underlying thoughts and perceptions that support these skills. The 12 questions are repeated below for review.

- What are social skills?
- What are the origins of social development? Is there an age when our social development stops?

- In what areas of social thinking do students with social cognitive challenges struggle? The ILAUGH Model remodeled
- What impact do weaknesses in social conceptual information have on learning the Common Core State Standards?
- When do we use social thinking and related social skills? How do we approach teaching them?
- How can cognitive behavior therapy address teaching social thinking and related social skills?
- Do all those with ASD-SCD benefit from the same teachings? The Social Thinking-Social Communication Profile (ST-SCP)
- Who is responsible for teaching social thinking and related social skills? Is the same set of teaching techniques relevant for all persons with ASD and related social learning challenges?
- What is a framework for teaching social thinking and related social skills?
- What are some guidelines for teaching social thinking and related skills to groups of students?
- How does social teaching fit into what we typically call "education"?
- What are evidence-based practices? How do they apply to teaching social thinking and related social skills?

We've put the cart before the horse by requesting and requiring evidence based social skill treatment methodologies before we fully understand the dynamic and synergistic nature of what constitutes the production of social skills. A call to action is made. We're challenged to recognize that we've yet to reach consensus on basic definitions in this emerging field of study and to actively engage in discussions that illuminate the pivotal role that social thinking plays not just in academics, but all areas of education, inside and outside the school environment. Furthermore, we have to recognize that our national educational policy, NCLB, doesn't explore education as a holistic process that engages both the social and academic minds, but instead as a singular construct—one that produces higher test scores on discretely taught academic lessons that may or may not prove to help the student prepare for living more successfully as an adult.

As logic prevails, it's recognized that there's more than one type of evidence-based practice. Educators, administrators, and parents should continue to value not only the "best scientific evidence available" but also other factors that have a direct influence on the success or failure of any instruction method—such as student and family values, cultural and environmental issues, preconceptions toward treatment, the expertise of the professional who delivers instruction in understanding and treating social thinking and social challenges, as well as the "art" teachers bring to the teaching experience. As we develop our teaching theories and methodologies that are heavily supported by the research on social development and learning, we call these approaches theory-driven practices. It's important to keep in mind that every new idea that eventually demonstrates effective treatment results had to begin as an unresearched methodology that needed to be explored prior to the research being completed.

The paramount purpose of this book is to encourage those adults who work and live with persons with social learning challenges such as ASD and ADHD to think more deeply about the lessons we're teaching our students—at school, at home, and in the community. Instruction that neglects to take into account the complex nature of social thinking and social skills and their relationship to mental health issues, stages of social development, and one's temperament disrespects our students' needs and constructs a cycle of repeated failure, rather than ongoing success. Programs that achieve the success we hope for start by asking these fundamental questions: "What are social skills?" "How do we teach them to a student in light of her individual presentation of strengths and weaknesses?" And more importantly, "How can we teach deeper social thinking skills as the foundation of a comprehensive effort to bring about social understanding in our higher functioning students?"

Finally, we must acknowledge that social thinking and social skills are fluid, changing, responsive skills, dependent upon factors internal and external to the student. Our programs must be equally fluid and responsive, guided by teachers who possess the innate personality and social curiosity that allow them to step outside conventional teaching curricula and explore new avenues of social instruction that are meaningful and motivating to these students. In doing so, we expand our current idea of education to encompass instruction geared not just to students who present with neurotypically developing social systems but to all students. In the long run, that's a worthy goal indeed.

References

Abell, F., & Hare, D. (2005). An experimental investigation of the phenomenology of delusional beliefs in people with Asperger syndrome. *Autism, 9*(5), 515–531.

Adams, C., Green, J., Gilchrist A., & Cox, A. (2002). Conversational behaviour of children with Asperger syndrome and conduct disorder. *Journal of Child Psychology and Psychiatry, 43*(5), 679–690.

Adolphs, R. (2003). Investigating the cognitive neuroscience of social behavior. *Neuropsychologia, 41*(2), 119–126.

Allman, W. (1995a). *The Stone age present: How evolution has shaped modern life—From sex, violence, and language to emotions, morals and communities.* New York, NY: Simon and Shuster.

Allman, W. (1995b). Storming the citadel. In W. Allman *The Stone age present: How evolution has shaped modern life—from sex, violence, and language to emotions, morals and communities.* New York, NY: Simon and Shuster.

American Psychiatric Association. (2000). Diagnostic and statistical manual of mental disorders (4th ed., text rev.). Washington, DC: Author.

American Speech-Language-Hearing Association. (2005).
Evidence-based practice in communication disorders [Position Statement]. Available from www.asha.org/policy.
doi:10.1044/policy.PS2005–00221.

Anderson, S., & Morris, J. (2006). Cognitive behaviour therapy for people with Asperger syndrome. *Behavioural and Cognitive Psychotherapy, 34*(3), 293–303.

Aspy, R., & Grossman, B. G. (2008). *The ziggurat model: A framework for designing comprehensive interventions for individuals with high functioning autism and Asperger syndrome.* Shawnee Mission, KS: Autism Asperger Publishing Company.

Arwood, E. L., & Kaulitz, C. (2007). *Learning with a visual brain in an auditory world: Visual language strategies for individuals with autism spectrum disorders.* Shawnee Mission, KS: Autism Asperger Publishing Company.

Attwood, T. (2003). Cognitive behaviour therapy (CBT). In L. Holliday Willey (Ed.), *Asperger syndrome in adolescence: Living with the ups and downs and things in between* (pp. 38–63). London, England: Jessica Kingsley Publishers.

Attwood, T. (2006). *The complete guide to Asperger's syndrome.* Philadelphia, PA: Jessica Kingsley Publishers.

Ayres, J. (1979). *Sensory integration and the child*. Los Angeles, CA: Western Psychological Services.

Barkley, R. (2012). *Executive functions: What they are, how they work and why they evolved*. New York, NY: The Guilford Press.

Baron-Cohen, S. (1995). *Mindblindness: An essay on autism and theory of mind*. Cambridge, MA: MIT Press.

Baron-Cohen, S. (2000). Theory of mind and autism: A fifteen-year review. In S. Baron-Cohen, H. Tager-Flusberg, & D. Cohen (Eds.), *Understanding other minds: Perspectives from developmental cognitive neuroscience*. New York, NY: Oxford University Press.

Baron-Cohen, S. (2009). Autism: The empathizing–systemizing (E-S) theory. *Annals of the New York Academy of Sciences, 1156*(1), 68–80.

Baron-Cohen, S. (2010). Empathizing, systemizing, and the extreme male brain theory of autism. *Progress in Brain Research, 186,* 167–175.

Baron-Cohen, S., Baldwin, D. A., & Crowson, M. (1997). Do children with autism use the speaker's direction of gaze strategy to crack the code of language? *Child Development, 68*(1), 48–57.

Baron-Cohen, S., Leslie, A. M., & Frith, U. (1985). Does the autistic child have a theory of mind? *Cognition, 21*(1), 37–46.

Beaumont, R., & Newcombe, P. (2006). Theory of mind and central coherence in adults with high-functioning autism or Asperger syndrome. *Autism, 10*(4), 365–382.

Beebe, D. W., & Risi, S. (2003). Treatment of adolescents and young adults with high-functioning autism or Asperger syndrome. In M. A. Reinecke, F. M. Dattilio, & A. Freeman (Eds.), *Cognitive therapy with children and adolescents: A casebook for clinical practice* (2nd ed., pp. 369–401). New York, NY: Guilford Press.

Bellini, S. (2004). Social skill deficits and anxiety in high-functioning adolescents with autism spectrum disorders. *Focus on Autism and Other Developmental Disabilities, 19*(2), 78–86.

Bellini, S., Peters, J., Benner, L., & Hopf, A. (2007). A meta-analysis of school-based social skills interventions for children with autism spectrum disorders. *Journal of Remedial and Special Education, 28*(3), 153–162.

Bondy, A., & Frost, L. (2002). *A picture's worth: PECS and other visual communication strategies in autism.* Bethesda, MD: Woodbine House.

Briers, S. (2009). *Brilliant cognitive behavioural therapy.* London, England: Pearson International.

Bronson, M. B. (2000). *Self-regulation in early childhood: Nature and nurture.* New York, NY: Guilford Press.

Brooks, D. (2011). *The social animal: The hidden sources of love, character, and achievement.* New York, NY: Random House, Inc.

Brown, G., & Yule, G. (1983). *Discourse analysis.* Cambridge, England: Cambridge University Press.

Buron, K. D. (2007). *A 5 is against the law! Social boundaries: Straight up! An honest guide for teens and young adults.* Shawnee Mission, KS: Autism Asperger Publishing Company.

Buron, K. D., & Curtis, M. (2003). *The incredible 5-point scale.* Shawnee Mission, KS: Autism Asperger Publishing Company.

Buschbacher, P. W., & Fox, L. (2003). Understanding and intervening with the challenging behavior of young children with autism spectrum disorder. *Language, Speech, and Hearing Services in Schools, 34*(3), 217–227.

Capps, L., Losh, M., & Thurber, C. (2000). "The frog ate the bug and made his mouth sad": Narrative competence in children with autism. *Journal of Abnormal Child Psychology, 28*(2), 193–204.

Carlson, S. M. (2009). Social origins of executive function development. In C. Lewis & J. I. M. Carpendale (Eds.), *Social interaction and the development of executive function. New Directions in Child and Adolescent Development, 123*, 87–97.

Carnahan, C., & Williamson, P. (2010). Quality literacy instruction for students with autism spectrum disorders (pp. 125–160). Shawnee Mission, KS: Autism Asperger Publishing Company.

Centers for Disease Control and Prevention. (2012). Autism Spectrum Disorders (ASDs). Retrieved from http://www.cdc.gov/ncbddd/autism/data.html

Chawarska, K., Klin, A., & Volkmar, F. (2003). Automatic attention cueing through eye movement in 2-year-old children with autism. *Child Development, 74*(4), 1108–1122.

Colombi, C., Liebal, K., Tomasello, M., Young, G., Warneken, F., & Rogers, S. J. (2009). Examining correlates of cooperation in autism: Imitation, joint attention, and understanding intentions. *Autism, 13*(2), 143–163.

Crooke, P. J., Hendrix, R. E., & Rachman, J. Y. (2008). Brief report: Measuring the effectiveness of teaching social thinking to children with Asperger syndrome (AS) and high functioning autism (HFA). *Journal of Autism and Developmental Disorders, 38*(3), 581–591.

Delsandro, E. (2010). *We can make it better!* San Jose, CA: Think Social Publishing, Inc.

DePape, A. M. R., Hall G. B. C., Tillmann, B., & Trainor, L. J. (2012). Auditory processing in high-functioning adolescents with autism spectrum disorder. *PLoS ONE, 7*(9), e44084.

Dettmer, S., Simpson, R. L., Myles, B. S., & Ganz, J. B. (2000). The use of visual supports to facilitate transitions of students with autism. *Focus on Autism and Other Developmental Disabilities, 15*(3), 163–169. doi: 10.1177/108835760001500307.

De Villiers, J. (2000). Language and theory of mind: What are the developmental relationships? In S. Baron-Cohen, H. Tager-Flusberg, & D. Cohen (Eds.), *Understanding other minds: Perspectives from developmental cognitive neuroscience.* New York, NY: Oxford University Press.

Diehl, J. J., Bennetto, L., & Young, E. C. (2006). Story recall and narrative coherence of high-functioning children with autism spectrum disorders. *Journal of Abnormal Child Psychology, 34*(1), 83–98.

Dobson, K., & Dozois, D. (2001). Historical and philosophical bases of the cognitive-behavioral therapies. In K. Dobson (Ed.), *Handbook of cognitive behavioral therapies* (pp. 3–39). New York, NY: Guilford Press.

Durlak, J. A., Weissberg, R. P., Dymnicki, A. B., Taylor, R. D., & Schellinger, K. B. (2011). The impact of enhancing students' social and emotional learning: A meta-analysis of school-based universal interventions. *Child Development, 82*(1), 405–432.

Eslinger, P. J. (1996). Conceptualizing, describing and measuring components of executive function: A summary. In G. R. Lyon, & N. A. Krasnegor (Eds.), *Attention, memory, and executive function* (pp. 367–439). Baltimore, MD: Brookes.

Farroni, T., Csibra, G., Simion, F., & Johnson, M. H. (2002). Eye contact detection in humans from birth. *Proceedings of the National Academy of Sciences, 99*(14), 9602–9605.

Farrugia, S., & Hudson, J. (2006). Anxiety in adolescents with Asperger syndrome: Negative thoughts, behavioral problems and life interference. *Focus on Autism and Other Developmental Disabilities, 21*(1), 25–35.

Field, T. M., Woodson, R., Cohen, D., Greenberg, R., Garcia, R., & Collins, K. (1983). Discrimination and imitation of facial expressions by term and preterm neonates. *Infant Behavior and Development, 6*(4), 485–489.

Flavell, J. H. (2004). Theory-of-mind development: Retrospect and prospect. *Merrill-Palmer Quarterly, 50*(3), 274–290.

Franke, L., & Durbin, C. (2011). *Nurturing narratives: Coaching comprehension and creating conversation.* Shawnee Mission, KS: Autism Asperger Publishing Company.

Frith, U. (1989). *Autism: Explaining the enigma.* Massachusetts: Basil Blackwell, Inc.

Frith, U., & Frith, U. (2010). The social brain: allowing humans to boldly go where no other species has been. *Philosophical Transactions of the Royal Society B: Biological Sciences, 365* (1537), 165–176.

Gardner, H. (1993). *Multiple intelligences: The theory in practice.* New York, NY: Basic Books.

Gaus, V. L. (2007). *Cognitive-behavioral therapy for adult Asperger syndrome.* New York, NY: Guilford Press.

Goleman, D. (1995). *Emotional intelligence: Why it can matter more than IQ.* New York, NY: Bantam Books.

Gopnik, A., Meltzoff, A. N., & Kuhl, P. K. (1999). *The scientist in the crib: What early learning tells us about the mind.* New York, NY: Harper Perennial.

Gray, C. (1994). *Comic strip conversations: Illustrated interactions that teach conversation skills to students with autism and related disorders.* Arlington, TX: Future Horizons.

Gray, C. (2010). *The new social story book*. Arlington, TX: Future Horizons.

Gray, C., McAndrew, S., & White, A. L. (2002). *My social stories book*. Philadelphia, PA: Jessica Kingsley Publishers.

Green, S. A., & Ben-Sasson, A. (2010). Anxiety disorders and sensory over-responsivity in children with autism spectrum disorders: Is there a causal relationship?. *Journal of Autism and Developmental Disorders, 40*(12), 1495–1504.

Greenspan, S. I., & Wieder, S. (2003). *Engaging autism: The floortime approach to helping children relate, communicate and think*. Jackson, TN: Perseus Books.

Gutstein, S. E. (2001). *Autism/Aspergers: Solving the relationship puzzle: A new developmental program that opens the door to lifelong social & emotional growth*. Arlington, TX: Future Horizons.

Hale, C. M. & Tager-Flusberg, H. (2005). Social communication in children with autism: The relationship between theory of mind and discourse development. *Autism, 9*(2), 157–178.

Happé, F. G. (1994). An advanced test of theory of mind: Understanding of story characters' thoughts and feelings by able autistic, mentally handicapped and normal children and adults. *Journal of Autism & Developmental Disorders, 24*(2), 129–154.

Happé, F. G. (1997). Central coherence and theory of mind in autism: Reading homographs in context. *British Journal of Developmental Psychology, 15*(1), 1–12. doi: 10.1111/j.2044–835X.1997.tb00721.x.

Happé, F., Booth, R., Charlton, R., & Hughes, C. (2006). Executive function deficits in autism spectrum disorders and attention deficit/hyperactivity disorder: Examining profiles across domains and ages. *Brain and Cognition, 61*(1), 25–39.

Happé, F., & Frith, U. (2006). The weak coherence account: Detail-focused cognitive style in autism spectrum disorders. *Journal of Autism and Developmental Disorders, 36*(1), 5–25.

Hawken, L. S., Vincent, C. G., & Schumann, J. (2008). Response to intervention for social behavior: Challenges and opportunities. *Journal of Emotional and Behavior Disorders, 16*(4), 213–225.

Hedley, D., & Young, R. (2006). Social comparison processes and depressive symptoms in children and adolescents with Asperger syndrome. *Autism, 10*(2), 139–153.

Henry, S. A., & Myles, B. S. (2007). *The comprehensive autism planning system (CAPS) for individuals with Asperger syndrome, autism and related disabilities: Integrating best practices throughout the student's day.* Shawnee Mission, KS: Autism Asperger Publishing Company.

Hill, E. L. (2004). Evaluating the theory of executive dysfunction in autism. *Developmental Review, 24*(2), 189–233.

Hirsh-Pasek, K., Golinkoff, R. M., & Eyer, D. (2003). *Einstein never used flash cards: How our children really learn - and why they need to play more and memorize less.* Emmaus, PA: Rodale Press.

Hume, K., Loftin, R., & Lantz J. (2009). Increasing independence in autism spectrum disorders: A review of three focused interventions. *Journal of Autism and Developmental Disorders. 39*(9), 1329–1338.

ImprovEverywhere. (2008, January 31). *Frozen Grand Central* [Video file]. Retrieved from http://www.youtube.com/watch?v=jwMj3PJDxuo.

Individuals with Disabilities Education Improvement Act, 20 U.S.C. § 1400, Pub. L. 108–446 (2004). Retrieved from http://idea.ed.gov/explore/view/p/%2Croot%2Cstatute%2C.

Jones, E. A., & Carr, E. G. (2004). Joint attention in children with autism: Theory and intervention. *Focus on Autism and Other Developmental Disabilities, 19*(1), 13–26.

Jones, W., Carr, K., & Klin, A. (2008). Absence of preferential looking to the eyes of approaching adults predicts level of social disability in 2-year-old toddlers with autism spectrum disorder. *Archives of General Psychiatry, 65*(8), 946–954.

Justice, L. M., & Fey, M. E. (2004). Evidence based practice in schools: Integrating craft and theory with science and data. *The ASHA Leader, 9*(17), 4–5 and 30–32.

Kent, R. D. (2006). Evidence-based practice in communication disorders: Progress not perfection. *Language, Speech, and Hearing in Schools, ASHA, 37*(4), 268–270.

Klin, A., Jones, W., Schultz, R., & Volkmar, F. (2003). The enactive mind, or from actions to cognition: lessons from autism. *Philosophical Transactions of the Royal Society of London Series B: Biological Sciences, 358*(1430), 345–360.

Koegel, R. L., & Kern Koegel, L. (2006). *Pivotal response treatments for autism: Communication, social, and academic development.* Baltimore, MD: Brookes Publishing Company.

Kuhlmeier, V., Wynn, K., & Bloom, P. (2003). Attribution of dispositional states by 12-month-olds. *Psychological Science, 14*(5), 402–408.

Kuusikko, S., Pollock-Wurman, R., Jussila, K., Carter, A. S., Mattila, M. L., Ebeling, H., ... & Moilanen, I. (2008). Social anxiety in high-functioning children and adolescents with autism and Asperger syndrome. *Journal of Autism and Developmental Disorders, 38*(9), 1697–1709.

Kuypers, L. (2011). *The zones of regulation.* San Jose, CA: Think Social Publishing, Inc.

Landa, R. J. & Goldberg, M. C. (2005). Language, social, and executive functions in high functioning autism: A continuum of performance. *Journal of Autism and Developmental Disorders, 35*(5), 557–573.

Lane, K. L., Wehby, J. H., & Cooley, C. (2006). Teacher expectations of students' classroom behavior across the grade span: Which social skills are necessary for success? *Exceptional Children, 72*(2), 153–167.

Levett, S., & Dubner, S. J. (2005). *Freakonomics: A rogue economist explores the hidden side of everything.* New York, NY: William Morrow.

Levine, M. (2002). *A mind at a time: America's top learning expert shows how every child can succeed.* New York, NY: Simon and Schuster.

Lopata, C., Thomeer, M. L., Volker, M. A., & Nida, R. E. (2006). Effectiveness of a cognitive-behavioral treatment on the social behaviors of children with Asperger disorder. *Focus on Autism and Other Developmental Disabilities, 21*(4), 237–244.

Lord, C. (1993). The complexity of social behaviour in autism. In S. Baron-Cohen, H. Tager-Flusberg, & D. Cohen (Eds.), *Understanding other minds: Perspectives from autism* (pp. 292–316). Oxford, England: Oxford University Press.

Losh, M., & Capps, L. (2003). Narrative ability in high-functioning children with autism or Asperger's syndrome. *Journal of Autism and Development Disorders, 33*(3), 239–251.

Loukusa, S., Leinonen, E., Kuusikko, S., Jussila, K., Mattila, M. L., Ryder, N., ... & Moilanen, I. (2007). Use of context in pragmatic language comprehension by children with Asperger syndrome or high-functioning autism. *Journal of Autism and Developmental Disorders, 37*(6), 1049–1059.

Lovaas, O. I. (1987). Behavioral treatment and normal educational and intellectual functioning in young autistic children. *Journal of Consulting and Clinical psychology, 55*(1), 3–9.

Loveland, K. A., McEvoy, R. E., Tunali, B., & Kelley, M. L. (1990). Narrative story telling in autism and Down's syndrome. *British Journal of Developmental Psychology, 8*(1), 9–23.

Marans, W. D., Rubin, E., & Laurent, A. (2005). Addressing social communication skills in individuals with high-functioning autism and Asperger syndrome: Critical priorities in educational programming. In F. R. Volkmar, A. Klin, and R. Paul (Eds.), *Handbook of autism and pervasive developmental disorders* (3rd ed.). New York, NY: John Wiley.

Marshall, P. J., & Fox, N. A. (Eds.). (2006). *The development of social engagement: Neurobiological perspectives.* New York, NY: Oxford University Press.

Meltzoff, A. N. (1995). Understanding intentions of others: Re-enactment of intended acts by 18-month-old children. *Developmental Psychology, 31*(5) 838–850.

Miller, L., Gillam, R., & Pena, E. (2001). *Dynamic assessment and intervention: Improving children's narrative abilities.* Austin, TX: Pro-Ed, Inc.

Minne, M. P., & Semrud-Clikeman, M. (2011). A social competence intervention for young children with high functioning autism and Asperger Syndrome: A pilot study. *Autism: The International Journal of Research and Practice, 16*(6), 586–602.

Mundy, P., & Acra, F. (2006). Joint attention, social engagement and the development of social competence. In P. Marshall & N. Fox (Eds.), *The development of social engagement neurobiological perspectives* (pp. 81–117). New York, NY: Oxford University Press.

Murray, D. S., Creaghead, N. A., Manning-Courtney, P., Shear, P. K., Bean, J., & Prendeville, J. A. (2008). The relationship between joint attention and language in children with autism spectrum disorders. *Focus on Autism and Other Developmental Disabilities, 23*(1), 5–14.

Myles, B. S., Cook, K., Miller, N., Rinner, L., & Robbins, L. (2000). *Asperger syndrome and sensory issues: Practical solutions for making sense of the world.* Shawnee Mission, KS: Autism Asperger Publishing Company.

Myles, B. S., Hilgenfeld, T. D., Barnhill, G. P., Griswold, D. E., Hagiwara, T., & Simpson, R. L. (2002). Analysis of reading skills in individuals with Asperger Syndrome. *Focus on Autism and Other Developmental Disabilities, 17*(1), 44–47.

Myles, B. S., Trautman, M., Schelvan, R. L. (2004). *The hidden curriculum: Practical solutions for understanding unstated rules in social situations*. Shawnee Mission, KS: Autism Asperger Publishing Company.

National Governors Association Center for Best Practices & Council of Chief State School Officers. (2010). *Common Core State Standards for English language arts and literacy in history/social studies, science, and technical subjects*. Washington, DC: Authors. Retrieved from www.corestandards.org/assets/CCSSI_ELA%20Standards.pdf

No Child Left Behind (NCLB) Act of 2001, Pub. L. No. 107–110, § 115, Stat. 1425 (2002).

Norbury, C. F., & Bishop, D. V. (2002). Inferential processing and story recall in children with communication problems: A comparison of specific language impairment, pragmatic language impairment and high-functioning autism. *International Journal of Language and Communication Disorders, 37*(3), 227–251.

Norbury, C. F., & Bishop, D. V. (2003). Narrative skills of children with communication impairments. *International Journal of Language & Communication Disorders, 38*(3), 287–313.

Ozonoff, S., & Griffith, E. M. (2000). Neuropsychological function and the external validity of Asperger syndrome. In A. Klin, F. Volkmar, and S. Sparrow (Eds.). *Asperger syndrome.* New York, NY: The Guilford Press.

Parish, P., & Parish H. (2009). *An Amelia Bedelia celebration: Four stories tall.* New York, NY: Greenwillow Books.

Pellicano, E. (2010). Individual differences in executive function and central coherence predict developmental changes in theory of mind in autism. *Developmental Psychology, 46*(2), 530–544.

Perner, J., Frith, U., Leslie, A. M., & Leekam, S. R. (1989). Exploration of the autistic child's theory of mind: Knowledge, belief, and communication. *Child Development, 60,* 689–700.

Perner, L. (Ed.). (2012). *Scholars with autism achieving dream.* Sedona, AZ: Auricle Ink Publishers.

Perry, A., & Condillac, R. (2003). *Evidence-based practices for children and adolescents with autism spectrum disorders: Review of the literature and practice guide.* Ontario: Children's Mental Health.

Pine, D. S., Guyer, A. E., Goldwin, M., Towbin K. A., & Leibenluft, E. (2008). Autism spectrum disorder scale scores in pediatric mood and anxiety disorders. *Journal of the American Academy of Child & Adolescent Psychiatry, 47*(6), 652–661.

Plaisted, K. C. (2001). Reduced generalization in autism: An alternative to weak central coherence. In J. A. Burack, T. Charman, N. Yirmiya, & P. R. Zelazo (Eds.), *The development of autism: Perspectives from theory and research* (pp. 149–169).

Prelock, P. (2006). *Autism spectrum disorders: Issues in assessment and intervention.* Austin, TX: Pro-Ed.

Prior, M., Dahlstrom, B., & Squires, T. L. (1990). Autistic children's knowledge of thinking and feeling states in other people. *Journal of Child Psychology & Psychiatry, 31*(4), 587–601.

Prizant, B. M., Wetherby, A. M., Rubin, E., Laurent, A. C., & Rydell, P. J. (2006). *The SCERTS™ model: A comprehensive educational approach for children with autism spectrum disorders. Volume II program planning and intervention.* Maryland: Brookes Publishing Company.

Rao, P. A., Beidel, D. C., & Murray, M. J. (2008). Social skills interventions for children with Asperger's syndrome or high-functioning autism: A review and recommendations. *Journal of Autism and Developmental Disorders, 38*(2), 353–361.

Rapin, I., & Dunn, M. (2003). Update on the language disorders of individuals on the autistic spectrum. *Brain and Development, 25*(3), 166–172.

Ratner, N. B. (2006). Evidence-based practice: An examination of its ramifications for the practice of speech-language pathology. *Language, Speech and Hearing Services in Schools, ASHA, 37*(4), 257–267.

Reaven, J. A., Blakeley-Smith, A., Nichols, S., Dasari, M., Flanigan, E., & Hepburn S. (2009). Cognitive-behavioral group treatment for anxiety symptoms in children with high functioning autism spectrum disorders: A pilot study. *Focus on Autism and Other Developmental Disorders, 24*(1), 27–37.

Repacholi, B. M., & Gopnik, A. (1997). Early reasoning about desires: Evidence from 14- and 18-month olds. *Developmental Psychology, 33*(1), 12–21.

Reynhout, G., & Carter, M. (2006). Social Stories™ for children with disabilities. *Journal of Autism and Developmental Disorders, 36*(4), 445–469.

Rooney Moreau, M. (2010). *Making connections! The language-thinking-social-connection.* In Book 2 from *The Autism Collection.* Springfield, MA: MindWing Concepts.

Russell, J. E. (1997). *Autism as an executive disorder.* New York, NY: Oxford University Press.

Saalasti, S., Lepistö, T., Toppila, E., Kujala, T., Laakso, M., Nieminen-von Wendt, T., von Wendt, L., & Jansson-Verkasalo, E. (2008). Language abilities of children with Asperger syndrome. *Journal of Autism and Developmental Disorders, 38*(8), 1574–1580.

Sabbagh, M. (2006). Neurocognitive bases of preschoolers' theory-of-mind development: Integrating cognitive neuroscience and cognitive development. In P. Marshall & N. Fox (Eds.), *The development of social engagement: Neurobiological Perspectives* (pp. 153–170). New York, NY: Oxford University Press.

Saulnier, C. A., & Klin, A. (2007). Brief report: Social and communication abilities and disabilities in higher functioning individuals with autism and Asperger syndrome. *Journal of Autism and Developmental Disorders, 37*(4), 788–793.

Simmons-Mackie, N. N., & Damico, J. S. (2003). Contributions of qualitative research to the knowledge base of normal communication. *American Journal of Speech Language Pathology, 12*(2), 144–154.

Simpson, R. (2005). *Autism spectrum disorders: interventions and treatments for children and youth.* Thousand Oaks, CA: Corwin Press.

Simpson, R. (2006). Evidence-based practices and students with autism spectrum disorders. *Focus on Autism and Other Developmental Disabilities, 20*(3), 140–149.

Sodian, B., & Frith, U. (1992). Deception and sabotage in autistic, retarded, and normal children. *Journal of Child Psychology and Psychiatry, 33*(3), 591–606.

Sofronoff, K., Attwood, T., & Hinton, S. (2005). A randomised controlled trial of a CBT intervention for anxiety in children with Asperger syndrome. *Journal of Child Psychology and Psychiatry, 46*(11), 1152–1160.

Spek, A. A., Scholte, E. M., Van Berckelaer-Onnes, I. A. (2010). Theory of mind in adults with HFA and Asperger syndrome. *Journal of Autism and Developmental Disorders, 40*(3), 280–289.

Stewart, M. E., Barnard, L., Pearson, J., Hasan, R., & O'Brien, G. (2006). Presentation of depression in autism and Asperger syndrome: A review. *Autism, 10*(1), 103–116.

Tager-Flusberg, H. (1995). 'Once upon a ribbit': Stories narrated by autistic children. *British Journal of Developmental Psychology, 13*(1), 45–59.

Tomasello, M., Carpenter, M., Call, J., Behne, T., & Moll, H. (2005). Understanding and sharing intentions: The origins of cultural cognition. *Behavioral and Brain Sciences, 28*(5), 675–690.

Toplis, R., & Hadwin, J. (2006). Using social stories to change problematic lunchtime behaviour in school. *Educational Psychology in Practice, 22*(1), 53–67.

Tovani, C. (2000). *I read it, but I don't get it: Comprehension strategies for adolescent readers.* Portland, ME: Stenhouse Publishers.

Truesdale, S. P. (1990). Whole-Body Listening: Developing active auditory skills. *Language, Speech, and Hearing in Schools, 21,* 183–184.

Twachtman-Cullen, D. (2000). More able children with autism spectrum disorders: Social-communicative challenges and guidelines for enhancing abilities. In A. M. Wetherby, & B. M. Prizant (Eds.), *Autism spectrum disorders: A transactional developmental approach* (pp. 225–249). Baltimore, MD: Paul H. Brookes Publishing.

Van den Broek, P., Rapp, D., & Kendeou, P. (2005). Integrating memory-based and constructionist processes in accounts of reading comprehension. *Discourse Processes, 39*(2–3), 299–316.

Vermeulen, P. (2012). *Autism as context blindness.* Shawnee Mission, KS: Autism Asperger Publishing Company.

Volkmar, F. R. (1987). Social development. In D. J. Cohen and A. M. Donnellan (Eds.), *Handbook of autism and pervasive developmental disorders* (pp. 41–60). New York, NY: John Wiley & Sons.

Volkmar, F. R., & Klin, A. (1990). Social development in autism: Historical and clinical perspectives. In S. Baron-Cohen, H. Tager-Flusberg, & D. Cohen (Eds.), *Understanding other minds: Perspectives from autism* (pp. 40–55). Oxford, England: Oxford University Press.

Walker, A. S. (1982). Intermodal perception of expressive behaviors by human infants. *Journal of Experimental Child Psychology, 33*(3), 514–535.

Westby, C. (2012, October 8). Theory of mind: Going to the heart of autism spectrum disorders and social communication disorder. Talk presented in Manchester, New Hampshire.

Whalen, C., Schreibman, L., & Ingersoll, B. (2006). The collateral effects of joint attention training on social initiations, positive affect, imitation, and spontaneous speech for young children with autism. *Journal of Autism and Developmental Disorders, 36*(5), 655–664.

White, S., Keonig, K., & Scahill, L. (2007). Social skills development in children with autism spectrum disorder: A review of intervention research. *Journal of Autism and Developmental Disorders, 37*(10), 1858–1868.

Williams, M. S., & Shellenberger, S. (1996). *How does your engine run? A leader's guide to The Alert Program for self-regulation.* Albuquerque, NM: Therapy Works, Inc.

Winner, M. G. (2000). *Inside out: What makes the person with social cognitive deficits tick?* San Jose, CA: Think Social Publishing, Inc.

Winner, M. G. (2005). *Think social! A social thinking curriculum for school-age students.* San Jose, CA: Think Social Publishing, Inc.

Winner, M. G. (2007a). *Social behavior mapping: Connecting behavior, emotions and consequences across the day.* San Jose, CA: Think Social Publishing, Inc.

Winner, M. G. (2007b). *Thinking about YOU, thinking about ME* (2nd ed.). San Jose, CA: Think Social Publishing, Inc.

Winner, M. G. (2007c). *Worksheets for teaching social thinking and related skills.* San Jose, CA: Think Social Publishing, Inc.

Winner, M. G. (2011). *Social thinking worksheets for tweens and teens: Learning to read in between the social lines.* San Jose, CA: Think Social Publishing, Inc.

Winner, M. G., & Crooke P. (2010). *You are a social detective! Explaining social thinking to kids.* San Jose, CA: Think Social Publishing, Inc.

Winner, M. G., & Madrigal, S. (2008). *Superflex... A superhero social thinking curriculum.* San Jose, CA: Think Social Publishing.

Wolfberg, P. J. (2003). *Peer play and the autism spectrum: The art of guiding children's socialization and imagination.* Shawnee Mission, KS: Autism Asperger Publishing Company.

Yeager, M., & Yeager, D. (2013). *Executive function & child development* (p. 39). New York, NY: W. W. Norton.

Zaks, Z. (2008). Interventions for children with autism spectrum disorders: Major issues, major choices. *Autism Asperger's Digest Magazine,* January-February 2008. Arlington, TX: Future Horizons.

Zunshine, L. (2012). *Getting inside your head: What cognitive science can tell us about popular culture.* Baltimore, MD: The Johns Hopkins University Press.

Study Guide

Why Teach Social Thinking? attempts to raise awareness of the many complex and interrelated issues that are at the heart of teaching today's students social emotional information. Author Michelle Garcia Winner presents a provocative discussion about what it really means to teach social skills to students who struggle to understand our complex and highly context-driven social world, whether or not they have a disability label or an IEP.

Through 12 questions that challenge us to think more deeply about how we view social intelligence, she illuminates the difference between teaching social *skills* (e.g., behaviors) and teaching students a *pathway of thinking about self and others as a means to problem solve whatever social situation they may experience.* Topics span various aspects of social learning, from the need for a com-

mon definition for "social skills" to understanding different "levels of the social mind", from evidence-based practices and how they apply to teaching social awareness and social skills, to best practice guidelines for teaching her Social Thinking® Methodology.

These Study Guide questions can be used by individuals, or study groups, to crack open their thinking and assumptions about what our students know about the social world. The book and study guide questions are targeted to educators, therapists, clinicians, school administrators, family members, state and federal policy makers, and health-care professionals. Individuals who work with or design educational and/or treatment programs for individuals of all ages, as well as academic professionals who prepare educators and clinicians to work with students with social learning challenges, will find these probing questions especially useful in appreciating the complex process involved in assessing students' social learning needs and designing relevant, and effective, programs to help students in any setting.

Discussion concepts apply to all people, children through adults, who struggle with social learning, whether or not they have a diagnosed disorder such as ASD, NVLD, Social Communication (Pragmatics) Disorder, ADHD, or other related disorders.

Content and Suggestions

- Self-Assessment Form to be completed before reading the book, by an individual, or as a group discussion, to explore existing knowledge, thoughts, and assumptions related to social emotional learning, social skills, and social awareness.

- Study Guide Questions for each chapter.

- Post study Self-Assessment Form to be completed after reading/discussing the entire book.

Note: A downloadable PDF of the entire Study Guide is available at the Social Thinking website, www.socialthinking.com. Find it on the product page for the *Why Teach Social Thinking?* book.

Suggestions for Using the Book and Study Guide Questions

- *School educators* interested in promoting the concepts, vocabulary, and materials that make up the Social Thinking Methodology can use this book and the study questions to reinforce the idea that social learning helps everyone; it's not just reserved for students with social learning challenges. The questions can be used to spearhead discussions among teachers and administrators about the importance of including social emotional learning instruction within the teaching day and illuminate the roadblocks in doing so.

- *Parents* of children with social challenges can use many of the questions and descriptive text to educate themselves about the broader concepts involved in the social learning process, and in making a case for Social Thinking and/or other social teaching programs to be incorporated into a child's IEP.

- At the *college/university* level, the 12 questions in the book and the Study Guide can be a springboard for graduate and post-graduate level classroom discussions related to social learning, social intelligence, and/or social treatment program design and instruction.

- *Policy makers/program planners* can use the 12 questions and Study Guide for round- table discussions about best practice strategies for teaching social emotional curriculum within an education and/or treatment setting.

Why Teach Social Thinking?
Getting Started:
Self Assessment Form

People have many different ideas about what it means to "be social" and the role social intelligence plays in later success in life. The following questions probe your own (or a group's) existing knowledge and ideas related to social emotional learning and social skills.

How do you define "social skills"?

_____

_____

What factors determine whether an individual exhibits "good social skills" vs. "bad social skills"?

_____

_____

Is there currently a common definition of "social skills" within Federal education legislation (IDEA, NCLB, etc.)? ☐ Yes ☐ No

List 3 social skills that you think are weak and/or lacking in today's students entering kindergarten?

1. _____
2. _____
3. _____

True or false: Social expectations change with age? ☐ True ☐ False

Using the rating scale that follows, to what extent do you believe that:

_____ social emotional skills can be effectively taught using behavior-based methods

_____ academic intelligence is more important than social intelligence in a student's later success in life

_____ all children can learn good social emotional skills by watching others who exhibit these skills

_____ all children arrive to school with the same innate social abilities

_____ children know what they're doing when they exhibit inappropriate social behaviors

_____ teachers should not be responsible for teaching social emotional skills to students beyond the preschool level

_____ social scripting is an effective strategy for teaching social skills

_____ social intelligence is directly linked to IQ

_____ social emotional skills are mainly used outside the classroom/academic instruction, such as in making friends, playing with others, etc.

_____ children with the same diagnosis will benefit equally from the same social learning treatment plan

_____ social emotional skills can be taught to mastery

_____ students can still get a "good education" without teachers attending to their social learning needs

_____ social behavior is culturally driven

Rating Scale:
**5 = Strongly agree; 4 = Mildly agree; 3 = No opinion;
2 = Mildly disagree; 1 = Strongly disagree**

Why Teach Social Thinking?
Post Study:
Self Assessment Form

Provide responses below that reflect your own (or the group's) understanding, changed perceptions, and/or new ideas related to teaching Social Thinking and social emotional learning as a result of reading this book. Discuss or reflect on the ways your ideas and opinions have/have not changed and why.

Has your definition of "social skills" changed? If so, how?

_____

_____

Prior to reading this book, what beliefs or assumptions did you hold about how social learning occurs? Did anything in this book change those assumptions? How?

_____

_____

Using the rating scale that follows, to what extent do you now believe that:

_____ social emotional skills can be effectively taught using behavior-based methods

_____ academic intelligence is more important than social intelligence in a student's later success in life

_____ all children can learn good social emotional skills by watching others who exhibit these skills

_____ all children arrive to school with the same innate social abilities

_____ children know what they're doing when they exhibit inappropriate social behaviors

_____ teachers should not be responsible for teaching social emotional skills to students beyond the preschool level

_____ social scripting is an effective strategy for teaching social skills

_____ social intelligence is directly linked to IQ

_____ social emotional skills are mainly used outside direct classroom instruction, such as in making friends, playing with others, etc.

_____ children with the same diagnosis will benefit equally from the same social learning treatment plan

_____ social emotional skills can be taught to mastery

_____ a student can still get a "good education" without teachers attending to his/her social learning needs

_____ social behavior is culturally driven

Rating Scale:
**5 = Strongly agree; 4 = Mildly agree; 3 = No opinion;
2 = Mildly disagree; 1 = Strongly disagree**

To what extent in your own thinking, or that of your school/district, did you, or do you still, hold that a behavior-based method of instruction is "more important/valuable" than one based on social cognitive concepts? Has your opinion changed as a result of reading this book? If so, how?

_____

_____

Do you agree or disagree with the author's notion that teaching social skills without teaching the underlying structure of social thinking is insufficient in meeting our students' needs?

_____

_____

To what extent have you assumed that your students' inappropriate behaviors are willful or intentional? Has that opinion changed as a result of reading this book? If so, how and why?

_____

_____

How important is it to model the social thinking you hope to teach your student(s)? Why?

_____

_____

The author suggests that by becoming more cognitively aware of our social processing and the social strategies we choose in situations, we are better able to teach social emotional concepts. To what extent do you agree/disagree with this idea?

_____

_____

What factors (budgetary, time, teaching emphasis) affect your ability as an educator to place more emphasis on teaching Social Thinking to your students?

_____

_____

Describe 2 keys ways in which your own perceptions toward teaching social emotional skills have changed as a result of reading this book. How will that affect your teaching approach?

_____

_____

If you passed this book along to another educator, what main point(s) would you be sure to mention in describing the book?

_____

_____

Introduction to Social Thinking and Social Skills

1. How does familiarizing ourselves with the literature related to cultural anthropology, sociology and linguistics help educators and counselors develop treatment plans for students with social learning challenges?

2. When encouraging a student to use better social skills, explain why this author thinks it is important to teach social learning/ thinking as a mandatory part of this process.

3. Identify a social skill that might be taught to encourage students to greet another person.

   a. Prior to answering the following sub-questions, observe people in your community greeting each other.

      i. Explain at least three different types of behaviors you observed that were interpreted to be greetings.

      ii. Explain why people do not use one uniform type of greeting.

      iii. Consider and explain what would be meant by a person "over-greeting" another person.

      iv. Explain why the answers to the above questions can shape how you develop a treatment plan.

   b. Describe how you would literally teach a student to perform this skill.

   c. Explain how the use of that social skill affects the thinking of others who observe the greeting.

    d. Explain the expected social mindset of the person who is producing the social skill, which helps to motivate that person to use the skill.

    e. Use information from your answers to a, b and c to create a treatment plan for teaching a student how to greet another person.

    f. Describe how this treatment plan may be different from those developed simply to teach the social skill of producing a response that is interpreted by others to be a "greeting."

4. When you teach a social skill, to what extent do you include a discussion of why this skill is important and how it may generalize outside the classroom setting? Can you think of ways to incorporate this type of teaching more actively into your overall curriculum?

What Are Social Skills?

1. One approach to teaching social skills, commonly used with persons with social learning challenges, is the "social skills script." When "scripting" the social skills teacher will teach a social skill such as greetings and then have students follow the exact same script each time they see a person they are told to greet, at times greeting the same person multiple times in a day. Describe why this approach can create new social dilemmas for our students when faced with using the same script in different contexts.

2. How does the authors' statement that, "Social expectations evolve in nuance and sophistication with age" affect the development of treatment plans to encourage students to use better social skills?

3. When sitting in an IEP meeting, the special education teacher was not sure how to respond to her principal's statement that the student should only need two years of social skills goals and related lessons and that any social skills teachings should only be done during social time, which he defined as "recess time." Assume the voice of the special education teacher, to explain to all those in attendance at the IEP meeting why the principal's logic is not supported by the evidence and state it in a manner which does not embarrass the principal.

4. List three assumptions you hold about innate social processing and social learning. How do those assumptions affect the way you relate to and teach your students?

5. Create a list of 5–10 examples of how you define "good social skills"? Review your list: how many examples are behavior based and how many reflect the thinking skills that precede the behavior? What does that tell you about your approach to teaching social skills?

What Are the Origins of Social Development? Is There an Age When Our Social Development Stops?

1. Around one year of age children follow others' eyes to notice what they are looking at and they also point to show others what they are interested in. This author thinks parents should throw a party to celebrate this developmental accomplishment.

   a. What is the name of this developmental accomplishment?

   b. How does this basic developmental milestone lend itself to language development in that same child?

2. This author talks about the development of social, emotional and behavior regulation skills as necessary pre-cursors to the child being able to develop cooperative play skills.

   a. How are social, emotional and behavior regulation skills related to cooperative play?

   b. If a child has not learned to play cooperatively by age five, do you think we can teach the child to cooperate by writing a goal that states the child will learn to cooperate 80% of the time by the end of the year? Yes or No?

      i. Support your answer with an overview of a treatment plan you might develop.

3. Give an example of your own use of narrative language when you were recently talking to someone.

    a. What type of thinking did your mind engage in to decide what information to share and what information not to share with the person you were talking to?

    b. Describe what you considered about the other person's knowledge to decide what to say/not say.

    c. What if you told the person every possible detail you could picture in your mind as you told the story; how would that affect the communicative process?

    d. Why is narrative language considered a critical part of social skills?

4. Do you teach current/up-to-date social thinking and related social skills that will help students blend in with their peers? For instance, does your social pragmatics program address everyday peer slang, common peer body language, etc.? If not, why?

5. Discuss at least three ways in which your school's social skills/ social emotional programs can be made more flexible to adapt to changing social conventions within society, peer groups, etc.

288

Chapter **4**
Study Guide

. . . .

In What Areas of Social Thinking Do Students with Social Cognitive Challenges Struggle? The ILAUGH Model Remodeled

1. Recall a time you had to give a presentation in front of an audience or class. Describe how each of these processes assisted you in the development and presentation of that talk.
   a. Central coherence theory
   b. Joint attention/Theory of mind
   c. Executive functioning
   d. Emotional process and emotional regulation
   e. Sensory integration
2. Why don't most teachers directly teach the information conveyed through the ILAUGH Model of Social Cognition?
3. Many students who score extremely well on academic testing and IQ tests still struggle to demonstrate competencies related to the ILAUGH Model. Why?
4. The process of "listening to the teacher" while seated amongst other students in the classroom requires more than simply hearing the words. Describe how each of these concepts helps a child to "listen":
   a. Listening with eyes and brain
   b. Abstracting and Inferencing

      c. Understanding Perspective

      d. Gestalt Processing

5. Discuss the commonly held idea that IQ and social processing abilities go hand in hand. As a result of reading this chapter has your perception changed?

6. Discuss how weak or strong perspective taking skills affect academic learning. Discuss how they affect test scores.

What Impact Do Weaknesses in Social Conceptual Information Have on Learning the Common Core State Standards?

1. Describe how reading comprehension relates to social learning.
2. Describe how written expression relates to social learning.
3. Describe how working in a science lab relates to social learning.
4. An administrator in a school district has been told that IEP goals are to be written based on the Common Core State Educational Standards. She has interpreted that to mean that she is to write the Common Core Standards which the child does not appear to be on track to meet as the IEP goal itself.
   a. Explain why her reasoning is faulty.
   b. Explain how to encourage the IEP team to write goals that are more basic than the expectations implied in the Common Core Standard.
5. To what extent to you believe that our educational curriculum is predicated on the idea that all children arrive at school with fully functional social brains?
6. To what extent in your own thinking, or that of your school/district, is the assumption made that students with ASD,

Social Communication (Pragmatics) Disorder, or other disorders involving social processing can learn better social skills by 1) being in the presence of and watching others with good social skills, and/or 2) through social skills modeling? How has this assumption helped or hindered your community's understanding of social skills program development for students who struggle with social learning?

When Do We Use Social Thinking and Related Social Skills? How Do We Approach Teaching These Skills?

1. What does the author mean when she suggests that observing others is the "glue that ties together actions and environment"?

2. Why should classroom behavior regulation problems not necessarily be thought of by the educators as simply problem behavior?

3. How is a behaviorally-based intervention which rewards the student for doing an appropriate behavior different from a Social Thinking intervention?

4. Discuss how social emotional thinking is involved in learning subjects such as math, chemistry, or affects a student's ability to engage in extracurricular activities such as individual/team sports, choir, drama, etc.

5. Discuss the differences between "social skills performance" and "social competence." Why is teaching social competence more effective overall in helping our students?

6. As a whole, do you/does your school advocate a behavioral approach or a social cognitive approach to teaching social skills? Discuss the pros and cons of each.

7. Select a social skill you teach. Describe three ways in which a Social Thinking approach could be integrated into a behavior-based program for teaching this skill.

Chapter 7
Study Guide

. . . .

How Can Cognitive Behavior Therapy Address Teaching Social Thinking and Related Social Skills?

1. Think of a situation in your own life where you struggled to make yourself do something you did not want to do, but in the end you were able to get yourself to do the dreaded behavior. Give an example of:

    a. How your cognitive activity (thinking) affected your behavior.

    b. How your cognitive activity (thinking) was monitored and altered.

    c. How your desired behavior change was affected through cognitive change (changing your thoughts).

2. Think of a situation in your own life where you have not succeeded in altering your behavior (e.g., you may drive too fast or not exercise enough, etc.). Describe how your current mindset discourages you from changing your behavior.

    a. How is your cognitive activity maintaining the current behavior, even if it is a behavior you wish you did not have?

    b. How can you try and change the way you think about the behavior to motivate yourself to change it?

3. Does your classroom/school curriculum include cognitive behavior teaching strategies? If not, should it? Discuss possible perceived roadblocks that exist in incorporating CBT into your program.

Do All Those with ASD-SCD Benefit from the Same Teachings? The Social Thinking-Social Communication Profile (ST-SCP)

1. Describe why this author thinks that diagnostic labels do not provide adequate information for creating treatment plans.

2. Why do the authors of the ST-SCP discourage discussion of a prognosis before third grade? Once a prognosis is given from third grade on, how can this help with treatment planning?

3. Why do the authors feel there is a need to categorize students' social learning abilities? How do these categories assist in treatment planning?

4. Why are students we perceive as being more "awkward and odd" more apt to be mentored by their neurotypical peers than our students who have nuanced social challenges?

5. How do you think a person's natural "social radar abilities" relate directly to their ability to abstract and infer information?

6. Describe possible perceived challenges that could prevent a school from assessing and grouping children according to the ST-SCP when designing treatment programs.

Who Is Responsible for Creating and Teaching Social Thinking and Related Social Skills? Is the Same Set of Teaching Techniques Relevant for All Persons with ASD and Related Social Learning Challenges?

1. Why should people who provide Social Thinking teaching not be limited to one field of practice?

2. Why is it important for any persons involved with teaching social emotional learning to acquire knowledge about the social developmental learning process?

3. Why is it important for any person involved in teaching social emotional learning to acquire knowledge of basic principles related to behaviorism?

4. How is multidisciplinary teaching different from interdisciplinary teaching? Why does this author recommend interdisciplinary teaching for staff involved with teaching social emotional thinking?

5. The author believes all professionals can assume some responsibility for learning and teaching social processing and related social skills in any situation. State your opinion about this.

6. What perceptual, educational, or financial conditions exist that may preclude a school from adopting this viewpoint and putting this idea into practice?

Chapter **10**
Study Guide

· · · · · · · · · · · · ·

What Is a Framework for Teaching Social Thinking and Related Social Skills?

1. How do the Four Steps of Communication and the Four Steps of Perspective Taking guide teachers in treatment planning? How do they guide students in learning concepts involved in social engagement?

2. How does Social Thinking Vocabulary help teachers guide students differently than using more common vocabulary such as "cooperate", "pay attention" and "show respect"?

3. How does use of the terms "expected behaviors" and "unexpected behaviors" :
    a. Differ from teaching students to be "appropriate" rather than "inappropriate"?
    b. Encourage students to observe the social situation?
    c. Encourage students to seek the hidden rules?

4. The Four Steps of Communication was developed because it was noticed teachers spent the bulk of their time teaching social language rather than social communication. In the Four Steps of Communication, language between conversational partners occurs only at the last step. Compare/contrast this way of teaching social communication compared to teaching social language that you/your school currently uses.

What Are Some Guidelines for Teaching Social Thinking and Related Skills to Groups of Students? Best-Practice Teaching Guidelines for Social Thinking

1. Why is it considered a "best practice" to evaluate a student's social learning level on the ST- SCP prior to selecting other students who will be part of the group?

2. How can teaching neurotypical students the Social Thinking Vocabulary help them be stronger social mentors?

3. Why is it important for a student to be accountable for his or her social learning despite having been diagnosed as having a social challenge? Should the diagnosis allow the student to be excused from our social expectations?

4. Why does this author describe friendship as requiring "work" on the part of each person in the friendship?

5. The author lists 14 "best practice" guidelines to use when teaching students. Are there any you disagree with? Are there any others you would add?

How Does Social Teaching Fit Into What We Typically Call "Education"?

1. Why does this author state "it is our students' ability to adapt to a variety of social contexts that best prepares them for independence and adulthood and increases their chances for success in our society at large?"

2. Why does this author feel there is a need for an educational team to define what is meant by the term "education" prior to their development of the IEP or treatment plan?

3. A teacher insisted that a student was receiving a good education because the student passed all the tests given by the teacher with a B or above, even though she allowed the student to work independently since he seemed to cause problems when he worked with his peers in a group. Was he getting a "good education"?

4. Debate this statement: High test scores indicate greater success in adult life.

5. Explore a mission statement from a public school. Discuss the disparity between what the mission statement implies it is teaching students and what the classroom teachers are told they should teach students. Discuss public policy and the focus on test taking as the hallmark of success rather than the school's mission statement.

What Are Evidence-Based Practices? How Do They Apply to Teaching Social Thinking and Related Social Skills?

1. Why is the research on teaching social skills, to date, somewhat inconclusive?

2. How does today's media interfere with the public's interpretation of research?

3. Why is it difficult to acquire Scientifically Based Research to study the efficacy of treatment plans to encourage social emotional learning and social skills development?

4. Why, in this author's opinion, is it difficult to do research on social skills programs if we do not know the student's social functioning level?

5. How do you/does your school define "evidence based practices"?

6. What criteria do you use/does your school use when assessing treatment efficacy? As a result of reading this chapter, have you expanded your framework to include anything different?

7. Given that social learning is subjective, fluid and changes from one context to the next, discuss how feasible it is to gather research evidence on social skills performance.

8. How do you resolve the mandate for using evidence-based methods in a classroom with the difficulty in generating research on social skills and social learning, which because of its complex nature and varied conditions, does not lend itself to be studied through conventional research methods?

9. To what extent does your school take into consideration the values, beliefs or ideas of your students and their immediate family when formulating treatment goals? List three ways in which you could implement this more in your everyday operations.

Index

An *f* after a page number indicates a figure; a *t* indicates a table.

A

ABA. *See* Applied behavior analysis (ABA)
Abstract and inferential language/
    communication
    with ASD-SCD, 49–50
    curriculum requirements, 52–53
    interpretation, 50–52
    as prerequisite for social skills, 53–54
A Five Is Against the Law! (Buron), 89
Applied behavior analysis (ABA)
    behavior improvement, 12
    inadequacy for social skills teaching, 15
    uses of, 11
ASD. *See* Autism spectrum disorder (ASD)
ASD-SCD. *See* Autism spectrum disorder with
    social communication disorders
    (ASD-SCD)
Attwood, Tony, 115
Autism as Context Blindness (Vermeulen), 36
Autism spectrum disorder (ASD)
    eye contact, 48
    incidence of, 230–231
    social impairment, 1
Autism spectrum disorder with social com-
    munication disorders (ASD-SCD)
    different learning styles, 12–13
    lifelong disorder, 19

B

Baron-Cohen, Simon, 178–179
Behavioral based social skills teaching
    criticisms of, 75
    as impediment to social competence, 81
    strengths of, 76–77
Best Practice teaching guidelines
    accountability, 198
    age appropriateness, 202
    appreciation of complexity, 204–205
    assumptions, avoiding, 195–196
    definition of social thinking and social
      skills, 201–202
    evaluation of social thinking, 193–194
    flexible thinking, 196
    group social learning experiences, 203
    inclusion, neurotypical students,
      199–200
    interaction skills, 200–201
    meaningfulness to student, 198–199
    multisensory learning opportunities, 194

    tailoring teaching to client, 194
    team oriented approach, 196–197
    training, continuing, for educators,
      205–206
    work ethic, friendship, 203–204
Brooks, David, 8

C

Carol Gray's Social Stories, 88
CCT. *See* Central coherence theory (CCT)
CEC. *See* Council for Exceptional Children
    (CEC)
Central coherence theory (CCT)
    concept formation, 34–35
    definition, 6
    and executive function, 41–42
    generalizations and applications, 35–36
    understanding perspective, 55
    weaknesses in, 34
Challenged Social Communicator (CSC),
    130–142
    areas of concern, 137–138
    assessment, 137
    characteristics, 130–136
    effective teaching strategies, 138–141
    prognosis, 141–142
    strengths, 136
    theory of mind, 131–132
Cognitive behavior therapy (CBT)
    with Asperger's Syndrome, 87
    Carol Gray's Social Stories, 88
    cognitive interventions, 87
    Comic Strip Conversations, 88–89
    definition, 86
    Five Is Against the Law! (Buron), 89
    Incredible 5-Point Scale, The (Buron and
      Curtis), 89
    Social Behavior Mapping, 89–90
    Superflex® ... a Superhero Social Thinking®
      Curriculum (Winner), 90
    as treatment for ASD, 86–87
Comic Strip Conversations, 88–89
Common Core State Standards, 59
    language arts educational standards, 63*t*
Council for Exceptional Children (CEC),
    207–208
CSC. See Challenged Social Communicator
    (CSC)

D

Diagnostic and Statistical Manual of Mental Disorders, Fifth Edition (DSM-5), 94, 163, 164, 235

E

EF. *See* Executive function (EF)
Emerging Social Communicator (ESC)
    areas of concern, 125–126
    assessment, 125
    characteristics, 117–123
    effective teaching strategies, 126–129
    prognosis, 129–130
    strengths, 123–125
    theory of mind, 121
Emotional Intelligence (Goleman), 8
Emotional processing/emotional regulation
    with ASD-SCD, 43
    definition, 42–43
Empathizing-systemizing (ES) theory, 178–179
ES theory. *See* Empathizing-systemizing (ES) theory
Evidence-based practice. *See also* Scientifically based research (SBR)
    allied health professionals, 233–234
    behaviorists, 233
    cognitive-behavioral techniques, 235–236
    limited availability for ASD-SCD, 15
    and NCLB requirements, 215
    questions about, 17–18
    reasons for, 18
    redefining, 16–17
    requirement, 14
    Social Thinking development, 234
    teacher role, 236–237
Executive function (EF)
    and central coherence theory, 41–42
    definition, 5
    empathizing-systemizing (ES) theory, 178–179
    and joint attention, 6
    and perspective taking, 111
    skills, 40, 41
    and social mind, 41
    and theory of mind, 5
    in Weak Interactive Social Communicator (WICS), 112
Eye contact
    with ASD, 48
    with behaviorally based instruction, 78–79
    and joint attention, 48
    role of, 77

F

Four Steps of Communication, 179, 182–183
Four Steps of Perspective Taking, 179–182

Framework for instruction
    behaviors, agreement about, 175–176
    common vocabulary, 175
    empathizing-systemizing (ES) theory, 178–179
    explicit instruction, 178
    Four Steps of Communication, 179, 182–183
    Four Steps of Perspective Taking, 179–182
    intact brain fallacy, 177
    mislabeling, 176
    vocabulary, 184–191*t*
Frith, Uta, 34–35

G

Gardner, Howard, 7
Gestalt processing/getting the big picture, 55–56
Goleman, Daniel, 8
Gray, Carol, 88, 115
Guidelines for teaching. *See* Best Practice teaching guidelines

H

Humor and human relatedness, 56

I

IDEA. *See* Individuals with Disabilities Education Act (IDEA)
ILAUGH Model of Social
    A = abstract and inferential language/communication, 49–54
    creation of, 45–46
    framework, 57*f*
    G = gestalt processing/getting the big picture, 55–56
    H = humor and human relatedness, 56
    I = initiation of communication, 46–47
    L = listening with eyes and brain, 47–49
    U = understanding perspective, 54–55
Incredible 5-Point Scale (Buron and Curtis), 89
Individuals with Disabilities Education Act (IDEA), 211–212, 243
Initiation of communication, 46–47
Intact social brain fallacy, 177, 242
Intelligence quotient (IQ), and social development, 9
IQ. *See* Intelligence quotient (IQ)

J

Joint attention
    development of, 6
    and eye contact, 78
    as pivotal, 9
    and theory of mind, 36

L

Language arts educational standards, 60–63t
Listening with eyes and brain, 47–49

M

Multiple intelligences, 7

N

NCLB. *See* No Child Left Behind (NCLB)
NCS. *See* Neurotypical social communicator (NCS)
Neurotypical
    central coherence theory, 34
    development, social mind, 37
    joint attention, 78
    nuances, 13
    social development, 2–3
    and ST-SCP, 94, 98
Neurotypical Social Communicator (NCS), 102–103
No Child Left Behind (NCLB)
    and Common Core State Standards, 59
    policy, 243
    and social conceptual information required, 60–63t
    and social teaching, 210–211, 212
Nuance Challenged Social Communicator, 103–104

P

PBIS. *See* Positive Behavior Intervention Support (PBIS)
Perspective taking
    central importance of, 83
    in communication, 161
    definition, 185
    and executive function, 111
    Four Steps of Perspective Taking, 179–182
    and gestalt processing, 57f
    human relatedness, 56
    range of skills, 55
    and theory of mind, 132
    weaknesses in, 38–39, 55
Perspective Taking Scale, 98
Positive Behavior Intervention Support (PBIS), 173

R

Resistant Social Communicator (RSC)
    as alternative category on the ST-SCP, 149
    areas of concern, 153–154
    assessment, 152–153
    characteristics, 149–152
    effective teaching strategies, 155–157

    emotionally disturbed label, 152
    prognosis, 157–158
    strengths, 153
Response to Intervention (RTI) approaches, 213–214
Roles and responsibilities
    attitude, 165–166
    for clinical decisions, 167
    for grouping issues, 170
    input and insight, 164–165
    limits of profession, 161–162
    parents, 162
    for placement of students, 169
    in professional fields of study, 166
    research, lack of, 163
    in school districts, 164
    for social cognitive thinking, 167–168
    for system creation, 170–171
    training, lack of, 161
RSC. *See* Resistant Social Communicator (RSC)
RTI approaches. *See* Response to Intervention (RTI) approaches

S

SACS. *See* Socially Anxious Social Communicator (SACS)
SBR. *See* Scientifically based research (SBR)
SCD. *See* Social communication disorder (SCD)
SCERTS™ model, 115, 127, 148, 197, 235
Scientifically based research (SBR). *See also* Evidence-based practice
    age differences, 225–226
    complexity, 227–228
    control group problems, 228–219
    definition, 216–217
    errors in, 222
    evaluation of, 222–223
    formulation of research questions, 222–223
    inconsistencies in, 219
    limits for treatment of ASD, 217
    measurement over time, 227
    media interpretations, 222–223
    meta-analysis of research, problems with, 220–221
    progress rates, 229
    social emotional needs, 226–227
    standardization problems, 217–218
    subjectivity, 218
    sub-types, defining, 224–225
    unanswered questions, 230
    variables, 228–229
SCSC. *See* Significantly Challenged Social Communicator (SCSC)
Self-Regulation in Early Childhood (Bronson), 209

Sensory integration, definition, 43–44
Social Animal, The (Brooks), 8
Significantly Challenged Social Communicator (SCSC)
    areas of concern, 145–147
    assessment, 147–148
    characteristics, 142–144
    effective teaching strategies, 147–148
    prognosis, 148
    strengths, 144
    theory of mind, 146
Social Behavior Mapping, 89–90
Social communication disorder (SCD), with ASD, 10
Social conceptual information
    assumptions made about, 67–68
    developmental roots of, 64–66
    as prerequisite knowledge, 68–69, 71f
    remediation for, 70
    required for meeting Core Curriculum Standards, 60–63t
    social operating system assumption, 66–67
    teacher's role, 64
Social development
    with cognitive development, 29–30
    and cultural differences, 83–84
    developmental stages, 28–29
    narrative thinking, 30
    origins of, 27–28
    successful programs for, 31–32
Social development theory
    central coherence theory, 6
    complexity, 4–5
    executive function (EF), 5
    and neurological development, 3
    theory of mind (ToM), 4
Social intelligence
    definition, 7
    erroneous assumptions of, 9
    importance of, 8
Socially Anxious Social Communicator (SACS
    areas of concern, 105
    characteristics, 104–105
    effective teaching strategies, 106
    prognosis, 106
    strengths, 105
Social radar system, 96–97
Social skills
    abstract and inferential language/communication, 53–54
    effective adaptation, 24–25
    nuances, 25–26
    problems with, 23–24
Social skills instruction
    applied behavior analysis (ABA), 11
    for ASD individuals, 8
    discrete skills versus generalization, 10

    focus needed, 20–21
    history of, 10–12
    lack of, 2
    limitations of, 82–83
    need for, 10
    for neurotypical populations, 3
    nuance and sophistication of skills, 13
    with social rules, 12
Social teaching and education
    defining education, 211
    Individuals with Disabilities Education Act (IDEA), 211–212
    integration into instruction, 207–208
    in kindergarten, 209
    labels, limited value of, 210
    mission, 214
    and NCLB, 210–211, 212
    recess instruction versus classroom instruction, 208
    Response to Intervention (RTI) approaches, 213–214
Social thinking
    versus behavioral response emphasis, 74–75
    with delayed social development, 81
    as evidence-based teachings, 234
    eye contact, purpose of, 79–80
    for inappropriate behavior, 74
    necessity, 73–74
    rationale for instruction in, 80
    sophistication of, 82
    transferable skills, 75–76
    tree, 71f
    uses, 72–73
    vocabulary for, 184–191t
Social thinking-social communication profile (ST-SCP)
    age considerations, 95
    background, 94
    categories, 99
    Challenged Social Communicator (CSC), 130–142
    conclusions, 158–159
    criteria, 99
    diagnostic profile, confusion about, 92–93
    Emerging Social Communicator (ESC), 117–130
    neurotypical base line, 98
    Neurotypical Social Communicator (NCS), 102–103
    Nuance Challenged Social Communicator, 103–104
    Perspective Taking Scale, 98
    predictions for student academic learning challenges, 97
    predictions for transition to adulthood, 97–98

purpose, 94–95
  rationale for, 93
  Resistant Social Communicator (RSC), 149–158
  self-awareness, 95–96
  Significantly Challenged Social Communicator (SCSC), 142–148
  social learning abilities versus diagnostic labels, 91–92
  Socially Anxious Social Communicator (SACS), 104–107
  social radar system, 96–97
  uses, 100–101
  Weak Interactive Social Communicator (WICS), 107–117
ST-STP. *See* Social thinking-social communication profile (ST-SCP)

T
TEACCH model, 139, 148
Teachers
  and evidence-based practice, 236–237
  successful, 238
Teaching guidelines. *See* Best Practice teaching guidelines
Theory of mind (ToM)
  in Challenged Social Communicator (CSC), 131–132
  definition, 4
  delays, 38–39
  discrepancies with intellect, 39
  emergence of, 37
  in Emerging Social Communicator (ESC), 121
  evolution of, 37
  and executive function, 5
  and joint attention, 36
  and perspective taking, 132

  in Significantly Challenged Social Communicator (SCSC), 146
  stages, 38
  understanding perspective, 54
  weaknesses in, 37
Think Social! (Winner), 183
ToM. *See* Theory of mind (ToM)
Treatment, successful, participants
  educators, 236–237
  parents, 237–238
  students, 238

U
Understanding perspective, 54–55

V
Vermeulen, Peter, 36
Vocabulary for Social Thinking, 184–191*t*

W
Weak Interactive Social Communicator (WICS)
  areas of concern, 113–114
  assessment, 111–113
  characteristics, 107–108
  effective teaching strategies, 114–116
  executive function skills, 112
  masking of symptoms, 110–111
  prognosis, 116–117
  in social situations, 108–109
  strengths, 112–113
  theory of mind tests, 109–110
WICS. *See* Weak Interactive Social Communicator (WICS)

Z
Zaks, Zosia, 217–219

SocialThinking℠ has so much to offer!

OUR MISSION

At Social Thinking, our mission is to help people develop their social competencies to better connect with others and experience deeper well being. We create unique treatment frameworks and strategies to help individuals develop their social thinking and related skills to meet their academic, personal, and professional social goals. These goals often included sharing space effectively with others, learning to work as part of a team, and developing relationships of all kinds: with family, friends, classmates, co-workers, romantic partners, etc.

ARTICLES

100+ free educational articles and treatment strategies

CONNFERENCES, eLEARNING & CUSTOM TRAINING

Courses and embedded training for schools and organizations

PRODUCTS

Books, games, posters, music and more!

CLINICAL RESEARCH

Measuring the effectiveness of the Social Thinking Methodology

TREATMENT: CHILDREN & ADULTS

Clinical treatment, assessments, school consultations, etc.

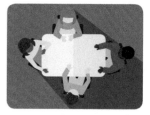

CLINICAL TRAINING PROGRAM

Three-day intensive training for professionals